You Called My Name

The Hidden Treasures of Your Hebrew Heritage

Rabbi Esther Ben-Toviya, MA

O

BOOKS

Winchester, U.K.
New York, U.S.A.

First published by O Books, 2006
An imprint of John Hunt Publishing Ltd., The Bothy, Deershot Lodge,
Park Lane, Ropley, Hants, SO24 0BE, UK
office@johnhunt-publishing.com
www.o-books.net

USA and Canada
NBN
custserv@nbnbooks.com
Tel: 1 800 462 6420
Fax: 1 800 338 4550

Singapore
STP
davidbuckland@tlp.com.sg
Tel: 65 6276
Fax: 65 6276 7119

Australia
Brumby Books
sales@brumbybooks.com
Tel: 61 3 9761 5535
Fax: 61 3 9761 7095

South Africa
Alternative Books
altbook@global.co.za
Tel: 27 011 792 7730
Fax: 27 011 972 7787

Text copyright Esther Ben-Toviya 2006

Design: Jim Weaver Ltd
Cover design: Book Design, London

ISBN-13: 978 1 905047 79 6
ISBN-10: 1 905047 79 7

A CIP catalogue record for this book is available from the British Library.

Printed by Maple-Vail, USA

Table of Contents

Acknowledgements

Rabbi Rami Shapiro penned the idea that no book is written by just one person. Each book is an amalgamation of the many teachers in the life of an author, as well as the fresh inspiration coming through the author. This is certainly true in the writing of this book, *You Called My Name*.

I have been very gifted by the teachers who have come into my life. They have called forth from within me that which I could not see in myself, and challenged me to go higher, move beyond, and explore the unknown. This book is a tribute to the part they have each played in my life. Their voices can be heard in the words of *You Called My Name*, echoing through the voice of my own Soul.

I acknowledge John Hunt, my publisher, who had the spiritual vision and courage to publish this book. Thank you, John. My deep gratitude goes out to you.

I thank Christina Lunden for sharing so much on the journey with me, and suggesting I send my book to John Hunt.

I honor my parents, Ernest and Ruth Ann Reed and grandparents who shared their faith and their heritage with me.

I honor Rabbi and Freda Brod who walked hand and hand with me from my first days in Judaism through the maturity of these many years hence. My Abba and Ima, they have nurtured me and supported me with their unconditional love and wisdom. And, I honor my beloved mentor and the deep friend of my Soul, David, who first challenged me to share the treasures in this book with Christians.

I thank my Rebbe and friend, Rabbi Zalman Schachter-Shalomi, who saw my Soul, guided me and initiated me into the Rabbinate with smicha (ordination). I was privileged to intern under Rabbi Rami Shapiro whose wisdom guided me and helped me to become simply the Rabbi I am created to be. Thank you, Rami.

Thank you to my beloved friend and healer of the bereaved, *Cornelius J. van der Poel, CSSP., former professor of pastoral theology and pastoral training at Barry University, Miami, FL.* Your words of wisdom touching the common bond of the human experience and the Infinite Value of each of us ring throughout this book.

Thank you to my friend, birthday mate, and colleague, Rabbi Suzanne Carter, for encouraging me and helping me to rise above and soar with the truth of my Soul, regardless.

The Talmud states that we can learn something from each person we meet. This is especially true for the high caliber of professors and teachers of my formal education, graduate, post graduate and seminary, as well as each member of the congregations I have served and the families I have been privileged to be with in the hospice setting. Each person has touched me in a unique and particular way.

At the risk of waxing bold, I honor the mystics and wisdom keepers from Abraham down through the ages of four thousand years, who have held sacred the traditions and teachings and who offered their shoulders upon which to stand that we in this generation may see farther.

Thank you to my wonderful sisters, Majel and Elizabeth, who love me "no matter what". We always find something to laugh about, thereby nurturing our Souls and keeping ourselves from becoming too serious. We will always be there for each other.

And most preciously, I honor my children, Lee and Atticus. Thank you for the journey we have shared together; through all the phases, through all the major changes. You have walked in miraculous spiritual experiences, some shared and some your own. You carry the Light in your own wonderful and unique way in your generation on the planet. Life is the sweeter for your presence in my life. I saved you for last because you are my heart.

Foreword

This is an invitation to all Christians to search in the Hebrew tradition for the foundations (roots) of their spirituality. This invitation is not new. We read the same in Matthew 5: 17-20, where Jesus says:

> Do not think that I have come to abolish the law or the prophets. I have come not to abolish but to fulfill. Amen, I say to you, until heaven and earth pass away, not the smallest letter, or the smallest part of a letter will pass from the law, until all things have taken place. (NAB, 1986).

Jesus went back to the roots of religious and human values. Too many leaders of the people had left their roots and got stuck in externals. It is a very human tendency to be guided by what we can see and touch. Spiritual meanings easily fade into the background and human life may attach itself exclusively to the material. Jesus came to unveil again the original meaning of the Hebrew tradition and to guide it to perfection.

Rabbi Esther Ben-Toviya does an excellent job in researching for us the spiritual richness that is contained in the Hebrew writings. She points out that Jesus spoke from that treasure-trove and, very correctly, admonishes every one, Hebrew and Christian alike, to grasp the meaning of God's revelation preserved and formulated in the Hebrew tradition.

In reading this, one concept in particular kept returning to me, namely, "created in the image of God". In other words, humanity expresses God's life as communicated (creation is self-communication and sharing of self) to and shared with creatures. God's inner Self is brought within human reach in humanity. Hence, the spiritual dimension is an inseparable and indispensable requirement for the fullness of being human.

"Being created in the image of God" brings us back to the original call of humanity and pre-dates the Hebrew scriptures. However, no other religious approach is known that describes and integrates spiritual values into human existence as do the Hebrew traditions. For Jews and Christians alike they are a progressive, ever deepening invitation to search for the human expression that indeed reveals the image of God in humanity. This image can only be recognized when we grasp the spiritual perspective and meaning of everyday life.

Rabbi Esther Ben-Toviya digs deep into the meaning of spiritual disciplines and shows how they portray the human as a spiritual-material existence, or as a wholeness that touches earth and heaven. She describes the unifying spiritual power of seasons and community celebrations that in the final analysis gather all together into the people of God.

However, membership of and participation in a community does not take away personal responsibility. In the end, each individual must make the choice of how one's life can become the honest expression of God's loving presence in the world in which we live. It is the burning bush experience in which each person must know oneself and answer when God calls him/her by name to fulfill the task of one's life.

You Called My Name is an outstanding guide toward a deeper understanding of the roots of spirituality for all people, since all are created in the image of God. It is a great contribution toward a deepening insight into the meaning of "being human," and a source of unity in which Hebrews and Christians can search together and listen when God calls their name.

Cornelius J. van de Poel, cssp

Key to
Hebrew Pronunciation

Hebrew is written in letters (characters) that are different from the English alphabet characters and some letters are pronounced with sounds that are not in the English alphabet. Hebrew is read right to left. For ease of reading I have transliterated the Hebrew words in this book, which means Hebrew words are written phonetically using English letters. When Hebrew letters are not being used, transliterated Hebrew words may vary in spellings. For example, you may have seen the winter holiday the Feast of Dedication written as: Hanukkah, Chanukah, Hannukah, in the public domain. There is no one set rule for spelling words in English that are written in different characters in the original language. The following guidelines will help with the pronunciation of the Hebrew written in this book:

The accent generally falls on the last syllable:
Sha-BBAT
Ta-LLIT
Me-zu-ZAH

"Ch" is guttural and pronounced as in "Bach".

(It is <u>not</u> the sound of "ch" as in "chair".)

"Tz" is pronounced as in "pizza" and "matzah".

"Kk" is pronounced as a hard "k" as in "kite".

The Hebrew letter *het* is a softly aspirated sound in Hebrew and I have simply used the letter "h" to indicate where it is used.

Example: *Ruah*, spirit, breath, wind, is pronounced Roo-**ah**, with a "breathed" *h* at the end. It is not pronounced Roo-a.

To indicate a word is Hebrew I have italicized it the first time it appears in the text. Thereafter it will appear in normal format for ease of reading.

I use the English letters **YHVH** to indicate where the Hebrew text uses the ineffable or unspoken name of God. **YHVH** stands for the Hebrew letters *Yod, Hey, Vav, Hey*. **YHVH** is the emanating "Breath of Life" or "Power-flow of Life" aspect of God that is usually translated "Lord" in the King James Version Bible. I translate **YHVH** as "The Holy One".

Introduction

Welcome to the treasure room, the roots of your Christian faith. Your Hebrew heritage is the inheritance of your spiritual rebirth as a Christian. Your legacy of peoplehood, daily spiritual practices, and mystical teachings increases by 2000 years as you open these pages.

This book has been written for your Christian life enhancement. You already know the Rabbi from Nazareth. It is reasonable to believe that you learn about him in your church. However, as you begin to explore the knowledge, wisdom, and spiritual guidance of the ages handed down through the oral and written traditions of the Hebrews, (which Jesus knew, understood and taught at a deeper level), you will add a new depth and breadth to the power of your faith. As Jesus spoke with his disciples, taught the masses and sat in study with priests and rabbis at the Temple he was speaking as a Jew, to Jews, about Jewish concepts. He was continuing in the tradition of the prophets to call the Hebrew people to a deeper experience of their intentions to answer the call: "be Holy for I AM Holy" and to be a "kingdom of Priests, a Holy Nation" (Exodus 19). How do we live up to this calling? What are the Sacred Ways?

There are many instances in the New Testament writings where Jesus refers to, but does not spell out a particular Hebrew concept, whether it is about God or the meaning of a spiritual practice, because his disciples were Jewish and knew that to which he was referring. His followers lived the customs and culture of their Hebrew faith. Two thousand years later, as the Christian religion has developed in the Gentile world some of the deep and rich meanings have been lost, as the Hebrew understanding of these practices and concepts were not taught. However, these concepts and practices are still available to you as part of your Christian identity. The purpose of this book is that you may learn some of the Jewish concepts and practices that your ancestors hand down to you through your spiritual inheritance. As you integrate these concepts and practices with relevance to your life, they will enrich your spiritual growth and give roots to nourish your Christian journey.

This text is by no means an exhaustive account of all Hebrew spiritual and mystical practices. However, this book provides a place to start, a beginning that enables you to explore the spiritual pathway of your Hebrew roots.

As Isaiah the Prophet teaches, we learn "precept upon precept, line upon line, here a little, there a little." As we learn a new spiritual principle and seek to incorporate it into our lives, it takes the experience of the concept, the actual "doing" of it, to integrate it into our thoughts, feelings and spirit. It is through the "doing" that it becomes familiar to us and part of us. **Through the doing comes the understanding.**

As you learn and apply some of the concepts and practices in this book, such as the principles of faith and the fulfillment of faith through *Mitzvot* (Sacred Ways), the use of the *Tallit* (Prayer Shawl), and the sounding of the *Shofar* (Ram's Horn) they may seem strange to your conscious mind, yet your Spirit may leap within you. Your Soul may feel at home.

For thousands of years our people have sought ways to express the spiritual principles given to us that we may experience God's Presence in our daily lives and create harmony not only in our lives but in the world. These Sacred Ways belong to you as a follower of the Rabbi from Nazareth. As you seek holiness in your life, wisdom will be revealed to you and opportunities will arise for you to practice sacred living in love.

I invite you to accompany the reading of this book with a prayer that the Holy Spirit may guide you in truth and into all understanding. May you be blessed with peace and love.

Rabbi Esther Ben-Toviya, MA

1
Meeting God at the Burning Bush of Faith

Your Biblical Roots in Faith and Mitzvot

"And now, Israel, what does The Holy One your God require of you, but to always experience awe of The Infinite One, your God, to walk in all of the Sacred Ways, and to love the Creator of the Universe, your Intimate Friend, and to serve the Source of Life with all your heart and with all your Soul, to be a keeper of the Sacred Ways of the Fountain of All Life and the statutes through which I bring you into God – Consciousness this day that it may be good for you."

DEUTERONOMY 10:12

Faith within Hebrew thought is inseparable from action; the "doing" of the Sacred Ways. Deuteronomy 10:12 links the experience of standing in the "Awe of God's Presence" to doing the Sacred Ways. As the word "Awe" is used here it indicates a special state of Grace, a state of an opened consciousness, a blinding to the separateness of existence, but a vision of Truth of the oneness and connectedness of all that exists. It is beyond the sense of separate Self with a brief glimpse of "no-self" consciousness. This consciousness cannot be sustained and still be acted upon in the physical world of action. However, by doing the Sacred Ways of loving kindness we sustain that sense of The Divine Presence in every day life. The Sacred Ways fulfill the experience of "meeting God" in a state of Awe. A consciousness of the constant Presence of the Holy One in daily life is brought about through performing the Sacred Ways given in Torah, (the first five books of the Bible) in everything we do.

These Sacred Ways are called *Mitzvot* (*Mitzvah* in the singular) in Hebrew. These have been translated as "commandments" of God to the Hebrew people in the English King James Version Bible. A more accurate way of understanding them from the mystical traditions is as Sacred Ways of our people. They are Sacred Ways of staying in harmony with Creation and those parts of Creation which are outside or above the physical world. These Sacred Ways carry a sense of command to them, however, the commanded-ness must come from within our hearts, not from outside of us. The commanded-ness is a compelling from within to act outwardly from our awareness of The Divine Presence.

Faith is the energy that flows from Spirit, (in-spiration) from within us. This flow moves through to our thoughts and ideas, becomes empowered by our emotions and finally is acted out in the drama of our lives, through our actions. These actions are an end result of our faith, the flow of Spirit through us – which is not complete without the action. We prove what we have faith in through our actions. Faith is the fuel of manifestation in our lives. Through our actions we can create an enlightened world: "as it is above, so it is below."

Which do you think is more important, the knowledge of what

the Sacred Ways are or the actual doing of the Sacred Ways? Take a moment to answer both ways. Consider a person who studies God's words and takes them to heart, but does not do them. What good has this knowledge brought to the world? Now consider one who has not studied the Sacred Ways, does not know what they are, but is very busy doing things he or she believes God desires. How high is the probability of missing the mark of harmonious living? How will that person know what Sacred Ways to choose for any particular situation? Knowledge and study is completed in the action. Each needs the other. It is through our faith that we study and reach into God's Torah, book of enlightenment, in order to make informed choices for our actions.

The Letter of James clearly states this Hebrew understanding of faith and mitzvot in the following passage:

> But – obey the message; be doers of the Word and not merely listeners to it, ...
>
> JAMES 1:22, THE AMPLIFIED BIBLE

> ...being not a heedless listener who forgets, but an active doer, he shall be blessed in his doing.
>
> JAMES 1:25, THE AMPLIFIED BIBLE

We set our intentions to fulfill our faith when we say a blessing before we begin each action. It is an ancient tradition to do this from the moment we awaken to consciousness in the morning by repeating the *Shema*, a prayer which is the watchword of our faith. The Shema reminds us that God is "All One" and thus we, as creations of God are part of The Oneness.

When we lay our head on the pillow at night, just before falling asleep, we again repeat the Shema, reminding our Soul that it is still "All One." The actions of the day in between the two recitations of the Shema are to be based upon the concept that whatever we do to someone or something else, we do to ourselves and to God as well, for it is "All One."

This concept of "Oneness" is the essence, core and basis of the faith of Abraham. That is why the Shema is our "watchword." This is the Hebrew faith – that God, our own being and all of Creation is "All One." The Shema, the prayer that simply states this esoteric and universal Truth, the watchword of our Faith is as follows:

"Shema Yisrael, Yah Eloheinu, Yah Echad."
"Hear, O Israel, The Holy One is our God,
The Holy One is Oneness itself."

FAITH OF THE ANCESTORS

The concept of God as Oneness, as the Shema teaches us is the faith of Father Abraham, the first Hebrew. The covenant God and Abraham made was one of action:

"Lech lecha," – Get yourself out of your country and from your kindred and from your father's house to the land that I will show you: and I will make of you a great nation, and I will bless you and make your name great; and you shall be a blessing: and I will bless them who bless you and curse those who curses you: and all the families of the earth be blessed by you."

GENESIS 12:1-3

The Hebrew phrase, *lech lecha*, literally means "go to yourself" or "get to your Self." God established a covenant with Abraham to move him from where he was as a wealthy merchant prince to a role that more fully fulfilled his Soul's destiny as the Father of many nations of Souls who would be opening their consciousness to God through the understanding that "All is One." At this point in the story, Abraham's name was Avram, for God had not yet given him his new name of Abraham. The sages say that when our name changes so does our destiny (life). Abram made a covenant which changed his life and his change of name reflected that. He became the "father" of thousands of Souls who followed in the wisdom of his ways.

When Avram was a child his father, Terah, was in the business of making and selling idols. Avram was well acquainted with spirituality based upon worshipping many physical gods, each prayed to for a specific purpose. There is a story in our tradition that says that one day Terah left young Avram alone to watch the shop. While Terah was gone, Avram took a large hammer and smashed all the idols except the largest one. He laid the hammer at the feet of this idol. When Terah returned he found his shop in ruins. Furious, he asked Avram what happened. The young boy told him, "The large god over there was jealous of all the other idols so he smashed them all to bits." Livid with rage his father exclaimed, "You know that can't be true. These idols are only wood and clay, they cannot even move." To that Avram replied, "Then why do you sell them to people as gods who will act on their behalf when they pray to them?"

As an adult, Abraham fully gave himself over to The One God, Creator and Sustainer of All Life. This was not a God with physical form or human traits. Abraham made a covenant with the Eternal One; a covenant that has many meanings at different levels of our existence; which touches us in our faith and covenant with God today.

On the physical plane this covenant meant that Abraham must move away from his familiar country of birth and the household of his extended family (and their business). He must go to a land that God would lead him to and settle there with his family. The first action of the contract removes Abraham from the scene of his previous life.

Often, we too find ourselves in a new situation in life after reaching a place of personal commitment to God. Our friends may change, our perspectives change and the relationships we have built with others evolve into deeper and more meaningful relationships. Like Abraham, we find ourselves in a "new place" in life.

On the emotional level, Abraham was told to leave behind the culture and social ties of his childhood, his "tribe" and his place of security in the world to find out who he is by dwelling in his own heart space. He was to learn to relate to others and his own Self as one with The Holy One, the God of Eternal Love. He is invited to "lech lecha", "go to your Self" in love; and from that love to relate to other people, creatures and the earth in compassion and in love as part of the Greater Self. This new way of relating in love removes the dualistic ideas of God being "other" and expands the personal Self to be included in the Oneness of all Life. It then becomes possible to "love others as you love your Self."

On an intellectual level Abraham was challenged by a new way of thinking; he was learning to order his life according to faith in God's words of guidance, even if that guidance was not always logical in his mind. After all, an Unseen God with an Inaudible Voice is telling him to go to a place that he doesn't know about and there The Holy One will make him a great nation, when at this point Abraham didn't even have any children. Abraham was seventy-five years old. He and Sarah, his wife, were beyond their child-bearing years; they were mature and settled in business, their family and their ways. It was a challenge to change the way he had always thought, but after this eminent "meeting" with The Infinite One, Abraham's mind was opened to new concepts, thoughts and ideas of life. His first step of action was to replace the illusion of separation of his own Self from "others" with the truth that he was infinitely and essentially connected as part of The One. The One is presented as "other" in Creation as part of a necessary illusion so that we, The Many, may face and even "talk together" with The One of Creation. This is an abstract point for meditation. *Selah*, (Hebrew for "pause and meditate upon this".)

This covenant challenged Abraham in all aspects, but, most importantly, it challenged Abraham's Spirit in the commandment, "Lech lecha", "Go to your-Self." This can also be understood as "Go to the Divinity within your own Being." Once we begin to let this enormous concept of the "Oneness" get down into our consciousness everything in life changes for us. We are moved into a different consciousness of our existence. We no longer strive to impose our will and control on others, but we seek to work in harmony with what "is" for we are secure in our place as an indispensable part of the whole. When we understand ourselves as being a Spark of the Divine, an emanation of God Being, then we begin to understand ourselves as having Infinite Value; for we are a fraction of The Infinite Being; and any fraction of Infinity is still Infinity! Think of that! We are made of "God stuff." As such we have everything within us that we need to deal with life. We see the Divinity in our Selves and recognize it in others; other human beings, animals, nature, and all that exists. There is no duality.

This concept changes our world. God emanates Being, or Life-force, to create all that exists. God's emanation is Creation (including us). When we see the countenance or energy of that Life-force we call it "Light". When we feel the flow of Life-force we call it "Love". As emanations of God we are God's Love made manifest in this physical world. When we open our hearts and let ourselves feel the Eternal Love already flowing within us, it fills us from the inside to overflow onto others around us. We no longer seek love from others in order to feel loved and to fill the "empty place" within us, for we know we **are** love. When we perceive ourselves as Eternal Beings of God's Divine Love, our minds are expanded and enlightened to ideas beyond all boundaries, stretching out to unlimited borders of unity. We can imagine a world of peace, for we **are** at peace. It is All One. This is the heart of the covenant that Abraham, our Ancestor made. This is the first action: "Lech lecha", "Go to your Self" – implying – for you are One with Me. This is the covenant of your Ancestors. This is your Hebrew heritage.

The covenant that Abraham made with God was continued and passed down to the promised son, Isaac, and to his son, Jacob, and to his sons, the Twelve Tribes, (most specifically Joseph), generation to generation, down to the Children of Israel whom God delivered from the bondage of Egypt and met with at Mount Sinai. The covenant made at Sinai was no longer between one person, the leader of a family, but was made with a group of people. The covenant at Mount Sinai created "peoplehood" and for the first time, the Hebrews were a nation. This covenant is also action-oriented. It links the remembrance of the Sacred Ways and the "doing" of them to each individual's relationship to and walk with The Holy One.

> "If you walk in my statutes and keep my Sacred Ways (living in harmony), and do them, then I will give you rain in due season, the land will yield its increase, and the trees of the field shall yield their fruit.... And I will walk among you and will be your God and you shall be my people."
>
> LEVITICUS 26:1 – 12

The Hebrew faith is lived through actions. Identity of one who is in the Covenant is focused on actions, the Sacred Ways.

Today, there are many "beliefs" in Judaism, but what we believe does not give us our identity as a Hebrew. For instance, you can believe God exists or doesn't exist, you are still a Hebrew, and you still **do** Passover. The focus is on the actions, not on the beliefs.

The action of the covenant (doing the Sacred Ways) is the focus for Hebrew traditions, while the beliefs about God evolve in the individual heart as we learn and grow, in our relationship with The Infinite. During a lifetime of studying sacred writings, prayer and actions of loving kindness, we question and learn and expand our beliefs as we grow and develop spiritually in God's light.

Our basic concepts of God are action-oriented; we think of God as **a** transitive verb; the verb of Being. When Moses stood before the burning bush and God asked him to take the Children of Israel out of Egypt, Moses asked God "When I go to them who shall I say sent me?" God replied, *"E'heye asher e'heye"* which can be literally translated, "I will be that which I will be." God is not a noun in Jewish thought and is not named as a noun. God is a verb, the dynamic unfolding of Being – in the Universe and beyond.

There are many names for God within Judaism. However, the names for God do not name God as a noun, but the names point to a specific relationship with God. For instance, consider the relationship these names indicate:

Avinu – Our Father or Our Source
Ribbono Shel Olam – Guide (Master) of the Cosmos
HaMakom – The Place (which is no "place" – the non-place you "go to" in meditation, a consciousness)
Tzur Yisrael – Rock of Israel

Shomer Yisrael, Guardian of Israel

El Shaddai – The Nurturer

These are only a few names for God, of which there are many, many in Hebrew, each describing a different aspect of God.

In Jewish thought, God is the dynamic force that powers the Universe, constantly creating and giving the Life Force of Being to the Universe; and yet, God is beyond the Cosmos, all Universes and Dimensions. We cannot define God, for the moment we say, "God is this" then in the next nanosecond God is manifesting more, different, beyond. All of Creation is the outflow of God manifesting Being. All of Creation, including each human being, is God's love made manifest in this dimension. As such, humans are a particular creation, given the ability to transcend this dimension and to affect this dimension through our transcendence. We are the outflow of God's love in physical form. We are beings of love, made in the image of God in that we have the ability to give **and** receive, the desire to love and be loved. To be fully human means to experience all that is within us to the fullest. Because we have the spark of The Holy One within us, and our very body is the physical manifestation of God's love and energy of Being, we have everything we need within us to deal with life. Learning how to access all that is within us and fulfill that for which we were created is what Jewish life is about. The actions and practices within the Hebrew heritage are the exercises that teach us how to access the highest within ourselves. These Sacred Ways are called in Hebrew, the *mitzvot* (singular is *mitzvah*). These are the ways of our faith. These are the ways God has taught us to live in harmony with all of Creation, and to bring all of Creation into Oneness through harmony. This too, is part of the faith of your Hebrew heritage.

The Mitzvot – The Sacred Actions of Faith

And he (Moses) took the Book of the Covenant, and read in the hearing of the people: and they said, "All that The Holy One has said we will do and we will hear."

EXODUS 24:8

The covenant that was made at Sinai was an agreement between the Children of Israel and the God of their ancestors, the God of Abraham and Sarah, the God of Isaac and Rebecca, and the God of Jacob, Rachel and Leah. The provision of the covenant was that they would live enlightened lives by following sacred imperatives given by God. The unstated spiritual principle of the covenant was that through doing those imperatives, they would gain a deeper understanding of the Divine Oneness; that they would live their everyday life on earth with a higher consciousness of God. These imperatives teach humanity how to live in harmony with themselves, other people, all of Creation and with God. By the "doing" of these ways of harmony, they would come to understand the secrets of how the Universe manifests in physical form, the Infinite One Who is without form. When we enter this covenant, making it between ourselves and God within our own hearts, we open our consciousness to the love that is God flowing through us, giving us Being. When we experience this love our consciousness opens to the Awe of God and we desire to be ever closer to that Infinite Love. We recognize the Divine in all which has existence.

By practicing the Sacred Ways, our consciousness is further awakened to the Awe and we attain ever higher levels of God-awareness and a greater ability to stay in that Luminous Presence while living our daily lives. This ability to stay in the Luminous

Presence is called *d'vekut,* in Hebrew, which literally means "sticking to God." It is from this word's root, *davak,* which the word "glue" is formed from in Hebrew. The Sacred Ways of our Covenant help us to attain d'vekut, "sticking to God" when we might otherwise become so caught up in the immediacy of this world that we forget God the Eternal Presence. In that immediacy we might miss the Divine in the everyday and the wisdom that the "bigger picture" holds for us.

By practicing these Sacred Ways we gain divine wisdom, and open our consciousness to the deeper secrets of the cosmos that through us a higher level of Light may flow into this dimension, enlightening our world. This is our mission; to bring into manifestation the healing of our world, (*Tikkun Olam* in Hebrew) and the time of Peace and Enlightenment here on Earth.

How does this work? How do these Sacred Ways open our "God Consciousness" and bring us into d'vekut? There is a hint in the passage from Exodus at the beginning of this chapter. Take a moment to reread it and see if there is something that strikes your eye as "out of order". Why does it say, "we will do and we will hear?" Doesn't that seem backwards? Shouldn't it read "we will hear and we will do"? One of the wisdoms we learn from the way this text is worded is that through the doing of a mitzvah (Sacred Way) comes the understanding of it. It is similar to learning to ride a bike. You can learn all of the physics of how to keep the bike balanced, but you really don't understand it until you are actually pedaling your way down the street! Then you have a deeper understanding of it. Through the "doing" comes the "understanding." In the same way, when we do a mitzvah we gain a deeper understanding of what that mitzvah is teaching us about living in harmony with the flow of Divine Energy we call Creation. Each time we do a mitzvah with *kavennah,* (intentionality), we open ourselves to a new revelation of The Divine Presence in our life. The mitzvot, keep us in d'vekut, sticking close to God, and impart fresh revelations of spiritual wisdom.

By doing these Sacred Ways, or mitzvot, we learn to live a life of holiness. By doing the Sacred Ways, we support our spiritual life in the physical world by drawing ever closer to The Holy One who has given us the mission to "Be holy, for I am Holy." These Sacred Ways enable us to fulfill the prophecy, "You shall be a kingdom of Priests, a holy nation." These sacred acts refine our consciousness of "Oneness" by bringing together The One and The Many – by bonding us together in unity. As we reach out to others, doing a mitzvah for them, we extend our hearts in love. As the mitzvah is received with an open heart and hand, we are bound in unity together through the Divine Energy of God's love flowing through us.

Traditionally, there are 613 mitzvot, particular Sacred Ways, enumerated. However, these are only the beginning guidelines, to open divine awareness in certain areas of our life. As we grow in our desire to strengthen our d'vekut, "adhering" to God, and live in the conscious awareness of God's Divine love, we become more aware of all of our actions and intend them all to be mitzvot.

Just as the mitzvot bring us into a heightened awareness of God, so transgressions of the Sacred Ways separates us and blinds us to these fresh revelations. Therefore, we avoid transgressions for the sake of our d'vekut, rather than simply because we are told "Thou shall not..."

In his book, *Jewish Spiritual Practices*, Rabbi Buxbaum illustrates the purpose of the mitzvot through the teachings of Rabbi Yehiel Michal, the Zlotchover Maggid (Preacher/ Storyteller). Rabbi Yehiel explains that Abraham was able to keep all of the Torah, even before it was given:

"He was always conscious of God, and any action that would disrupt his attachment (consciousness) to God he refrained from doing; and any action that he saw would increase his attachment (consciousness) to God he realized it was a mitzvah, and that he would do."

(YESHUOT MALKO, P. 100)

Rabbi Yehiel further taught his *Chassidim* (faithful ones, or disciples):

"You should be attached (consciousness) to God continuously, and your love for The Holy One should be constant. The test to know what The Holy One's Divine Will, is this: If you want to do something, and see that this action will increase your God – Consciousness and love of God, then know that this is a mitzvah and God's Will. But, if you see that this action will decrease your love and God – Consciousness, then know that it is a transgression, and do not do it."

(YESHUOT MALKO, P. 19)

By this means, the Zlotchover Maggid taught his followers to measure every action they are about to take by the direction it will take their Souls and their consciousness – either toward God, or away from God. By this standard, they should even decide the most common daily activities; when to sleep and when to awaken, when, what and how much to eat, what to wear, where to go, what to do for work, what to pray, when to say a blessing and how to act in relationship to themselves and to others. This is a goal, an ideal to reach for in life. It becomes a desire of the heart the more it is practiced. Then truly all of life becomes sacred in the eyes of the mitzvah-doer. And all of life becomes an opportunity to share in the love of The Holy One.

A mitzvah is the fulfillment of service to God. This service to God begins with spiritual impulses of the Soul which give rise to inspired ideas and thoughts. When we open our hearts, our emotions attach power to these thoughts to become actions. Through this process, what started out as Spirit becomes inspired thought, is energized by the emotions of our heart and is birthed into the physical dimension of this world through our actions. A life spent in service to God includes all four dimensions, Spirit Being, Inspired Thought, Empowerment of Heart and finally, Sacred Action. In order for this process to become our natural way of living, we must practice it with *kavennah*, intentionality. Therefore, the Torah gives us mitzvot, sacred imperatives to learn how to live in God-Consciousness. The rest is up to us in the living of our covenant. The living of our covenant is no less than living the life of God in this world. In this sense we are not "doing Torah," but we are "Being Torah," the "Light Bearer."

The mitzvot teach us how to live a life of holiness. Living a life of holiness does not mean just following all the "rules," or being "right" or "moral." To live in holiness means to take a particular action at a particular time that restores and preserves harmony and wholeness to a situation. Holy actions affect the long term. Our actions also reach into other higher dimensions, where we affect worlds that we do not readily see with our natural eyes. How can we attain such a high standard? By being conscious of Spirit within, guiding and giving light to our thoughts which are "powered up" by our emotions which overflow and are expressed in our actions.

The vision comes from Spirit within us. We use our brain, intellect, and thought processes to order our steps to get to that vision. Our thoughts are "powered up" by the emotions that we attach to them. A thought is just a thought, with little energy to become an action until an emotion such as love, joy, anger or fear is attached to it. Then we use our body to express the flow of energy from our thoughts and emotions. We express ourselves in writing poetry, books, and music, saying a blessing, giving our help to others, doing the work of our vocation or profession, caring for our family, actions that manifest into this physical world of doing. This is the secret of how to manifest your vision. Faith and mitzvot unite to create the pathway of manifestation to enlighten our world. The Faith and mitzvot pathway is a way to "live in Holiness".

To manifest Holiness in our actions is a constant choice, for the same process that brings the light of our vision and inspiration into physical being can also be distorted to manifest our fears, bringing disharmony and inhibiting life. When we see the vision of our Soul and begin thinking about it our thoughts usually run in two directions in parallel with our emotions. We are excited and joyous at the prospects of where the vision may take us. Then the fear of where it might take us begins to fuel thoughts of a catastrophic fantasy. "If you try to do this ... then ... will happen" is often the theme of a new idea running amok! The fear of the responsibility begins to misdirect our feelings and we begin to think we are responsible for the success of the venture, rather than the doing of the vision. It takes a little practice, but you can experience great joy when you learn to let go of the outcome and allow your vision to take a life of its own. Your task is to start the work, it is God's to complete it!

Without even thinking the fearful thoughts out loud, the feeling the fears bring can become manifest and felt in our physical being in the pit of our stomach (we are trying to digest the situation) or in our *kishkas* – guts (we are trying to rid ourselves or push to the outside our thoughts). The feelings may be felt as a great weight on our chest (our heart is heavy from trying to restrict the flow of this feeling throughout our body), or on our neck and shoulders (we are weighed down by the load of responsibility and the "yoke" of our labor is too heavy).

In the same way, the feelings your love and joy bring can be manifest in your body and you experience a sense of enlightenment (higher Light), giddiness (childlike enchantment), a feeling of truly being alive! When people fall in love they experience these manifestations in the body. It is as if you see colors more brightly (your spiritual vision is clear), you notice the birds singing (your ears are open to hear the Divine) and you have a sense of well-being (you are aware that the entire world is within God's care).

This is the choice:

> "I call Heaven and Earth (Creation) to witness for you this day that I have set before you Life and Death, the blessing and the curse, therefore, choose Life!"
>
> DEUT. 30:19

To choose our actions from our fear is to choose death or the curse (of darkness). To choose our actions from love is to choose Life, the blessings of the vision. It is to act upon our inspired thoughts, which are empowered by our love and joy. Our actions become those of harmony, wholeness and peace. This is living a life of Holiness. This is living our faith through the Sacred Ways – the Mitzvot.

Moses exemplified this process of choice at the burning bush. God gave him a vision and mission to go to Egypt and bring the Children of Israel out of bondage. He is asked to bring them into the wilderness, to Mount Sinai to come into covenant with the God of their Ancestors. It is a great vision, a vision of high calling and enormous ambition! When Moses heard God's calling his fear rose up and Moses gave God excuses why he couldn't possibility do it. Understanding Moses' heart, God calmed his fears by giving him the support of his older brother Aaron, and God promised to be there with Moses. Together, and with the help of the Heavenly Host, the two brothers manifest the vision. Along with their sister, Miriam the Prophetess, they begin the journey of a lifetime, fulfilling the sacred pathway of their Souls.

God understands our fears, too. Remember the message of the watchword of our faith, the Shema – it is All One. Our fears are a signal to us, a way to remind us that we have a choice. God asks us to consciously choose the light, choose to feel the love flowing within us and move to acts of love and harmony in the face of our fears, which is true courage. Courage is not the absence of fear, but the ability to move in the face of fear. We are empowered by our gift of choice; we can choose to fulfill the Sacred Ways in holy service in the face of all that confronts us.

The Mitzvot falls into two categories: ethical and ritual. The ethical Sacred Ways also have two categories: mitzvot that are between you and others and ones that are between you and God. The Sacred Ways of ritual include such observances as that of *Shabbat* (Sabbath). However, there is much overlap between the ethical and ritual Mitzvot. For instance, while Shabbat is a Sacred Way of ritual, it is also a covenant held between each individual and God. This is a Mitzvah between God and us. One of the Sacred Ways to be observed on Shabbat is that we are not to let our family members or those we employ work on Shabbat. This is a Sacred Way between us and others. From this we learn that the Mitzvot teach us to be God-conscious in both our ethical behavior and in our sacred ritual, for they are intertwined and enmeshed in the fabric of life as one.

What are some of the Mitzvot that we are given in the *Torah* to bring us into God-Conscious living? An exhaustive list is not in the scope of this book (there are 613 mitzvot in the Torah); however, I will list a few major ones here that guide us in holiness as God's people of the Sacred Ways. For further reading see *Two Essays* by Rabbi Rami Shapiro, and *Jewish Literacy* by Rabbi Joseph Telushkin.

P'ru Ur'vu / "Be fruitful and multiply" – GEN 1:28

This is the first of the Sacred Ways that God gave to Adam and Eve in the Garden of Eden: to be fruitful and multiply, filling the earth and preserving her (the Earth). This verse is often translated to "subdue" or "dominate" the Earth and everything in it. However, the Hebrew word used is *chevshuha,* which also has the meaning to "preserve." The first mitzvah, was given <u>after</u> the creation of human beings. By this we understand that it is the obligation of **humanity** to care for the elements of the Earth, its animals of the land, sea, and air, and to preserve the Earth. This is the order of Creation. We are to continue the work of Creation, filling the Earth and caring for it. And how are we to do this? We do so by following the rest of the Sacred Ways, which teach us how to live in harmony, how to promote life, and how to enlighten our Earth by bringing the light of our vision into manifestation through our mitzvot, living in Holiness.

In order to insure that there will be a legacy care in the future we are obligated to replace both husband and wife by having (according to the traditions) at least two children. However, if having children will put the woman in danger for her life, then she is not obligated. And if a couple is not able to have children then their work (what they create in the world) is considered their "children" for it will continue on in the world after them.

Aseret HaDibrot / Ten Sacred Imperatives

These Sacred Ways have become known to the Western World as "The Ten Commandments" as translated in the Kings James version of the Bible. The Hebrew, *Aseret HaDibrot,* literally means the ten *(aseret)* sayings *(dibrot)*. We are given these sayings to live from our hearts; they are imperatives for living in harmony with the Divine Energy of God, which promotes and creates Life. If they are spiritual imperatives to direct our thinking, emotions and behavior, then they must be performed from a desire within; we are compelled to fulfill them. They may be thought of as "The First Ten of the Sacred Ways."

There is a pattern to the listing of these first ten of the Sacred Ways given at Mount Sinai by The Holy One. The first four Commandments deal with our individual relationship with The Holy One. The fifth Sacred Way is directed to our relationship with those who brought us into this world and cared for us as parents. The last four Commandments deal with our actions once we are in the world and how to maintain harmonious relationships between ourselves and others.

Volumes have been written on these Ten Imperatives, too vast to cover in this section, however, we will explore some of their unique guidance for wisdom in our lives. The meanings and nuances of each Imperative have been fuel for discussion among those seeking God's purposes for thousands of years. Here I will briefly describe the basic tenet, a seminal thought for further consideration and application in your life.

"The Ten Commandments"

1. I am YHVH your God Who brought you out of Egypt, the house of bondage. This seems to be God's calling card to The Covenant People. It reminds us of the purpose for which we were brought out of Egypt – to meet with our God in the Wilderness. This is our personal and communal life purpose – to come out of that which holds us in bondage, and meet with The Infinite in the Finite World.

The world can feel like a wilderness when we feel separated from the imminent Presence of the Holy One. We meet with God in the wilderness of the physical world as we see The Divine in the environment, in Creation and in each other. We meet with God in the Wilderness when we see the Divine within our own Being. It is then that we come into the same experience of Awe as when we have a transcending experience in prayer or meditation of The Oneness. In the experience of Oneness, even if only for a nanosecond, our consciousness opens to the truth that everything is all wrapped up in and part of God – and God is everything. This first of the Ten Imperatives is more of an invitation than an imperative. It is an invitation to enter a dialogue with The Holy One about the meaning of existence and life. It is the first premise by which we view the rest of the nine; for if we accept this first one as a lifetime goal to explore, then as we read further we find out how to meet with The Holy Infinite One Who brings us out of our bondage to meet with us in this lifetime, in this finite world.

2. You shall have no other Gods besides me. God is Mystery. God is Oneness itself. In the mystery of Oneness, if all is within

God, then to hold any <u>one</u> created thing as God would limit God in our consciousness. We see the Divine Spirit within trees, mountains, the skies, but we reserve the concept of God for the Infinite Mystery which is including, but beyond all we can know with the human mind.

3. You shall not carry the name YHVH in vain. This Sacred Way is often mistranslated as "<u>take</u> the name **YHVH** in vain" instead of "<u>carry</u>". The word in dispute is the key Hebrew word *tisa*, which comes from the root *nisa*, which means "to lift, to carry, bear, sustain, to endure, to take away, to receive, to forgive, to destroy and even to marry". From this list you can get a deeper understanding of what it means to say **YHVH** is your God, and to carry that name. **YHVH** is a powerful name to bear. To carry it is to marry it, sustain it, bear it before the world and creatures of the Heavenly Dimensions and to endure with it. To bear that name means to receive it and take it away with you wherever you go in life. To carry this name is to live the Sacred Ways that bring harmony into this world through our actions. As the saying goes, "If you are going to talk the talk, you must walk the walk."

4. Remember the Sabbath day and keep it holy. This Sacred Way is so simple, yet it takes enormous discipline to give ourselves this gift of one 24- hour period of rest for reflection and renewal every week. The Sabbath is our time of intimacy with "Papa" God, so to speak. Shabbat is a time when we stop the "doing" of the six-day work week and enter the blissful Sabbath day of just "Being". We don't have to **do** anything, just **be**. In so doing we are able to renew our true sense of Self, take time to reconnect our most important relationships, and revitalize our Spirits. Shabbat gives us time to integrate the "doing" of the week that we may be able to bring balance back to our lives.

Shabbat is the seventh day of the week. It is taken from the story of Creation in the first chapter of Genesis. For six periods of creation God was "doing", emanating the universe and the creatures of it. But, the work of creation was not finished until the seventh period of creation when God ceased from creating anything new and "rested". This period of creation allowed all that was created to blend together, integrate and come into full manifestation. You can compare this process to that of making a delicious spaghetti dinner.

When you "make spaghetti" you prepare the spaghetti noodles and the sauce in stages. You sauté the ingredients of the sauce in olive oil, onions, garlic, peppers, mushrooms in stages, each ingredient added at just the right moment. The sauce simmers for a long time, and then you serve it for dinner. After dinner you put the leftovers into the refrigerator for another meal. The next night you retrieve the spaghetti sauce from the refrigerator, make fresh noodles, reheat the sauce and enjoy a second meal. Only this time there is something a little different about the taste of the sauce. It may have tasted good the first night, however, after the ingredients have had 24 hours to sit together they blend their essences and the sauce now has a unique flavor that can only come from aging. It has had time to integrate and to create a new flavor altogether. The Sabbath is like a good spaghetti sauce the second night. The Sabbath gives you time to integrate all of the events and "doing" of the previous week. After Shabbat you are able to enter into the new week from a fresh perspective with a bright new flavor.

So how can you bring this special time into your week? Outside of Israel we must "make" Shabbat. We must make room for it in our busy week. In Jerusalem you do not have to "make" Shabbat, for

Shabbat simply happens. At noon on Friday the children get out of school to prepare with their families for Shabbat. By afternoon there is a flurry of activity at the grocers and stores, for everyone is buying their foods in preparation for their Shabbat dinner guests before the stores close, for they close early on Friday afternoon for Shabbat, not to open again until after sundown Saturday night. Families gather for Shabbat and friends are invited over to enjoy a day of peace and relaxation together. In Jerusalem just before sunset you may hear the sound of the *Shofar* (ram's horn) or Shabbat siren calling to everyone "Shabbat approaches – make ready!" By evening all the stores are closed, the cars and buses are still, families and friends are gathered together to greet Shabbat in their homes, the candles are lit and a gentle hush settles over the City of Gold, Jerusalem. The country is in Shabbat.

Outside of Israel Saturday is filled with activities, bustling malls, noise and traffic. So, we make Shabbat. It is a time for reconnecting with God in prayer, meditation and reflection. It is a time for re-Jew-vinating your Soul in the Hebrew Sacred Path, getting back to who you are on a Soul level, regaining your sense of your infinite value. It is a time for reconnecting with your friends and family members; having the time to look a little more deeply into the eyes of your beloved. On *Shabbat*, there is even a double blessing for making love on this special day. Why? Because uniting the physical bodies of two Souls through love symbolizes and manifests here on earth the Holy Union of The Creator One, the Source of All Life (masculine) with the *Shekhinah*, the feminine aspect of God's Presence in the world. United, these two aspects bring us into consciousness of **YHVH**, the power beyond all gender, naming and knowing.

When we celebrate the Sabbath the tradition says we bring *Olam HaBah*, the "World to Come" to earth for 24 hours. Selah, pause and meditate upon this – next Shabbat! Shabbat is your special day with your blessed and intimate Friend, God, The Eternal, your Self, and your loved ones in rest. The Divine Light in which you dwell on Shabbat is the Divine Light by which you will walk in the week ahead. Don't cheat yourself out of it! This too, is your Hebrew Heritage.

5. Honor your father and mother. The spirit of this mitzvah is that we honor our parents and their parents, and their parents and their parents and so on until we realize that this Sacred Way is saying "Honor your Ancestors with whom you came out of Ur of Chaldees in covenant with The Holy One, and out of the bondage of Egypt and with whom you stood at Mount Sinai, making a sacred covenant with God there." See the Divine in the ones who pass on to you physical Being, that you might bring Divine Light into this world through your life. The lives of your parents are the portals through which you came into this world. Honor that passage and those who were co-creators with God to make you possible.

Some people are raised by nurturing parents who honor their children. These are children who grow up to honor their parents for they have learned how to honor others at home. Others are raised by parents who have not learned how to honor themselves; therefore, they do not know how to honor their children or others. These children must experience being honored elsewhere. Sometimes a grandparent is the one who gives them this experience. Parents cannot teach their children what they themselves do not know. However, the experience of honoring can be learned from many sources.

This fifth Sacred Way is to honor the parent; however, honoring them does not mean having to agree with them or even like them. It simply says to see the Divine Spark of Life in their eyes and honor it. When you are truly filled with a sense of your own Infinite Value, and secure in your autonomy, you are able to let down the walls that block you from letting your parents be who they are and honoring them. By seeing the Divine in others, we are able to love them in peace. This is said in less than one minute, but it sometimes takes a lifetime to learn how to do.

A mystical and symbolic understanding of Father is "The Source of Life" and Mother is the Shekhinah, the feminine aspect of God, the Presence of God in this Dimension. This opens to us a deeper understanding of what it means to honor the parents. This Imperative teaches us to honor the Source of this world and The Divine Presence in this world as parents of all that is. The male and female energy is to be honored as life-giving. Male and female suggest wholeness. This wholeness is within each of us. The mystics say that first we must unite male and female within before we can unite it between us. The prerequisite for marriage in mystical terms is to gain the ability to access the male and female from within ourselves and then we will live in peace as husband and wife, male and female between us. Honoring that process is honoring the celestial Mother and the Father. Honoring that process leads us into the deeper truth of the nature of life as balance, wholeness and integration of the opposites of this world. We honor the opposites, the Mother and the Father, the parent and the child, the mature and the new growth. It is all necessary for existence. We honor the passageway of the opposites who create the portals of life.

6. **Do not murder.** Notice that the word used in this sixth Sacred Way is not "kill," but the Hebrew word, רצח "*retzah*" for "murder." The distinction lies in the intentionality of the act. To kill means

to cause life to cease, to destroy life. To murder is to kill with aforethought of malice. There are several levels of murder that can be committed against a person.

Murder on the physical level is obvious in its effect. However, the oral tradition teaches us that to publicly embarrass someone is also considered murder. It is considered to be "character assassination" and carries the consequences of destroying the person's life in the community. Therefore, even gossip is considered "murdering" another person.

When a person saves someone's life it is considered to be the same as saving of a whole world; for the person has also saved the lives of the descendants of that person. In like manner, if a person murders another it is considered that they have murdered a whole world, for the person murdered will not live to give life to his or her descendants.

Has anyone ever murdered your dream, or vision? Have you ever murdered another person's dream? If we speak words of condemnation against someone's dream until we have destroyed the life of it altogether, we are "murdering" the potential of that person's future. Their Soul may have come into the world to fulfill the good that dream brings to the world. We cannot judge the vision or dream of others. We cannot speak words of death to it regardless of whether we like the dream or believe in it or not.

It is particularly important for us not to destroy other peoples lives with our tongue, with aforethought of malice, for our words are as mighty as a sword to snuff out life. To spread malicious words about someone with our tongue is called *lashone harah* the "evil tongue". We have only to have it done to us to know the devastating effect it can have. A positive statement of this Sacred Way is: "Promote life and do everything to support it by your deeds and your words."

7. Do not commit adultery. Sexual relations are considered a holy act in the Hebrew tradition; therefore, it must carry the kavvenah, intentionality of honesty. Marriage in the Hebrew culture includes a spiritual covenant, the commitment of two Souls bonded as husband and wife. To engage in sexual bonds with someone else dishonors this covenant.

In Biblical times men were allowed to have more than one wife. Monogamy has since become the tradition. To step outside of that covenant by having an intimate relationship with another person destroys the honesty and integrity of the covenant. The covenant is broken. Further, this breach of covenant also affects the peace of the community.

It is said that 40 days before a baby is born a voice rings out in the Heavens that says, "The son of so-and-so will marry the daughter of so-and-so." Thus the "soul-mate" of a person is known in the Heavenly Realms even before birth. The marriage covenant is entered into by the Souls before they are born into human bodies. This covenant is sacred.

However, in the course of human events, it sometimes happens that a person who is in a covenant will violate (or desire to violate) the sacred bond of that covenant to be with someone else. To violate that bond is to impact the spiritual "body" of both the ones in the adulterous relationship and their covenant partner(s). While the ideal is that the marriage covenant is to serve the partners for a lifetime, there are times the covenant is to be broken. If so, there is a way to dissolve the covenant vows while maintaining the spiritual integrity of the partners. In order for married partners to be spiritually free from the vows taken in their marriage covenant, they must go through a spiritual ritual of the husband giving the wife a *get*, a Hebrew divorce. This ritual "cuts" all bonds between the husband and wife in all dimensions for all time. The two people are then free to go in their separate ways and enter a bonding covenant with someone else, if they so choose, both spiritually and physically. This is a powerful ritual that serves the human condition.

The effects of adultery cannot only destroy the harmony of a family, but it also impacts the community. It carries consequences of disharmony and destruction in the spiritual lives of all involved.

A positive statement of this Sacred Way might be: Honor your Self and your covenant partner with fidelity.

8. Do not steal. To take something of someone else's is to trespass their "energy boundaries" their sacred ground. As with all of the Sacred Ways this is understood to apply to all of the Four Worlds within and between us. We are not to steal another person's possessions of the physical world – things; we are not to steal from the world of their heart – dreams, hopes, feelings; we are not to steal from their mental world – ideas (from which we get the laws of copyright); we are not to steal from their spiritual world – their sacred vision, their sacred callings.

This Sacred Way calls us to a high obligation in community; that even if objects, or ideas are available, we are not to take and use them as if they are our own.

How can a person steal another person's spiritual vision? If God gives you a vision, and someone says it is "improper" or judges it as "not of God" and you abandon your vision, then you are giving that person your vision and greater authority in your life then you give God. If this is true of adults, then *al ahat cama v'cama*, "how much more so" for the children! There is a great responsibility upon us as adults to guide our children carefully, teaching them to hear and to confirm what they are hearing from the "still small voice" the sacred Voice of the Divine within them, lest we steal their "vision" before it blooms. To do this, we must be attuned to the "still small voice" within our own Being. Modeling this attunement by our own behavior is the greatest teacher to our children.

When we steal, we are denying the truth of the Oneness of God; for why would we steal from ourselves?

A positive statement of this Sacred Way is: Acknowledge and honor to whom something has been given.

9. Do not bear false witness. This Sacred Way is at the heart of our kavennah, our intentionality. Lying destroys communities, breaks down relationships and destroys our personal integrity. It denies the Sacred Truth that All is One in God, for it seeks to be hidden in the shadows of "untruth" as if it is separate. It is only to be revealed in the Light, in the world to come.

A positive statement of this Sacred Way is: Honor your words with the power of Truth.

10. You shall not covet ... for it leads to breaking any or all of the other Sacred Ways. To desire what is in someone else's given pathway may lead us to (9) lie, (8) steal, (7) commit adultery, (6) murder, and in so doing we dishonor our (5) parents (our ancestry), (4) carry the name of our God, **YHVH** in vain. We may not celebrate (3) Shabbat as a day for rest and reflection if we do not want to be confronted with ourselves before The Holy One. This indicates that our desire for something of someone else's has become a (2) "God" to us higher than The Holy One. Here we find ourselves back in the bondage of our own making, which denies that the Holy One, has brought us out of (1) Egypt (that which enslaves us). The last of the Aseret HaDibrot, the Ten

Sacred Ways is a key to the first nine, and the first nine will keep us from the tenth. The first is in the last, and the last, the first.

A positive statement of this ninth Sacred Way is: Thank God for the blessings bestowed upon others and yourself, for all things are in Divine Order.

These ten Sacred Ways bring harmony within us in spirit, mind, heart and body. They bring harmony between us and our world, and between us and our consciousness of God. They open our consciousness to the sacredness of all life and to our obligation to care for it; for within the finite of the world is hidden The Infinite. We continue now with more of the Sacred Ways given to us to bring harmony to us and to our world.

Bal Tashkit / **Not Harming The Earth**

Our obligation to the earth goes back as far as the dawn of human existence. In Gen. 1:15, the Creator put the human being in the Garden of Eden to "serve her and watch over her." The earth is part of the Oneness of All, as are we; therefore, we keep guard over how we live on the Earth, what happens to the Earth, and how to honor all of life as sacred.

There is a *Midrash* (story handed down in the oral traditions) gives us further information about the instructions the Creator gave Adam in the Garden of Eden. God was walking with Adam in the Garden pointing out the wonders of Creation. "Take care not to destroy this," God said, "for should you destroy it, there is none to come after you to repair it." From this we learn that the future of the Earth is in the hands of humanity. However we interact with our planet is how we will be supported by our planet to sustain life.

As a last thought, the first name given for humanity is *Adam*. It is derived and related to the Hebrew word for earth, the ground, which is *adamah*. The color red is *adom* relating to the red of the Earth's clay. It is easy to see from these related words that we are intrinsically related to the Earth in our very elemental makeup. We are eternal Souls housed in the elements of this planet, our body. We are taught in this Sacred Way not to harm the Earth, but to care for it, for it is part of our existence in this world.

Sh'mitah V'Yovel / Observing The Sabbatical Year

Among the ways to care for the Earth and live in harmony with it is the concept of letting the Earth rest every seventh and fiftieth year. Today, our agriculturists and farmers know that the land needs a time of rest to replenish its richness in nutrients in order to grow healthy crops.

This concept can be expanded, however, to anything having to do with Life and growing things. What in your life supports your Life? How do you give it rest? If the Earth needs a rest every seventh year and every fiftieth year how much more so do we human beings need a time of rest to reflect, integrate and replenish ourselves to promote Life during that time?

In preparation for the resting year, *sh'mitah*, God provides an extra abundance in the crops to feed the people, not only for one year, but for three years. The crop fed the people the year before the sabbatical year, the year during the sabbatical year, and then the next year while the new crop was growing and they were waiting for ripening and harvest season. During the sabbatical years the workers were free to study, rest, and renew their lives. It was a time to reconnect with family and rest from the labors of the growing season. Mother Earth would also yield up "volunteer" plants from the previous year's plantings, which they could use for their own purposes. But, they were relieved of planting and selling the harvest during the sabbatical year. Keeping this Sacred Way took trust in God from the people. That trust was planted within their hearts during the forty-year experience in the Wilderness after leaving Egypt. They ate *manna*, a miraculous sustenance given by God during each night. As they followed the Sacred Way of gathering it they had food continually.

All week manna would appear overnight on the ground. They were told to gather it for that day's sustenance only. (It is said that it was white like hoarfrost and tasted like sweet almond cakes.) If they tried to gather more than one day's worth during the week to avoid having to gather it the next day, it would turn to worms over night. The exception was on Friday when they were instructed to gather two days' worth in order not to gather (work) on the Sabbath, the seventh day. The manna remained fresh on Shabbat as if it was newly gathered. God provided for the time when they were to rest. In the same way, the year of resting the earth when there would be no crops was provided for during the year previous to the sabbatical year.

Have you ever had a time in your business when you were so busy you could hardly keep up with the demand? Then you might experience other times when there is a lull. You might begin to watch for a pattern of an abundance being given before a lull. It is an indication to you that you are being given a "retreat" time or time to rest. When you begin to trust God for the supply you need then you relieve yourself of worry during the "down' times, knowing your needs will be met in the divine timing of God.

Observing the sabbatical year is a way of expanding our

observance of Shabbat each week. Just as we give Sabbath time to ourselves to renew, rejuvenate and revitalize, we are told to give our land a rest, a Sabbath to renew the life it carries.

Pikuah Nefesh / **Preservation of Life**

The Sacred Ways ingeniously teach us guidelines that we can apply to the many unique situations in which we find ourselves in life. The mitzvot give us curbs, like the sides of a road, between which we can find our sacred pathway of Life. The concept of *Pikuah Nefesh*, the Preservation of Life, is an example of this safety curbing. On the one hand we do everything possible to preserve life. For example, if you are ill and there is a medicine which will promote your healing you are obligated to take it in order to preserve your life. Likewise, if someone in your town is held for ransom the community must come up with the ransom money to gain the captive's freedom. This idea of Pikuah Nefesh, preserving one's life, is a curb on one side of the road.

But this must be kept in balance, for there are times in life when we must consider the other issues. The curb on the other side of the path from Pikuakh Nefesh, which helps us keep balance, is the concept of the *Goses*. A Goses is a person who is within 72 hours (meaning within the process) of dying which is considered their Soul's sacred journey of transcending the physical being and returning to The Source of Life. We are obligated not to do anything to disturb this process or prolong it (holding onto them by trying to heal or cure them). We are not even to move their pillow if this will disturb them and detain them on their sacred journey. The truth that Pikuakh Nefesh and the Goses teaches is that when we are in life we are to live it fully; but when it is time to die, we are to do so in peace. It teaches us that birthing and dying are all life.

Tza'ar Ba'alei Hayyim / Prevention Of Cruelty To Animals

While the Hebrew traditions teach us that we are obligated to see to the just and compassionate treatment of all beings, animals included, *Tza'ar Ba'alei Hayyim* relates directly to caring for the life of animals. The Sacred Imperatives do not teach animals rights, but teach us that we are obligated. In a world based upon the **rights** of animals, the animal is in danger, for it cannot speak for itself and must depend upon the voice of a human being in order to be heard. How much safer it is for animals to live in a world filled with people who feel obligated before God to care for them? This is Tza'ar Ba'alei Hayyim, our obligation to prevent cruelty to animals and care for them with understanding and compassion.

For an example of this sensitivity to the life of an animal consider the sacred way that teaches us that we must feed and water our animals before we eat. Our animals (pets and domestic workers) cannot help themselves to dinner like wild animals, so we must fulfill their needs before we attend to our own.

Likewise, when we take the life of an animal for our sustenance, we are to do so in a way that causes the least amount of pain. This is why the neck vein must be cut with a knife of specified sharpness. Any animal that has died any other way may not be used. This sacred way prohibits taking an animal's life by violent means. By this Sacred Imperative we are sensitized to the life and suffering of animals. We are to promote their life and their comfort in life.

Kashrut / Ethical Eating

Rabbi Rami Shapiro gives the following concise definition for this Sacred Way:

> "A way of sustaining one's life without harming the natural environment or exploiting the labor or lives of other sentient beings."
>
> TWO ESSAYS, PG. 8

The Torah lists foods that were given to Adam to eat from the very beginning. These foods are listed in Gen. 1:29-31. The list does not include the eating of flesh, whether mammal, fowl or fish. However, after the flood, when a full growing season was necessary before crops would be available, the concession to eating meat was given. God gave specific instructions as to what meat could be used and how the life of the animal was to be taken. This made the meat *kosher*. The word kosher has many meanings: ritually fit, honest, wholesome, fitness, opportunity, and legitimacy. We understand "wholesome" to mean being in harmony with the Divine Energy of the Whole. We our own energy within us by what we put into our bodies.

The Torah teaches us not to "boil a kid in its mother's milk." To do so mixes the spirit of Death (the meat of the baby goat) with the spirit of Life (the milk of the mother goat, meant to give life to the kid and help the baby goat grow). This mixture of life and death is not in harmony together and will bring disharmony into one's body. This Sacred Way was given at a time when the human consciousness of the suffering of animals was so low that it was not uncommon for a person to cut off only the leg of a lamb (or goat) that would be needed for food and leave the animal alive, thereby preserving the majority of the rest of the meat (there was no refrigeration or freezing of meat). This is a repugnant and heinous idea to us today, precisely because we have had our consciousness raised by Torah teaching us to be sensitive to the life and suffering of all sentient beings.

If we are to kill an animal for its meat we are to do so in a manner that causes it the least amount of pain. The guidelines of *kashrut* (kosher methods) demands an extremely sharp knife be used to cut the jugular vein, rendering the animal unconscious very quickly. The meat must then be cleared of all blood before it coagulates in the veins and arteries. Meat taken in any other way is considered *traf*, which literally means "torn." Therefore, meat taken in hunting, an animal shot with a bow or rifle or from an animal found dead, is considered unfit for eating; the meat is traf, it is torn – a concept of violence – and is not ritually fit for use in the human being.

Many Kabbalists were and are vegetarians, preferring to eat according to the original intent for human beings as given in Genesis.

> Behold, I have given you every herb bearing seed, which is upon the face of all the earth, and every tree, on which is the fruit seed; to you it shall be for food. And to every beast of the earth and every bird of the air, and to everything that creeps on the earth, wherein there is life. I have given every green herb for food; and it was so.
>
> GENESIS 1:29

As you can see, there was no meat eaten in the original food chain. Mystics recognized that the energy of everything intended for food should be of a vibrational level to promote life within us, that we may use our energy to do the Sacred Ways. In that way, we actually raise the level of energy of our food, the vegetables, fruit, nuts, grains, herbs and even any meat that we eat to a higher level of energy through our Sacred Acts done with their energy and ours.

A *shohet* (one who does the ritual slaughter of animals) who adheres to Kabbalistic practices would say a prayer to the Soul of the animal before the animal is slaughtered. The shohet would say prayers honoring the animal, asking forgiveness from the animal for taking their life and thanking them for the use of their body to give life to human beings. When the meat of this animal is eaten, and it gives the human being strength to do a mitzvah, one of the Sacred Ways, then the life of the animal is raised also, for they, too, have sacrificed for the doing of the Sacred Way.

How can we expand the concept of eating that which is wholesome today? Are additives such as food coloring, artificial flavors, MSG, and aspartame kosher, wholesome on an energy level? Do genetically engineered foods (apples that contain a rat gene) maintain their pure energy for use in our human energy system? The Sacred Ways of kosher teach us to be responsible consumers, giving us guidelines to help us consume our food/fuel in a way that is to our highest good, while maintaining harmony with the world around us. Keeping kosher means we become conscious of what we consume, how we consume and how our consumption affects the world.

G'milut Hesed / Loving Acts of Kindness

The *G'milut Hesed*, Loving Acts of Kindness are a special category of Sacred Ways, in that they are altruistic acts, done without expectation of reward or for any personal gain. The act of visiting the sick would be one of these special Sacred Ways. When we perform *g'milut khassidim* (plural) we are often unaware that we have done anything special, for the nature of this sacred way is so pure and flows so naturally from a loving heart that it would seem that we could have done nothing else. This is when we are doing loving acts of kindness.

Bikur Holim / Visiting The Sick

This Sacred Way is considered to be one of life and death. Consider the following story from our Oral Tradition, the Talmud:

> "Rabbi Helbo fell sick. No one visited him. Rabbi Kahana rebuked the sages: "Did it not happen once, that one of Rabbi Akiva's disciples fell sick and the sages did not visit him? So Rabbi Akiva himself visited him, and because he had the floor swept and washed, the sick man recovered. 'My Master (Rabbi),' the sick man said to Akiva, 'you have revived me.' Rabbi Akiva went out and taught, 'He who does not visit the sick is like a shedder of blood.'"
>
> NEDARIM 39B-40A

Visiting one who is sick is a Sacred Way of supporting each other by our presence. We help their healing process by standing beside them during their time of difficulty or illness, showing our love and compassion. This positive and supportive presence promotes healing on many levels; mental, emotional and spiritual, which aides the physical healing process, manifesting wholeness on the higher levels. At the same time that we ourselves extend our compassion, we draw compassion unto ourselves and experience healing within our own lives. We do not visit the sick with self healing as the goal, for then our goal is self gain, not truly extending compassion. However, receiving healing and compassion is a consequence of giving of the same. It is as if when we draw down compassion from the higher realms through ourselves to others, some of it sticks to us through grace. It is a beautiful mystery of the Sacred Ways.

When we visit the sick we are told to enter the room cheerfully, not allowing shock to be shown on our face at the condition of the patient, for the ill monitor others for any hint of the danger their life may be in. A visit always includes a prayer for the sick that The Holy One may extend a complete healing, or *refuah sheleimah*. This includes all of the four worlds within the person, not only their physical, but their emotional, mental and spiritual body and well-being. It is not expedient to tell an ill person bad news, of violence in the community or the death or illness of a loved one, for this extra burden of worry may rob them of the energy they need for their own healing. "Leave your *tzuras* (troubles) at the doorway of the room of the sick one."

Bikur Holim is such a strong Sacred Imperative that one is permitted to travel to great distance on Shabbat (travel on Shabbat is limited to that which does not become "work") to visit a sick loved one.

In the story of the three angels who visited Abraham (Genesis) they were not only delivering their messages from The Holy One (the job of angels), but we are taught that by their presence God visited Abraham during his time of healing from circumcision, as he was sitting in the sun at the opening of his tent. See Gen. 18:1. In imitation of God, so we too visit one another at the time of illness.

To visit the sick is to open ourselves to the possibility of bringing healing. To bring healing we restore our world to wholeness. This is the work of Holiness.

Love Your Neighbor As Yourself

LEVITICUS 19:18

This is another seminal Sacred Way that could change our world and the physical nature of this planet if only we could grasp it from our souls and manifest it fully into our consciousness and behavior. To truly understand this Commandment we must explore who we are as human beings. One of the basic traditional prayers, the Shema, gives us a place to start.

The Shema (Hear O Israel, The Holy One is our God, The Holy One is Oneness itself), confirms to us that all that exists is one in The Holy One. The Hebrew tradition teaches that all of Creation is an emanation of The Infinite One. The Life force of The Infinite One goes through many Dimensions until it comes into physicality. If the Creator (God) is Infinite, then any fraction of Infinity (Creation) is still Infinity. When we begin to understand ourselves as being part of that Divine Infinity, then we begin to have awe for our own infinite value as sacred, both body and Soul. If The Infinite is emanating Divine Love, then we have Divine Love flowing through us, we are love. We are made of "God stuff" and we have everything we need within us to deal with Life. When we open our consciousness to this deep understanding we begin to have awe of The Holy One in our own physical and spiritual form – a human being – that which we see in the image in the mirror and that which we see looking back at us. It is all God. It is then that we are able to see God in others and in all of Creation – all that exists.

When we are in awe of our own being as miraculously and wondrously made as the Psalmist says, then we are able to be in awe of the miracle and wonder of others. We recognize that love is already flowing through us for that is the nature of our existence and we are able to consciously tap into that Divine Love – love for The Holy One, love for ourselves and love for others. This Sacred Way reminds us to have a daily consciousness of the flow of that Divine Love and embrace it.

There was a rabbi from Nazareth who is a master of that Love. He knew that the Mitzvot, the Sacred Ways, teach how to stay in that mind set of awe, and to understand through the doing and thereby to live a life of Holiness. After his Sermon on the Mount he taught his listeners about Holiness:

> "Whoever then breaks or does away with or relaxes one of the
> least of these Sacred Ways and teaches other to do so shall
> be called least in the kingdom of heaven; but he who practices
> them and teaches others to do so shall be called great in the
> kingdom of heaven.
>
> MATT. 5:14-19

Jesus taught the Jewish tradition that what we do in our life and the Holiness to which we aspire affects our Soul as it ascends back into the Source of All Life in its "nearness" or proximity to The Source, The Holy One. Our desire and love of God expressed here enables us to be ever closer to our God when we are no longer embodied and have returned to Spirit form.

> "And He said to him, "Why do you ask me about the perfectly
> and essentially good? One only there is Who is good —
> perfectly and essentially; God. If you would enter into the Life

(Holiness) you must continually keep the Sacred Ways."

MATT. 19:17

Here the Rabbi is playing with words and concepts, for, as the Shema teaches us, God is the Oneness of all. In Genesis, after the completion of each of the six periods of creation God pronounced that which was emanated to be "good". So how can there be an essential good? It is all God. However, as we move according to the Sacred Ways in this Dimension, we carry a higher Light, and open our consciousness to The Holy One, Source of All Light. Therein, we are in "closer" communion with The One.

As the text in Matthew continues, after these words the person inquiring of the Teacher asks which Sacred Ways (for he understands Jesus to be speaking of the Hebrew mitzvot) are the ones needed, and Jesus answered him:

"Honor your father and your mother, and, You shall love your neighbor as yourself.

MATT. 19:19

Refer back to number five of the Ten Commandments earlier in this chapter to gain fresh insight on honoring your father and mother, the first part of what Jesus replied. Now link that concept to the ideas of how we can only love others in the same way as we love ourselves, ideally being in awe of their (our) unique and infinite value.

The man asking the question does not understand that Jesus is also speaking in mystical language; Father referring to "God, The Source in the Heavenly Realms" and Mother as "The Shekhinah, the Presence of God within this World". Jesus is asking him to embrace the Divine Union which produces Life, i.e. the union and indwelling of the **spirit** with the **physical**.

Still refusing to hear what Jesus was telling him, the inquirer pressed Jesus further. At that Jesus addressed the man's state of mind (and heart). He tells him that he must sell everything (give over his life) and follow him (Jesus), learning from him how to live life through the doing as well as the study. Remember, "through the doing comes the understanding." By instructing the man to sell everything Jesus challenged the man to choose which is more important to him, obtaining new wisdom, or keeping his current possessions.

In order to gain new wisdom all of us must hold loosely in our hands the wisdom we possess, for the new Light of wisdom may go beyond our current knowledge, either altering it or changing its boundaries in order to illumine the unknown in our minds. Potential can only become actualized in the fertile field of an open mind. Jesus was asking the man to let go of what he "possessed" and to open his mind, heart and life to the wisdom Jesus was teaching him.

Jesus was teaching the Torah, preaching the Torah, studying with his followers the heritage of the Torah, the "Light Bearer." In the Hebrew tradition "study" is a form of worship. Study encompasses all discussions of the Torah, the teachings. But, the main way of studying the spiritual and hidden meanings of the Torah, the Light Bearer was in the "doing" of it. This is why Jesus says "follow me," (and learn from my actions).

Jesus said, "You are the Light of the world" (Matt. 5:14). Through living the wisdom of Torah, you come to know the awe of that statement down in your Soul and become able to say of yourself, "I am the Light of the world." It is a statement that brings with it a sense of awe. And in living from your Light you are following the Rabbi of Nazareth, a master of Love.

Jesus also brought this teaching together for his disciples in his intimate farewell talk with them when he gives them instructions to live by after his death:

> I have loved you [just] as the Father has loved me; abide in my love – continue in His love with me.
>
> JOHN 15:9, THE AMPLIFIED BIBLE

In order to love others as you love yourself, you must first come to a profound awakening to the awe of your own Being as an emanation of God. From that awakening you will find an infinite fountain of love flowing from your heart. Then, from that infinite flow of love in your heart you will unconditionally love others. God creates you through the Divine flow of Love, and God loves others through your Life.

2

Sacred Practices for Miraculous Living

The Power of Ritual

The spiritual practices, rituals and ancient symbols of your Hebrew heritage imply deep meanings that are hidden or often only understood through the experience of the practice or using the symbol. Some of these practices have been carried into Christian tradition and may also carry additional meanings attached to them by the church. In other instances some of these practices may be very new to you. I invite you to open your experience to the sacred practices of your inheritance. Embrace the gifts these new practices may hold for you.

As you read about the *shofar* (Ram's Horn), the *mikveh* (immersion) or the kindling of candles on Shabbat you may feel there is a familiarity with these sacred practices, even though you have not experienced them in your lifetime. It may be that your Soul "remembers" in Sacred Memory, the collective of "all time" and "all space." The spiritual practices are faint memories of "home" in the Heavenly places which your Soul aspires to return

47

to after this lifetime. When you engage in the sacred practices you not only ascend to that most holy consciousness, but you bring that consciousness back into this world through your actions of the practices. It is a way to bring "Heaven on Earth". It is also a way to reveal Heaven hidden here on Earth. After exploring these sacred practices write in your journal which practices are your favorite ones for bridging the Dimensions in your life.

Rituals within the Hebrew traditions are spiritual practices that bring change into our world. Through performing a ritual we convert a spiritual power or energy into an action that that gives it effect in the physical world. The physical world is the world of action.

The physical world is called the World of Action because everything in this world is in motion. Our scientists explain how even the chair in which you sit is actually made of tiny particles, molecules and atoms, which are in rapid and constant motion. In order for something of spirit to exist in this physical world we must turn it into an action. A ritual is an action that we have made sacred by saying a blessing before doing it, thereby setting our intention. By setting our intention and doing the action we translate that spiritual intention into a reality in the physical world, creating change. A bride and groom set their intentions at the wedding ceremony, and turn their intention of covenant into an action with the giving of a ring, the symbol for their intentions. At the birth of a child we consecrate its life to the Sacred Light of Torah, and turn that intention into an action by giving the baby a Hebrew name. We welcome and begin the spiritual day of Shabbat by our actions when we kindle the Shabbat candles. As you read about the rituals in this chapter see if you can identify the intention brought into this world through action.

Rituals are real and do commit change in this world, but they are truly only as powerful as the sacred intentions with which we do them.

Shofar – Ram's Horn
The "Wake-up Call of the Soul"

> And Moses brought the people out of the camp to meet with God; and they stood at the foot of the mountain. And Mount Sinai smoked in every part, because The Holy One descended upon it in fire: and the smoke of it ascended like the smoke of a furnace, and the whole mountain quaked greatly. And then the voice of the shofar sounded louder and louder; Moses speaks and The Holy One answers him by a Voice.
>
> EXODUS 19:17-19

The *shofar*, or ram's horn, is known as the "wake up call of the Soul." Truly, hearing the sound of the Shofar stirs the heart and awakens the spirit to ancient memory. The clear, clean notes of the shofar still speak to our Souls today, calling our hearts in the direction of our Destiny.

In ancient times the shofar was used in many ways. It was used for assembling the people, as in the story in Judges 3:27, when Ehud is gathering Israel to follow him. The shofar is the signal to gather together the tribes. The shofar is also used to announce a transition, such as at the new moon which marks the new month, the new year on Rosh HaShanah, or when announcing liberty in the Jubilee Year. (Leviticus 25:9).

In Jerusalem before sunset on Friday afternoon, you can hear the sound of the shofar calling across the neighborhoods announcing the coming of Shabbat. It announces that it is time to transition from the business of the work week to the peace and rest of the day set apart for God.

The blowing of the shofar at a funeral announces the transition of the Soul from being embodied as a human being to returning to the Source of All Life, as an eternal Being of Light.

I remember the first time I heard the notes of the shofar before I converted to Judaism. It was the season of Rosh HaShanah, the New Year, and a guest Rabbi came to blow Shofar at our church. As I heard the Rabbi blow a long, piercing blast, I was immediately transported in spirit to Jericho. It was as if I had stepped back in time to the story of Joshua 6:4, the taking of the city of Jericho by Joshua's army. I heard the sound of the seven *shofarot* (plural of shofar), felt the chaos! I saw the people running, the dust rising – choking our throats and lungs – and I heard the thunderous sound of the walls cracking and crashing to the earth. I could feel the ground tremble beneath our feet. I was sitting in a congregation in the twentieth century, yet I was transported in sacred time and sacred space to experience in sacred memory this powerful event. I was taken back on the waves of a voice; the mystical Voice of the shofar, calling my Soul to come home.

The shofar is blown at Rosh HaShanah to announce the transition from one year into the next. (See Numbers 29:1) The shofar calls us to make right any wrongs between us and another person during the ten days between Rosh HaShanah and Yom Kippur. On Yom Kippur, the Day of Atonement, the Day of At-One-ment, all of Israel comes before The Holy One as one people to renew our relationships in Holiness and mend any tears in the fabric of our community. The shofar calls us to this holy work of community.

At the end of the day on Yom Kippur, after all prayers and supplications have been raised and we have all sought God's eternal compassion and love for our world and ourselves, we listen to one long blast of the shofar just as the sun is setting, the time of the closing of the Gates of Heaven. It is a time of transition into renewal. We begin living together as spiritual community renewed in forgiveness of ourselves and of each other, revitalized by our love and the spirit of our Oneness.

In Psalm 98:6 the psalmist urges us to sound our praises with the shofar. By our songs and praises we raise our consciousness, lifting the veils that hide God from our awareness in everyday life. When we sing praises and lift our spirits with words or joy and the sound of the shofar, we are transported to an awareness of The Presence that is with us always.

> And it shall come to pass on that day, that a great shofar shall be blown, and they shall come who were lost in the land of Ashur, and the outcasts in the land of Mitzrayim, and shall worship The Eternal One in the holy mountain at Yerushalyim.
>
> ISAIAH 27:13

In the end times – not at the end of our world – but at the end of this time of the hiddeness of the Divine Light, the shofar will announce the coming of the Messiah. Isaiah 27:13 speaks of the voice of the shofar being heard throughout the Dimensions, calling our Souls from the corners of the earth to the ingathering, the time of the Messianic Age when the Light will abound and all of creation will be enlightened, *"Baruch HaShem"*, which means Blessed be The Holy One! May this time come soon and in our time!

No wonder our Souls leap within us at the voice of the shofar! It was the sound of our redemption in the past and it is the promise of the redemption of our world in the future!

What are the transitional times of your life? When would you like to hear the shofar in your spiritual community and in your rituals? You can find a shofar to purchase in Judaic stores, catalogs or in many places in Israel if you are visiting there. Your shofar becomes a personal instrument as you learn to blow it and play the sounding notes on it. It can even serve as an opening for meditation as you listen to its vibrations echoing in your heart. While hearing it, listen to the words of the "still small voice" within you to hear its messages to you.

May you be blessed in the Life transitions of your Soul and in hearing the Voice of the shofar.

The shofar symbolizes: transition, ingathering, joy, redemption, Messianic Age, and awakening.

Tallit and Tzitzit
Wrapping Yourself in a Prayer Tent

The Holy One spoke to Moses saying, "Speak to the Children of Israel and say to them, 'Make for yourselves tzitzit (fringes) for the corners of your garments, to all generations. And give to the tzitzit, fringes, a thread of tekhelet (indigo blue). And they will be for you gazing fringes (for meditation); and you will see them and remember all the Sacred Ways of The Holy One, and do them. And (when you see them) you will not seek after what your heart feels, or what you see, which has led you astray in the past. Therefore, you will remember and do all my Sacred Ways and those ways will make you Holy. For I AM, your God, which has delivered you from Egypt to be your God. I AM, The Infinite, your God.

NUMBERS 14:37-40

In fulfillment of this mitzvah, or "Sacred Way" given to Moses during the wanderings of the Children of Israel in the desert, we began to wear a *tzitzit*, or fringes, on each of the four corners of our garments. At that time garments were made on a loom, and were, therefore, square or rectangular in shape. The fringes were attached to the "four corners" of the garment. However, as time passed clothing styles changed, and we no longer wore the tunics and the cornered robes of Biblical days. Therefore, we took a rectangular piece of cloth and placed fringes, tzitzit, on the corners, that we could still fulfill the sacred way of wearing the fringes when we pray. When we see the fringes – we remember. But, what are we to remember?

In the Torah (the Five Books of Moses: Genesis, Exodus, Leviticus, Numbers and Deuteronomy) the instructions to wear tzitzit (fringes) comes directly after the story of the 12 witnesses, who were to go into the land of Canaan and see what the conditions were there, for our people had just come out of Egypt, and were ready to enter the Promised Land, (Numbers 13, 14).

This was the first 40-day tour of Israel. Ten of the witnesses came back impressed by the good of the land but their hearts were filled with fear and terror of the people who inhabited the land and the strong fortifications of the walled cities. Two witnesses, Joshua and Caleb, saw the same obstacles, but their hearts remained focused upon the faithfulness of The Holy One to bring them into the land successfully. However, fear from the negative report of the frightened ten men took root in the hearts of the people. Even though two men, Joshua and Caleb came back with joyful and encouraging reports of a land "flowing with milk and honey" the people were swayed in fear. They were afraid and would not trust the words of The Holy One. That entire generation who came out of Egypt, (except for the two who loved God more than they feared humans, Joshua and Caleb) had to pass away before the next generation, born in freedom, free from the mindset of slavery, were able to cross over into the Promised Land.

Directly after that incident in the Torah, in compassion and love, God extended to us a Sacred Way; a way that would help us whenever we see fearful things, to remain focused upon our love and the greater power of The Holy One of Blessing. It is the mitzvah of wearing fringes. One of the purposes of the tzitzit is to be a reminder of God's Promise to deliver us. How do these simple fringes remind us of that higher consciousness?

The Hebrew words used in this text reveal a deeper meaning. Tzitzit comes from a Hebrew root that means "fringe", but it is also the root for the word meaning "to gaze." The concept is more than just a glance and to remember God's ways. It means far more. The tzitzit are to be used as "gazing fringes", in visual meditation. When we enter prayer, we look at the symbolic windings and knots of the fringes and allow our thoughts to quiet while we follow our Soul to the heights of transcendence in the Presence of the Holy One. It is in that place of prayer that our heart is filled with the love and awe of The Holy One, Creator of the Universe, and intimate Friend. No matter how frightening or impossible our situation in life may look to our natural eyes and no matter how fearful our hearts may feel, we are steadied there in the gaze of The Holy One, our Rock. At times in life when something happens that is upsetting to us, we can look at our fringes and we are able to connect with what we experience in prayer; we are re-grounded in the love and awe we experienced there. Our Souls are moved to trust in God.

Some people wear a small tallit, a *tallit katan*, which is worn on the inside of our clothing, while the fringes may hang to the outside as a spiritual reminder of God's loving Presence. This fulfills the Sacred Way at all times in our lives; and the vision of the tzitzit is before us always.

The tallit (prayer shawl) has also been likened to a prayer tent, our *Ohel Moed*, (tent of meeting), a place where we meet with our higher selves and with God. It is our sanctuary, where we commune with God. When I wear my tallit I feel secluded with God and protected beneath the wings of Holy One, surrounded by Divine Light shining there.

Why are we told to add a thread of indigo-blue to the fringe? In the mystical teachings of our sages we are told about the Four Worlds; the World of Spirit, the World of Intellect, the World of Emotion and the physical world of Action. Each world is symbolized by a color. The color blue is symbolic of the World of B'riyah, the World of Intellect; it is the power of thought. When we see the indigo-blue thread, we are reminded to "see" with the higher vision of spirit, rather than what our natural eyes show us in this world. In this way our thoughts are inspired. Some people call this spiritual vision. When we see the thread of blue we are reminded to look further, see deeper, gain the Wisdom of our Inner Guidance, to guide our minds and thoughts to a higher consciousness. Encouraged by enlightened thoughts, our hearts are kept in love and not fear.

When we see the blue thread, we are reminded of the blue of the ocean, the reflection of the blue of the sky, which makes our eyes look up to the Guide of the Cosmos, and to lift our thoughts to the Divine. Even our language in English seems to connect the color blue with thoughts. We have all heard it said, "It came to me out of the blue!" In this way the fringes keep our hearts and eyes from leading us astray by what we see and fear.

The Sacred Way of wearing tzitzit (fringes) on the corners of our garments is actually a spiritual tool given to us to help us keep our eyes on The Holy One and our focus on the Oneness of all life. When we see the fringes we remember God's care and compassion for us and the world.

As a devout Jew and spiritual leader, Jesus, too would have worn tzitzit. Do you remember the story of the woman who touched the hem of Jesus' garment, that she might be healed? (Matthew 9:20, Luke 8:44) She knew that the fringes of his garment carried the power of his prayers and meditations, and that if she could only touch them, she would be made whole. In Mark 6:56, we read that many received healing from this practice of touching the fringes of his garment. They knew the power in the fringes, tzitzit, worn by a holy man.

The Sacred Way of wearing a tallit, prayer shawl with the tzitzit on the corners, is also part of your spiritual heritage. Is this a spiritual practice that you would like to try?

When you put on your tallit, state your intention, your kavennah, by saying a blessing beforehand. The ancient way of doing this is to hold your tallit before your eyes and say the following blessing:

> "Blessed are You, O Holy One, our God, Guide of the Cosmos, Who sanctifies us by Your Sacred Ways, and instructs us to wrap ourselves in tzitzit."

In Hebrew:

> Ba-ruch a-tah Yah, E-lo-hei-nu me-lekh ha-olam, a-sher kid-sha-nu b-mitz-vo-tav v-tzi-va-nu l-hi-ta-tef b-tzi-tzit.

Then put the tallit around your shoulders. Some people like to wear the tallit draped over their heads. Experiment with your tallit and see how Spirit leads you in this practice.

As you put on your tallit, meditate upon entering the Divine Light of The Holy One as the "wings" of the tallit enfold you.

It is natural to wind the fringes, tzitzit, around your fingers as you pray. This too was the habit of the Kabbalists, for in the *Gematria* (Kabbalistic numerology) the number of the windings and knots of the four fringes has the same numerical value as the Hebrew words "*Adonai Echad*," "The Infinite One is Oneness itself." Therefore, when we wind the fringes around our fingers we "bind" the work of our hands in unity with God.

As you wear the fringes, what do you feel? What new spiritual concepts are revealed to you? Enjoy exploring this most personal practice of the Sacred Ways of The Holy One.

The tzitzit symbolize: spiritual focus, Divine Unity, Divine Protection, Divine Guidance, Sacred Ways (mitzvot), B'riyah, the World of Thoughts, prayer, sanctuary.

Today: The Israeli flag is fashioned after the tallit and its thread of blue in the tzitzit. The flag has a white field with a blue stripe across the top and the bottom with a blue Star of David in the center of the white field. Whenever we see our Israeli flag our hearts and eyes are not deceived by fearful sights, but we remember. We remember God's Presence and God's faithful Love.

In Practice

Thousands of years of wearing tzitzit has given us much wisdom on the spiritual meaning of this practice. The following meditation and reflection for setting your intentions before donning your tallit may help you to explore the true meaning of wearing fringes.

Meditation Before Putting on the Tallit

Barchi Nafshi – Bless The Infinite One, O my Soul;
The Eternal One of love, You are very great;
You have donned majesty and splendor;
cloaked in Light as with a garment,
stretching out the Heavens
like a curtain of the Dimensions.

Declaration of Intention When Putting On The Tallit

With the intention of the unification of The Holy One Beyond and the Shekhinah, the feminine Divine Presence in this Dimension, in Awe and in love, to unify The Name in perfect unity, I AM ready to wrap my body in tzitzit, that my Soul and my physical form be wrapped in The Illumination. Just as I cover myself in this world, so may I wrap my Being in the World-To-Come in Infinite Light and Endless Love. Through the Sacred Way of the tzitzit may my Life-Force, Spirit, Soul, and prayer be kept safe from external forces of harm. May this tallit spread its wings over them and uplift them like an eagle rousing her nest, fluttering over her eaglets as she takes them and bears them upon her wings. May my intention be fulfilled with love and in unity with the Sacred Harmony of the Universe. Amen.

Selah (stop and meditation upon this)

Mikveh and T'vilah
Immersion into the Spiritual Birthing Waters of Life

And Aaron and his sons you shall bring to the door of the Tent
of Meeting, and shall wash them with water."

EXODUS 29:4

Aaron and his sons were about to enter the priesthood. They were
changing their status from common labors of life to consecrating
their lives to service in the Temple. They were instructed to prepare
themselves and mark the event by the ritual of *t'vilah*, immersion
in water. The ritual washing of the body for purification is fulfilled
by immersing oneself in a *mikveh*, a spring or pool, three times,
allowing the water to touch every part of the body with each
immersion. According to our traditions, this ritual has been used
throughout the millennia for purposes of purification and to mark
the transitions of our life since the times of Abraham.

Purification in this sense, however, does not mean to cleanse
one from filth, but relates to a change in status. Purification, therefore, means to ascend or change our spiritual status, rather than
to physically cleanse our body. There are many times of transition
in our lives when this ritual is performed. The spiritual meanings
abound as this is an intimate and powerful spiritual practice that
binds the human heart to God in *d'vekut* – "sticking" to God.

The Hebrew word mikveh means "a collection of water, a
pool." The mikveh is that place, whether a spring, river, or pool,
which has been set aside for the sacred purpose of t'vilah, ritual
immersion for purification. The verb means "to collect, to gather
(as in the waters)." There are specific times in our lives when we
are instructed to completely immerse ourselves in the waters of
the mikveh to mark our change in status.

The Hebrew word mikveh has a second meaning. It is also the word for "hope, the Source of Hope, and trust." From the root of this word, *kavah,* we form the verb, "to hope, trust" but only in the present tense. This is an important distinction that we will explore later. It is from this root that the word *"tikveh"* comes, as in *HaTikveh*, "The Hope" which is the title of the national anthem of Israel today. When we enter the waters of the mikveh we immerse ourselves in hope and trust that God will purify our hearts, transitioning us to a new and higher state of being.

The two meanings point us to the physical and spiritual meaning of the ritual of mikveh. In a physical sense we are washing our bodies in water, immersing ourselves in an environment (water) in which we cannot survive for any length of time. To do so we must employ our trust. We trust God to sustain our lives.

Spiritually, water symbolizes transition, change, and the creation of new life. It was from water that the rest of the Creation came forth in Genesis 1:1 as the Spirit of God hovered over the "face of the deep." We are immersing ourselves in the creative waters of life to be renewed, to transition to a higher spiritual state, to change our status from what was to what will be. Therein, while we are submerged in the waters of the mikveh, we are in the supreme moment of Now.

The twentieth-century Kabbalist Rabbi Aryeh Kaplan says: "The present is the womb in which the future is being born." It is the place of suspended Being – as the body is suspended in the waters. It is not the cessation of time, but the suspension of Now. What was **before** we entered the water is being "washed away," and it is no longer, and what **will be** as we emerge is not yet. We momentarily put ourselves in the experience of time as it relates to God – it is all "Now".

As we explore the different ways and times that we go to the mikveh, we will see how this practice symbolizes change in status and transcendence in hope and trust in The Holy One.

> And The Holy One said to Moses, "Go to the people, and sanctify them today and tomorrow, and let them wash their clothes, and be ready by the third day: for on the third day The Holy One will come down in the sight of all the people upon Mount Sinai."
>
> EXODUS 19:10, 11

In preparation for hearing God's Voice and powerfully experiencing The Presence as never before by a group of people, the Children of Israel are told to "wash their garments." What does the washing of garments have to do with the Sacred Way of mikveh?

Whenever the Torah instructs us to wash our bodies (immersion) for purification, it also mentions washing of our clothes. Therefore, where it mentions only the garments, it is a forgone conclusion in Jewish thought that immersion of the body is to precede. Our garments, the outermost clothes we wear for protection and adornment, symbolize the body as an outer garment for our Soul. The body encompasses all of the "inner garments" of our emotions, our thoughts and our spiritual vision, our Soul-life. All of the layers of our "garments" are to be relinquished to God's keeping in the waters of the mikveh. We are to let go of ourselves, our ego driven needs, even our self-will and float in the waters of the mikveh to be purified within and without.

In their three day preparation for meeting with God on Mount Sinai, the Children of Israel were preparing to change their status. They were changing from being a group of people to a nation. They were transcending **from** being a group of people seeking freedom from slavery, **to** their Destiny as *Am Yisrael*, the People of Israel, following a divinely inspired leader:

> "... and you shall be to me a kingdom of priests, and a holy nation."
>
> EXODUS 19:6

Just as Aaron and his sons prepared for their individual calling to be priests, the Children of Israel (and those to follow the covenant in the future) were to mark their readiness for their high calling, by washing themselves in the Waters of Life, the mikveh. There are also other aspects of the mikveh.

The element of water in the Hebrew heritage symbolizes the transitions of our life from birthing through dying, as well. Thus, the mikveh becomes both the grave and the womb. A baby passes through the birthing waters to be born. At death the body of one who has died is ritually washed for purification, preparing it and marking its' transition back to dust.

The mikveh is likened to a grave when we give ourselves over to trust in God's work of purifying us through the waters. However, there is another element that enters here, and that is the element of our intentions, our kavennah, which bears examination.

When we enter the water, we examine our lives, our actions, and the attitude of our heart to see where we might be out of harmony with God's Sacred Ways. When we remember a wrong we have committed, we seek The Holy One of Mercy and ask for forgiveness in God's great compassion. We die to our self-will and enter the uninhabitable environment of water, as if going down to the grave. As we immerse our self all that went before is washed away. We let go of whatever we have confessed trusting in God's words spoken through Ezekiel that we shall be cleansed"

"Then I will sprinkle clean water upon you, and you shall be clean…"

EZEKIEL 36:25

From this symbolism of the grave comes the interpretation that immersion is an enactment of death and resurrection. We cannot live without breath. When we enter the waters, we cannot breathe – it is as if we are entering the place of the non-living. When we rise up out of the waters we rise up in resurrection to breathe again unto new life.

As antithetical as these two ideas may seem, the idea of mikveh as the womb and the grave are actually two sides of the same coin. Death in this world is also a time of birthing our Soul back into the Source of All Life in the higher dimensions:

"The Holy One shall watch over you in your going out and in your coming in from this time forth and forevermore."

PSALMS 121:8

This verse alludes to two actions. In one sense it can mean coming and going from your house. But, the mystical meaning is hinted at by adding the word "forevermore" at the end which is a condition of Eternity. This condition of Eternity points to the idea that the verse is about "going out of and into this world" or being born and dying. So why does it mention "going out" first? You would think it would say "in your coming in and your going out".

However, from the viewpoint of God, when a Soul is born into human life, it is "going out" from the Eminent Presence of God, the Source of All Life. When that Soul is on its' journey of return, and dying to the life led on Earth, it is "coming in" to be reunited with the Eminent Presence of God. In a sense, what we call death is really another "birthing," as the Soul is birthing itself back into the Source of All Life from which it came. This verse tells us that in both instances, both going out and coming in, the Soul's journey is guarded and watched over by The Holy One, the Creator. Both birthing and dying are birthing processes that give Life. Going into the waters of the mikveh is symbolic of entering the birthing waters of Life.

The womb of a woman is the place of the waters of life. It is the place where life begins anew as a man and woman come together in unity. The womb is also the place of total mercy. The Hebrew word for compassion or loving mercy is *rechem*. The Hebrew word for the womb area is *beit ha-rechem* or literally the "house of mercy". Both "womb" and "mercy" stem from the same Hebrew root. Why? The developing fetus in the womb is in a place of complete mercy, for it does not have to breathe for itself, feed itself, eliminate for itself, sounds are muffled, its eyes are shaded in darkness to develop; it does not even bear its own weight, but floats in the amniotic fluids. It is in this state of mercy until it transitions from being potential life to actualized life, until it is born through the birthing waters.

The mikveh is symbolic of the womb of total mercy. The waters therein birth new life. Like the state of the fetus, the person in the mikveh undergoes a change that will bring them into a new status. The condition for this rebirth is, of course, a giving of our Soul back to the Source of All Life, for purification.

"The mikveh represents the womb. When an individual enters the mikvah, s/he is re-entering the womb, and when s/he emerges, s/he is as if born anew. Thus s/he attains a completely new status."

RABBI ARYEH KAPLAN, WATERS OF EDEN, P.13

When are the appropriate times to mark this rebirth by the ritual of mikveh? When are the times when you are marking a transition in your life, a change in your status? When these occasions arise, that is when you go to the mikveh.

It is traditional to go to the mikveh on Friday afternoon to mark the transition from the work week into Shabbat which begins at sundown Friday and lasts until sundown Saturday. In this way you are ready for this 24-hour day set apart for God. You clear yourself of the cares and worries of the week and readying yourself to receive the "Sabbath Soul," the eminent Presence of God which in Hebrew is called the Shekhinah.

Some people go to the mikveh before a Festival Day such as Passover, Sukkot (The Feast of Tabernacles) and Shavuot (The Feast of Weeks) or the Holy Days of Awe – Rosh HaShanah and Yom Kippur, thus transitioning into the holiness of the seasons.

It is traditional for women to go to the mikveh to mark the end of their time of menstruation. This symbolizes that the cycle of preparing the womb for creating life has ended and the womb is ready to begin the cycle of possibility again. The woman transitions from the clearing of one cycle to the possibility to another. Her womb changes status from fertile ground to sterile ground ready to become fertile again.

Closely related to the natural cycles of the female energy are the rhythmic phases of the moon. Some individuals mark the beginning of each Hebrew month by immersion in the mikveh, for each new month begins at the new moon. This is the time of month when the night sky is dark and void of the light of the moon. In chaos and void was Creation formed and birthed. This darkness symbolizes the mystery and birthing of the coming month. Yet just as we trust and hope in the coming of the full moon again, we hope and trust in the coming of the fullness of the Divine Light in our future.

Women gather together to experience this powerful ritual by going into the mikveh. The new month is called in Hebrew, *Rosh Chodesh*, the "head of the month." Traditionally, it is a Sabbath for women; women do not do any work on this day. Groups of women gather on Rosh Chodesh to experience a time of intimacy and feminine sharing in community. This is a time of sharing wisdom, teachings, experiences, poems, stories, and songs: and of course, food, without which it would not be a Jewish event! It is a time when women share their lives with each other and talk about the spiritual aspects of what happened to them during the last month and what they are looking forward to in the coming month. It is a time for sharing hopes, visions, concerns and overcoming their fears together. It is a time to help each other recognize fears that paralyze them and keep them from moving forward on their life paths. Through support, shared wisdoms and prayer they enable each other to move from fear to love, trust and vision. The group becomes close and their prayers become a powerful force as they pray together over the years, uniting their spiritual gifts of transcendence.

In modern times we have come to mark menopause as the fulfillment and maturity of our womanhood by the ritual of mikveh. At this time a woman ritualizes her change in status from Life-bearer to Life-giver. Just as she bore life by bringing children into the world, now she is giving spiritual birth to others around her by imparting her wisdom. In Proverbs 31, we read "who can find a woman of valor, for her value is far above rubies..." Note that this woman seems to have lived a full life; "her children rise up and call her blessed" indicates that her children are grown, she is an elder woman. She is called to be one of the Wise Ones, those who integrate lifelong learning and experience with their Inner Spiritual Guidance to impart the Wisdom of their Soul. She joins the Matriarchs, the Mothers; Sarah, Rebecca, Rachel and Leah, who gave birth to our People. She joins the women who gave great courage to our people such as Miriam, Deborah and Esther. Like these women who helped shape our Hebrew heritage of the past, she helps to shape our Hebrew heritage of the future. This ritual t'vilah marks her transition from the focus of giving life to her children through her body and the physical labor of caring for a young family to the broadened role of a Wisdom Keeper, giving life to those in the world community through Spirit. Women gather for this special immersion in the mikveh. If a woman is part of a Rosh Chodesh group for many years this is an especially meaningful event for the group. The female community of friends and family gather to celebrate this "graduation" with the woman. They may have a time of sharing when each woman speaks "Soul to Soul" to the new Wisdom Keeper the message that their Soul wants her to know for this part of her spiritual journey. After the mikveh ritual there is a time of celebration, schmoozing (talking together), eating and gift giving. It is traditional to bring chocolate as a new traditional food for this event to symbolize the sweetness of this time of Life.

Some brides and grooms go to the mikveh (separately), to mark the change in status from single to married, from "alone" to "two Souls bonded as husband and wife". It is a time for reflecting upon one's life up to this point and reflecting upon the hopes and dreams of life beyond this point.

However, while in the mikveh waters, time becomes suspended in the Now. It is a precious time of renewal, purification and re-unification with God. Then the bride and groom are ready for holy union with each other. Again, the bride may invite her friends for this ritual bridal mikveh which is followed by a time of sharing, celebration, delightful treats to eat and gift giving. The groom may do the same with his friends and male family members. The focus of the gathering, however, is on the spiritual aspects of fulfilling this Sacred Way in uniting with another Soul.

The powerful ritual of t'vilah also marks the transition of beginning life as a Jew for those who choose conversion. This is a once-in-a-lifetime mikveh event. As a Jew by choice, I remember my experience of going into the waters of t'vilah. Nothing could have prepared me for the feeling of exultation and yet quiet awe as I came forth from those birthing waters of new life, a new daughter of Israel.

It was November in Florida, which by a Floridian's standard is a nippy time to be going into the water. I had converted with an Orthodox Rabbi who came from a long line of Rabbis. He had been "steeped in *Talmud* (the oral Torah teachings) since childhood in Poland/Austria and is a Kabbalist, who studied for many years with his father-in-law a Rabbi and Kabbalist from Safed, Israel. He and his wife welcomed me and my family into Judaism by extending to us *mishpahah*, "family." Mishpahah is not just ordinary family by blood, but family as "those who create a warm and safe place in the world for you." They taught us Judaism by living it together, for the "understanding" comes through the "doing." After fulfilling our time of instruction and questioning the day came for us to "go to the water," and immerse ourselves in a ritual mikveh to mark our transition of becoming Jewish. We used the natural body of water, the Gulf of Mexico, as our Mikveh. It was a very beautiful way to be reborn.

It is considered that when one converts it is as if they have re-entered the womb and are reborn as a little child into this world. The tide was out and it seemed as if we would need to wade to

Mexico to get into deep enough water to immerse ourselves. The water was cold, but my excitement was so great I hardly noticed. At last I was ready. I said the appropriate blessings, and three times I went under the water, allowing it to completely cover my body. With each immersion, I concentrated upon a different part of my Being. First I transitioned from my physical Being (body) to my emotional Being in joy. With the second immersion I transitioned from the emotions to my intellectual Being in peace. With the third immersion I transitioned from the intellectual Being to my Spiritual Being in Shalom, wholeness. As I came up out of the water the third time I was, at last, a Daughter of Israel! I had brought my physical body into harmony with my heart, my mind and my spirit. I had changed my status to become a Jew as far as the world was concerned, but as far as I was concerned, I had transitioned into wholeness. I had come home. My destiny was now bound up with my people, Israel.

The ritual of t'vilah is what John the Baptist used when he was taking people into the water, immersing them and bringing them into a new spiritual status of life. They were already Jewish; however, he used this well known ritual to mark the commitment they made for a spiritual change in their lives. They trusted God and went into the waters of the mikveh to arise and be born anew. As Jews they were familiar with the mikveh and its symbolism of transition. Jesus taught Nicodemus in John 3:3 that a person needed to be "born of water and of spirit" not only mikveh, but also kavennah, the intentionality of mikveh, to experience personal enlightenment.

This is that once-in-a-lifetime ritual of *t'vilah*, "immersion," or Baptism in Christianity that marks a new status for the believer. Judaism is the cultivated olive tree in Romans 11:17, 18. A non-Jew coming up out of the waters of the *mikveh* receives the new status of the wild olive branch grafted into the cultivated tree, adopted into the Hebrew family covenant with God.

This spiritual family is to be *mishpahah*, that group of people who make a warm and safe place for you in the world. Jews worldwide acknowledge each other as family, kin, M.O.T. – Member of the Tribe. There is a kinship and peoplehood that comes as part of the Hebrew heritage. As in all families, this does not mean we are always in harmony, but it does mean we are always family, no matter what. So we can agree, we can disagree, we are still family. And that family extends itself to increase the quality of life to all of creation as we are told by the Prophet Isaiah:

> "Thus says God, The Holy One, the Creating One Who created the Heavens, and stretched them out; The One Who spread forth the Earth, and that which comes out of it; The One Who gives Soul-breath to the people upon it and Spirit to them that walk therein: I, the Holy One have called you in righteousness, and will give strength to your hand, and will gather you and give you for a covenant of the people, for a Light to the Nations; to open the blind eyes, to bring out the prisoners from the prison, and them that sit in darkness. I am יהוה, that is My Name..."
>
> ISAIAH 42:5-8

This is the calling of those entering the waters of t'vilah, the mikveh of Creation, to emerge as transformed beings, carrying the Light of The Holy One, that this world might be a brighter and more holy place. This is your Hebrew heritage in the mikveh.

How might you use the *mikveh* in your spiritual practices?
• You can begin your Sabbath with immersion to clear yourself of the *shmutz* (smudge and grime) of the cares of the work week.

- Purchase a Hebrew calendar and gather with other men and women at the new moon to mark the new month. Start a Rosh Chodesh group. Immerse yourselves for clearing the business of the old month and beginning the mystery of the new month together. Share your hopes, dreams, visions and intentions with one another. Support one another's requests in prayer throughout the month. Build your faith by sharing with one another the outcomes of your requests. This is traditionally a women's group, however, we are in the midst of learning to balance the masculine and feminine energies, so men could join these groups or form their own, as well.

- This year at Easter and Christmas Eve immerse yourself in preparation of the sacred celebration of that day.

- If you are considering Baptism, or Christening your child, or you will witness someone's Baptism, meditate upon the spiritual meaning of this ritual and ask God's blessing of Spirit for this change of status, the transition to a higher calling of service.

What can you use as a mikveh?

- Natural water is usually the most spiritual of settings, for it is there that all of creation witnesses your rebirth.

- If that is not possible, is there a church nearby that has a Baptism pool?

- Some people use their shower or hot tub as the place to do t'vilah when there is inclement weather.

- If none of these works you can use the mikveh of your imagination. Do a meditation where you walk into the waters of the mikveh and feel the water rising on your body. Immerse yourself three times, focusing on your kavennah, your intentions.

To make going to the mikveh a sacred occasion and not just any washing in water, say a blessing stating your intention:

> "Blessed are You, O Holy One, our God, Guide of the Cosmos, Who sanctifies us by Your Sacred Ways and instructs us to immerse ourselves."
> Ba-ruch a-tah Yah, E-lo-hei-nu me-lekh ha-olam, a-sher kid-sha-nu b-mitz-vo-tav v-tzi-va-nu al ha-t'vi-lah.

Do a meditation beforehand considering what you are letting go of, leaving behind and what you are changing to and becoming. Imagine the time in between as if you died and see yourself reborn as you come up out of the waters.

Make a statement of your intentions such as:

> "May it be Your Will, O Holy One, my God and God of my ancestors that just as I purify myself here Below in the water, so may you purify my Soul Above in your River of Light, engulfing me in your Endless Love."

The mikveh and t'vilah symbolize: transitions of death to life, the womb, new life, rebirth, transcendence, trust, dedication, purity.

Mezuzah
Power Symbol on Your Door

> "And these words which I command you this day, shall be in your heart ... and you shall write them upon the doorposts of your house and on your gates."
>
> DEUT. 6:4-9

The deeper meaning of this scripture is hidden within the diversity of the Hebrew words used in it. The word that is translated "doorposts" is *mezuzah*. Some scholars teach that this word is referring to the main tent pole at the center of a tent. In English the word "doorpost" refers to a permanent structure such as a house. At the time this was given to Moses, the Children of Israel were living in their tents in the wilderness of the Sinai Peninsula. Mezuzah at that time referred to the center pole, that central structure that gave strength and stability to their tents, their homes. In order to fulfill this Sacred Way, the actual words of God's instructions were carved into these poles for those in the wilderness.

During the epic of the Exodus from Egypt, the people were told to put the blood of the sacrifice upon their "doorposts" so they would be delivered from the last plague, the death of the firstborn. Now they are instructed to put God's words upon their doorposts so they would always remember to do the Sacred Ways transcending to a more holy way of living. The home is symbolic of "the dwelling place of the Soul". If these words are at the center of our homes, then how much more so should they be the center of our lives?

There is a connection between the word mezuzah and its Hebrew root, the word *azaz,* which means "to be or become strong, to be bold, to be courageous, and to encourage". Just as the main tent pole gives strength, stability and height to the tent so these words are to be the center of our hearts to give us strength and stability, to encourage us and to make us bold. God's Sacred Ways are to be the spiritual doorposts of our lives.

For future generations who would live in permanent housing in the Promised Land the words of the Sacred Ways were to be carved upon the doorposts, the openings of their homes and even on their gates, the extensions of their homes. When we follow this tradition, we remember in our going out and in our coming in, God's Sacred Ways. We center our lives on them both in our private lives (homes) and in the world beyond our gates.

The mezuzah also serves to remind us of God during the transitions from home to world, from private to public during the day. Often in the course of transitioning from home to the outside world, just by your change of activity, you may lose or forget your *d'vekut*, (literally, "sticking to God"). We call this God consciousness. When you pass by the mezuzah on your doorpost you maintain that God consciousness whether coming in or going out, while at work or at play, by touching or kissing the mezuzah. You do this special "touching" by putting your fingers on the mezuzah and then kissing your fingers. As you "kiss" the mezuzah you remember God and the Sacred Ways that enfold you in God's love. This causes you to pause and establish your mindfulness of what you are doing. It gives continuity to the flow of spirit in all that you do, wherever you are at home or away.

To those entering our homes the sign of a mezuzah is a blessing of peace, that the higher ways of The Holy One are observed here. It is a sign telling the guest Whom it is that this household serves. It is an extension of peace and harmony to all those who enter there.

Today, we fulfill the Sacred Way of the mezuzah by a scribe writing the words of The Holy One found in Deut. 6:4-9 and Deut. 11:13-21 on a small parchment. It is then rolled up and put into a "mezuzah case" (a decorative case made of metal, wood, stone, etc.) and affixed to the right hand side of the doorways as you enter the home or a room of the home. It is placed one third of the way from the top, slanting toward the center (heart) of the home, that it may be easily touched as a person walks past it. It is a way you mindfully draw the energy of the mezuzah's words to you. It is as if you are saying, "I love you, Holy One, and I embrace your Sacred Ways."

Touching your mezuzah as you leave and enter your home is also a way of re-grounding yourself in the peace of God, as you transition between your private domain and the public domain. It is a way of reminding yourself of the Presence and power of God when you leave your house, your place of nurturing, to go out into the world. When you return from the outside world and your interaction with community, you touch your mezuzah, you re-enter the intimacy of your home.

God's power and yet nurturing nature is brought to mind by the name *Shaddai*, שדי which is on the front of the mezuzah. Sometimes the letter *Shin*, ש which stands for the name Shaddai, is placed on the front of the mezuzah case. Shaddai or *El Shaddai* is one of the ancient Hebrew names for God. Our Hebrew names for God do not define God as a noun, but name the relationship we are having with God at that moment. The name Shaddai or El Shaddai is often translated as "Almighty One of Blessing" a powerful name for God.

The Hebrew root for the name Shaddai comes from the word *shad* שד which means breast, bosom, and also "source of blessing". *Shode* שוד means "mother's milk". The relationship presented by the name Shaddai is of God as the Source of Blessing, the mother's milk, the source of the blessing of life for the growth and health of the infant. Home is the place where we are nurtured and nourished, that we may go out into the world as a whole, balanced and healthy person. This is the ideal. We return to our home for respite, rejuvenation and re-centering in our lives. Our home is where we are supposed to first learn to love, to share and to experience who we are amongst others. Home is our first place of socialization and community. The mezuzah reminds us to keep our home as a sacred place for the name Shaddai, the Mighty Nurturer, to abide, and for us to nurture each other. The home with a mezuzah upon the doorposts and upon the gates offers to those living there and to those entering it, the nurturing power of God's Blessings. The doorway adorned with a mezuzah becomes an opening to the world to extend peace and unity, rather than a barrier, isolating us from the world.

The name Shaddai is also used as an acronym; each Hebrew letter stands for an entire word. Acronyms enjoy great popularity among mystical traditions, the Hebrew traditions being no exception! The name Shaddai is spelled with a *shin*, *dalet*, and *yud*, שדי. The shin ש stands for *shomer*, "guardian", the dalet, ד stands for *daltot*, "doors", and the yud, י stands for *Yisrael*, "Israel". Shaddai, שדי is the "Guardian of the Doors of Israel." Because of this concept of protection some people think of a mezuzah as an amulet of good luck as well as protection. However, it is much more than that. It is the "power point" with which we connect to "power up" as we go out into the world. It is the reset button that reminds us of the blessings of God as we return from the busyness of our day. It reminds us of who we are, Whose we are, and Who is watching over us!

Synagogues have a mezuzah in the doorway. On occasion I have seen one upon the doorposts of a church. Would you like to see one on your church? Speak with your pastor, minister or priest about fulfilling this powerful Sacred Way by placing a mezuzah on the doorway of your house of prayer.

Would you like to bless your home by placing a mezuzah on your door, thus fulfilling God's Sacred Way? You might choose a meaningfully decorated mezuzah case (containing a mezuzah) as a family together to go on your front door. A mezuzah is also placed upon the doorways within the home. Individual members of your family may want to choose their own mezuzah for their rooms. There are precious *mezuzot* (plural for mezuzah) for children's rooms and the nursery. One of my favorite nursery motifs is one that uses a Noah's Ark mezuzah case theme with all the animals poking their heads out of the Ark. A mezuzah is an appropriate wedding gift to give a bride and groom, to bless their new home with God's Presence of Peace.

After purchasing a mezuzah you may want to set a date to affix the mezuzah and consecration your home with your friends and family. Invite them over for the ritual of placing your mezuzah on your doorpost. After your guests arrive, gather at the doorway to affix your mezuzah. You may want to tell them what it means to you to affix this mezuzah to the doorpost of your home. Maybe you would like to tell why you chose the particular mezuzah that you did. Then say a blessing for affixing a mezuzah as you place it on your doorway (usually done with nails or screws). The traditional blessing is as follows:

> Blessed are You, O Holy One, Our God, Guide of the Cosmos, Who sanctifies us by your Sacred Ways, and instructs us to affix a mezuzah. Amen.
> Ba-ruch a-tah Yah, E-lo-hei-nu me-lekh ha-olam, a-sher kid-sha-nu b'mitz-vo-tav v'tzi-va-nu, l'k-bo-ah me-zu-zah.

Together say: "*B'ruchim Ha-ba-im.* **May all who enter be blessed."**

Then have each person (voluntary of course) offer a blessing from the heart upon your home. Very often after doing this ritual people like to go outside the door just so they can come in through the door, touching and kissing the newly affixed mezuzah.

After that it is time to enjoy wonderful treats and desserts, sing, dance, shmooze, (jovial chatting together) and to celebrate your home!

> May The Almighty Source of Nurture and Blessing
> guard the doors of your dwelling place
> and give all who enter there Peace.

The mezuzah symbolizes: love of God, nurturing, Source of Blessings, remembrance of Sacred Ways, to be strong, courageous and encouraging to others, Divine Protection, peace and sanctity of the home.

Incense
The Sweet-Smelling Savor unto God

> "And you shall make an altar for the burning of incense...
> And you shall overlay it with pure gold ...
> And you shall put it before the veil that is by the Ark of
> the Testimony ... where I will meet with you.
> And Aharon (High Priest Aaron) shall burn upon it sweet
> incense every morning ...
> And when Aharon lights the lamps at evening,
> he shall burn incense upon it, a perpetual incense
> before The Holy One throughout your generations."
>
> EXODUS 30:1-8

The burning of incense was a common practice both in private homes as well as in temples and places of worship in the Middle East. It remains a common spiritual practice for many world religions and some denominations of churches around the world. Incense is now found in the market place throughout the Western world since its resurgence in the 1960s when the young generation of that era began embracing Eastern religion and culture.

Incense was an important part of the Temple worship of our ancestors; so much so, that God instructed the Priesthood to keep it constantly rising to fill the air before the Ark of the Covenant. God even gave specific instructions in the Torah about which ingredients to combine in the making of sacred incense for use in the Temple. Because incense was used in homes the sacred recipe for Temple incense was guarded and consecrated for Temple use only. The scripture reads "throughout your generations" which tells us that the Sacred Way of burning incense is to be passed on from generation to generation. Why is incense so important? How can we use it in our worship today?

Incense is used when preparing a room for sacred activity. Its scent purifies the energy of the air in the same way that the water of the Mikveh purifies our body and spirit. By burning incense with the intention of consecrating it the room is "cleared" for sacred activity. The characteristics of incense hint at the reason why it is so effectual.

Incense fills and permeates a room with fragrance. Fragrance also carries with it memory – and in the case of the Temple incense, Sacred Memory. As the smoke of incense disperses and rises within a room it clears the energy of the room of whatever has gone on before and focuses the consciousness of those present. It is as if the veils of the Dimensions dissipate with the smoke of the incense as it rises.

What are some of your favorite smells? Of what do they remind you? The reason they are your favorite smells will be obvious to you when you link them to the memories they recall.

Try this exercise:

> List some of your favorite smells.
> Now make a list of what they remind you of when you smell them.
> For example, some of my favorite smells are:
> cookies baking
> a crackling fire
> mothballs
> roses
> fresh hay

Cookies baking:

Before I was school age, my mother and I would bake cookies and pies on rainy days, while my older sisters were in school. It was a special time for just my mother and me. The smell of cookies baking reminds me of the wonderful "alone" time I shared with my Mom.

A crackling fire:

I grew up in Florida and even though Florida is known for mild winters our home still had a cozy fireplace. On those rare occasions in winter, when it was cold enough and the temperature would dip below 60 degrees, my Dad would build a fire in the fireplace. It was cause for great excitement. It was my joy to help Dad carry wood into the living room for the fire. My sisters and I would huddle before the leaping flames, smelling the perfume of the freshly chopped pine kindling. Now, as everyone knows, pine is full of sap. This gave us cause to jump and squeal with delight and surprise whenever a pocket of sap burst and sent a shower of sparks up the flue and sometimes out into the room! It was fun and it was a "Daddy" thing. It was a time of warmth and it filled our home bright with soft firelight.

Mothballs:
Mothballs remind me of the smell of my Grandma Ferne's upstairs rooms, where she stored her blankets, linens and winter clothing in huge ancient and somehow curious chests. The linens and other mysterious items were, or course, stored in mothballs.

Grandma Ferne was a loving Grandma and a delight in my childhood. There were thirteen of us grandchildren. Grandma seemed to enjoy having us all in her large two-story, old-Florida home. Depending on how many of us were sleeping over, we would sleep in the four bedrooms, on couches in the living room and sometimes on daybeds on the "Florida sleeping porch" where we were lulled to sleep by the rhythmic songs of the crickets and other night creatures. The soft night air on the screened porch (before air-conditioning) gave relief from the heat of the Florida summer and offered waves of breezes perfumed with night-blooming jasmine and gardenias.

Regardless of how many children there were, or how many beds there were to be made, Grandma always had plenty of linens to go around in her big cedar chests upstairs. It seemed that the chests were so deep there might not be a bottom to them! She would very matter-of-factly make up our beds amidst a sea of giggling and excited children. As I snuggled deep into the clean, fresh sheets I could smell the mothballs she used in those chests. While mothballs are not exactly a sweet-smelling fragrance, the smell is dear to me because of the pleasurable memories that accompany it. The memory of the smell of mothballs is mingled with hearing my sisters and cousins saying their goodnights to each other. We were a happy lot – we were at Grandma's house.

Roses:

This same Grandmother had a huge rose garden. In the center of the rose garden was a large mango tree and around the edge of it was a thick row of bright red amaryllis. My sister gathered bountiful bouquets of roses from the garden even in the sweltering summer heat. She would bring her treasure of blossoms into the house, arrange them with great care and place them at the center of Grandma's big round dining room table. Every time I went past the bouquet of roses on the table I would catch a whiff of their fragrance. Their bright colors were a delight to my eyes. They meant joy, contentment and the cheery, carefree days of childhood. Roses still remind me of my sister and our shared love of flowers.

Fresh hay:

Many years ago I owned an equestrian center and trained horses in dressage. The rich alfalfa and timothy hay that we liked to feed the horses did not grow in the sandy soil of Florida so we had to ship it in from northern and Canadian regions. When a fresh truckload of hay would arrive we stacked the bales high. When I entered the barn to feed the horses in the morning I would be met by their soft nickering sounds and the fragrance of alfalfa, clover and timothy hay filling the barn like perfume.

You get the idea! Just smelling particular fragrances can bring back memories to you as fresh as if it were yesterday. And, interestingly, just recalling those occasions brings the smell to your "mind's nose" as if the fragrance still hangs in the air today.

A familiar fragrance can also bring a particular person to mind. Have you ever smelled a perfume on someone that someone special to you had always worn? Smelling their perfume brings that person to mind. One day a young man asked me what perfume I was wearing. I told him the name of the classic fragrance. He smiled very large and said, "That's the perfume my mother always wore when I was little." From the look on his face he was transported by the smell of that perfume to a good place with fond memories of his Mom. The smell of a fragrance has the power to transport you to a place outside of time and space.

If you had grown up smelling the incense of the Temple wafting through the streets of Jerusalem, then forever in your consciousness you would think of God and holiness and your experiences at the Temple when you smelled the unique fragrance of the Temple incense. If you grew up in a Catholic church where the incense is still used what memory does it bring to your mind when you smell that incense today? Are you immediately ready for Mass?

The Hebrew language gives us spiritual hints about the connection between memory and fragrance in the word *ruah*. Our memories connect us spiritually with events of the past, both in our individual lives and in our Sacred Memory of ancient days. Have you ever smelled something that had a precious and wonderful feel to it when you knew you had actually never smelled it before? That is a smell from Sacred Memory, for your Eternal Soul has experienced the essence before. The Hebrew word ruah means both wind and spirit. It is also our word for one of the five levels of the Soul. As we breathe air into our lungs, we not only bring life-giving oxygen to our body, but we inspire our Souls, bringing in fresh spirit. We are usually not aware of our breathing; we do not tell ourselves to breathe in and breathe out. It is an automatic response of being a living creature. In the same way we are "in-spirited" or inspired as an intrinsic part of our eternal being. However, we can consciously focus on our breath (wind) and our spirit, for meditation purposes. Incense makes us aware of our breath / spirit by giving us the signal through scent that we are, in fact, drawing in life, spirit. Thus, when we prepare a room (at home or at our place of worship) for prayer, meditation, Torah (Bible) study or any sacred activity by lighting incense, a sweet smelling fragrance, we become mindful of our breath, our in-spiring and we open our Being to Spirit, to enlightenment, to growth and to life.

Fragrance is a common link, the catalyst, for re-entering the spirit of a time, place or presence of a person. We can become in-spired by scent. When incense is used during meditation it can become a visual aid as well as a sensual aid to our prayers. As we watch the incense rise our Souls follow the smoke as it ascends leaving a curling trail as it makes its journey upward. As our prayers, our thoughts, words and feelings are formed and become convoluted together they rise with the smoke of the incense, until they finally dissipate into the oneness of the air. We are not even aware of ourselves as individuals, just a Holy Presence. It is there that we meet with The Holy One, in the midst of the "perpetual incense," the sweet smelling savor of Divine Union; that which is already One.

The smell of incense carries us back to this sacred place. If we use a particular fragrance for that purpose, then each time we enter a room prepared with incense we are immediately carried back in memory to the "place of meeting" we experienced before in our prayers and meditations. Our Soul is on alert, remembering the sweetness of our union and anticipating reunion.

Some people experience flashes of Sacred Memory beyond their own years, to a time when the Temple incense hung heavy in the air: frankincense, myrrh, spikenard, clove, balsam, saffron, cinnamon, costus, aromatic barks, galbanum, and cassia. These were the spices used in the Temple incense. Do any of their names catch your imagination and spirit? The fact that we were forbidden to use the exact recipe for the Temple incense in our homes indicates that the use of some type of incense during private worship in the home was common.

> "And The Holy One said to Moses, "Take for yourself sweet spices, storax, and onycha, and galbanum; sweet spices with pure frankincense: of each shall there be a like weight: and you shall make it a perfume, a confection after the art of the perfumer, mingled with salt, pure and holy: and you shall beat some of it very small, and put it before the Testimony in the Tent of Meeting, where I will meet with you: it shall be to you most holy. And as for the perfume which you shall make, you shall not make it for yourselves according to its prescribed composition: it shall be holy for the Eternal One."
>
> EXODUS 30:34-37

Incense was and continues to be used because it also has the power to relax your mind from distracting or straying thoughts as you breathe in the vapors. Just as a person who has fainted can be brought back to consciousness by smelling salts or ammonia capsules, so too, if we have been distracted by "mind chatter" or foreign thoughts while we are trying to meditate, we are brought back to the focus of our intentions when we inhale the fragrance of the incense. At the same time, if our consciousness has ventured very far into deep prayer, or very high in meditation, the smell of the incense helps us to recover consciousness in the physical world, and to regain full integration with our bodies. It can help us to become fully present in the physical world. Just as we follow the pathway of smoke up to the Higher Realms of our prayer, so too, are we able to follow the fragrance of the incense back to the consciousness of our physical world, as if it is our "breadcrumb trail" back to Earth.

In the section on Shabbat, the Sabbath, you will explore the spiritual significance of lighting candles to welcome the Sabbath. However, in preparation for lighting the candles, it is a spiritual practice to burn some incense in the room first.

> "Burn some incense before the arrival of Shabbat and give your room a pleasant scent for the honor of Shabbat."
>
> DERECH HAYIM, 6-42

> "What is it that the Soul enjoys yet does nothing for the body? A pleasant scent.
>
> BERACHOT 43

The rabbis teach that even though the body inhales the scent, it is not for the sake of the body (as in eating) but for the sake of the Soul. Again, the idea of the dual meanings of the word *ruah*, wind, breath, spirit, teaches us this spiritual principle. The scent "inspires" our Soul. Therefore, filling a room with fragrant incense is a practice in preparation for this most sacred day apart with God, the Sabbath. As you clear the room with incense in preparation for Shabbat, week by week, its smell links with memory and becomes familiar to you as a Sabbath smell. Soon just the smell of that incense in-spires your transition into the spirit of Shabbat.

How might you use incense in your own spiritual practices? Experiment with different fragrances of incense to find one that moves you spiritually. Try lighting some incense before you begin your prayers to prepare the room. Notice its fragrance as you breathe it in, set your intentions, and quiet your Soul for meditation.

You can say a blessing before kindling the incense to set it apart as a sacred act with the intention of drawing closer in your consciousness to God. The following blessing can be said:

> Blessed are You, O Holy One, Our God, Guide of the Cosmos, who has sanctified us by Your Sacred Ways and instructed us to kindle a sweet smelling savor.
> Ba-ruch a-tah Yah, E-lo-hei-nu Me-lech Ha-Olam, a-sher kid-sha-nu b'mitz-vo-tav v'tzi-va-nu l'had-lik rei-ah n'ko-ach.

Try using some incense in the room before you begin to study your Bible, or with your study group. It sets a special tone for study as a form of worship. Note: you might burn only a small part of a stick or cone of incense in order to keep from overpowering those to whom this practice is new or in sensitivity to those with breathing disorders.

Try meditating on the smoke as it rises. This can be done in your private meditation time or as a group. If you are in a group share your experiences with one another after your meditation.

The incense symbolizes: Service to God, purity, transcendence, spirit, breath, ascendance, Temple, embodiment, Sacred Memory.

Oil
Anointing of the Spirit for Light

> And The Holy One said (to Samuel the Prophet), "Arise, anoint him: for this is he. Then Samuel took the horn of oil and anointed him in the midst of his brothers: and the spirit of The Holy One came upon David from that day onwards."
>
> SAMUEL 16: 12,13

Oil has many uses in the history of our people. It symbolizes Divine blessing, appointment and transition. It is also a symbol for wealth, honor, joy and purity. Most significantly it represents the Holy Spirit, Ruach HaKodesh, in Hebrew.

In ancient times the oil used was olive oil, processed according to sacred instruction when it was to be used for holy purposes. Oil was considered one of the three necessities of life, along with food and clothing (includes shelter).

Oil was used for to represent the Divine Light in the Temple, (Ex. 35:8), for anointing the kings and prophets, healing the sick, and it was used in cosmetics and perfumes. Oil was a commodity to use in export as part of the bounty of the country. As such, it was part of the blessing given to the people in abundance by God as a natural result of living in harmony with God's Sacred Ways and expressing loving faithfulness to The Holy One (Deut. 11:13,14).

The spiritual aspects of oil are boundless. It was used only in sacrifices that were celebrative and joyful, such as occasions of thanksgiving, the completion and release of a vow, including the Nazarite vow. It was used in priestly ceremonies and in thanksgiving when a natural disaster (famine) had abated.

When a leper or person with a disease came to the Priests for healing, he or she was anointed with oil as a symbol of life, a symbol of their healing. In Leviticus 14:15-18, the Israelites are given specific instructions from God about how to anoint the sick with the sacred anointing oil for clearing of the illness and healing. In the Letter of James, following the sacred Hebrew practices (he was a Hebrew) he gives instructions to the spiritual guides to anoint any who are sick with oil.

When someone was changing their status in life they were anointed with oil to symbolize their transition. This included prophets, kings and priests. Even the holy places and the Temple objects were consecrated by ritually anointing them.

Anointing oil had to be made from a specific "recipe" given by God in Exodus 30:23-25. The spices used were specific to their unique properties and what they each brought to the mixture. However, along with the instructions on how to make the anointing oil came the warning that this mixture was sacred and to be used only for sacred purposes. It was to be used only by the Priesthood and for the purposes of consecration and healing as directed by God. As with the incense, since there is an admonition to use this particular blend of oils only for sacred purposes this tells us that oil was commonly used among the people.

The word *Mashiah*, which has become Messiah in English, literally means "the one anointed with oil". In Hebrew, The Mount of Olives is called *Har HaMishhah*, from the root word *masiah*, "to anoint, smear, oil".

A person was ritually anointed by placing or pouring oil upon their head. That ritual set them apart as consecrated to a sacred purpose, blessed by God. Oil is synonymous with God's Divine Blessing.

Oil was used in the *Ner Tamid*, the Eternal Light, in the Holy Place in the Temple, as well as in the six-branched lamp, the *menorah*. It was used in the lamps kindled on Shabbat (before candles) and in the *hanukiah*, the nine-branched lamp used at Hanukah.

The light burning from sacred oil is the Jewish symbol for the Divine Light of the Presence of the Holy One. That Presence is manifested both as the *Shechinah* (the feminine aspect of God's Presence in the physical world) and the indwelling Holy Spirit, the *Ruah HaKodesh*. As the oil was poured upon the head of the young shepherd, David, the Holy Spirit filled him and remained with him to guide him in the pathways of God all of his days. When a prophet (anointed to speak God's words to the people) prophesied, it was understood that s/he did so by the power of the Holy Spirit. Read the story of Bilaam (Balaam in English) to see how even a non-Hebrew who was hired to curse Israel was filled by the Spirit of God and instead of spewing out curses, he poured out blessings upon the Israelite people, three times (Numbers 24:2).

The Presence of God known as the *Shechinah* guides us and is with us, just as David sang in the 23rd Psalm. It is the Shepherdess guiding and guarding us. It joins with our Soul on Shabbat in holy union to give us an "extra Sabbath Soul." You can read more about this in the section on Shabbat.

The Ruach HaKodesh indwells us to speak words or do works beyond our natural ability. David's strength, courage and cunning that he used against Goliath was the work of the Holy Spirit. His son, King Solomon, ruled in wisdom imparted by the Holy Spirit and wrote such wisdom books as *Kohelet*, which is Ecclesiastes in English. The gifts of the Spirit abound in signs and wonders beyond our natural experiences.

Oil is the symbol for these manifestations of God. So too is the Light of the menorah and the *Ner Tamid*, Eternal Light, both fueled by especially prepared olive oil, symbolic of God's Presence in the Temple. Oil is also one of the central themes for the story of *Hanukkah*, (found in the book of Maccabees), the Festival of Light.

At the holiday of Hanukkah we retell the story of The Miracle of the Oil. It teaches us that when Israel was rededicating the Temple (desecrated by the Greeks), they could only find one bottle of consecrated oil to use in the Ner Tamid, the Eternal Flame. It was only a day's worth. It would take eight days to correctly process more oil. But, in faith (and by some miracle) they kindled that one cruse of oil, one day's worth, and lighted the lamp. Every day when they checked the lamp, instead of the oil running out, the oil had been multiplied by God, and the lamp continued to shine brightly in the Temple. It reassured the people of God's Presence with them. This continued for eight days until at last, they had the oil ready. They filled the lamp with the newly consecrated oil. When we let the symbolism of this story speak to our hearts we are reminded that just as God multiplied the oil in the story, by God's grace the Holy Spirit is multiplied greatly among us as we work together to bring our Divine Light into the world. It is a partnership. Like our ancestors, we work like it is all up to us and we pray like it is all up to God. This is what it means to light your lamp with one day's oil, while you busy yourself making the new oil, trusting God to supply your needs for the days ahead.

Hanukkah is celebrated at the darkest time of year, in the winter, when the days are short and the nights are long. Oil for the light is a symbol central to celebration of this holiday today. Hanukkah is also called the Festival of Lights and the Feast of the Dedication because the tiny army of revolutionaries, winning their great victory over the Greek army, restored and reconsecrated the Temple in Jerusalem which had been desecrated by the Greeks. (You can read more about it in the chapter on Holidays and the section on the historical holiday, Hanukkah.)

The traditional foods eaten at Hanukkah are symbolic of the importance of oil to this holiday. They are foods that are cooked in oil; *latkas* (potato pancakes) and *sofganyot* (something like a jelly-filled doughnut).

At Hanukkah we are reminded by the oil for the lights and even the foods that we eat that during our darkest moments we can trust and have faith that God's Light is within us and present all around us. We don't have to understand how it will happen; all we need is the oil of our willingness. God will provide the rest.

Dew is a symbol used for oil. It is Nature's anointing oil – the symbol used in the prophetic scriptures for blessing, purity and consecration after the coming of the Age of Enlightenment and Peace, The Age of the Messiah. Read Psalm 133:3 and Proverbs 19:12 to see the poetic use of dew in parallel with the oil of anointing. Read Hosea 14:5 and Zechariah 8:12 to learn more about the link between dew and oil in the Day of the Lord's blessing upon the Earth.

What are the ways you use oil in your spiritual practices? Does your church or spiritual community use oil when an individual dedicates his or her life or work to sacred service? Have you been anointed for specific purposes? Have you ever anointed particular objects for sacred use in your rituals and worship? Have you ever used oil to anoint the sick and infirmed?

Do you have an "altar" in your home, a place where you can go to worship, meditate and pray in solitude? How could you use your anointing oil in that room to consecrate it? Ask for guidance from Ruah HaKodesh, the Holy Spirit, on how to anoint your holy objects for sacred use.

Next Hanukkah, you may want to celebrate the bringing of the light during the dark winter season with your friends and family. Together, discuss how the oil, symbolic of the Holy Spirit of God, brings freedom. Think about how the Divine Light illumines the darkest of places. The Hanukiah, the candelabra used at Hanukkah, has eight lights; one for each of the eight nights of Hanukkah. But, there is a ninth light as well. It is the *Shammash*, or servant light. The Shammash is kindled first and from its flame all the other lights are kindled. Who or what is the Light that gives you Light?

The use of oil is a sacred practice of your Hebrew heritage. Enjoy it!

The oil symbolism: Holy Spirit, purity, Divine Light, anointing, joy, blessing, Messiahship, favor, holiness, wealth, Divine appointment, Kingship, transition, healing, honor, Life and consecration, appointment.

Candles
Honoring the Light of the Soul

The human Soul is the candle of The Holy One searching all the inward parts of her being.

PROVERBS 20:27

One of the symbols that the flame represents in Judaism is that of the human Soul; for just as the flame, which is energy, must cling to something physical, (the wick), to exist in the physical world, so too, the Soul, the non-physical energy, must cling to the physical, the body, to exist, exert its influence and dwell in this world.

The flame of the Soul symbolizes the Light and Love that we each bring to the world as a spark of the Divine. The flame clinging to the wick is a symbol of the spirit clinging to the physical to be present and bring light into this world.

Some say that you should always keep a few emergency candles and matches in the car if you live in cold climates. It is said that if a car is stranded in the snow, the flame from a single candle can keep the air temperature in a car just high enough to keep the occupants from freezing. While I wouldn't want to test this theory, I understand the underlying principle that becomes evident when we exchange the symbolism of the flame of the candle for the human Soul. It is true that the Divine Love flowing from just one Soul is enough warmth to inspire others in our community from freezing in their fear. Even a small spark of the Divine Light can bring enlightenment to a hopeless and darkened mind. Just as the flame from one candle can bring light to a darkened room, it is true that one Soul can bring light to a darkened place in the world. It is the Divine Light within each of us that the flame represents.

There is a ritual we call *Havdalah* which is done at the close of the Sabbath to transition into the new week. (See the section on Shabbat for more information about Havdalah.) In this ritual we use a special braided candle to represent the Light and the Love of The Holy One. This ritual implies a powerful spiritual truth and links the Divine Light with the flame of fire. The blessing that we say over the Havdalah candle when we use it is:

> "Blessed are You, O Holy One, our God, Guide of the Cosmos, Who creates fire from the Light."
> Ba-ruch a-tah Yah, E-lo-hei-nu me-lekh ha-o-lam, bo-rei m'o-rei ha-eish.

This blessing states that from the Divine Light, (Divine Energy flowing through the Dimensions) fire is created in this Dimension. So fire reminds us of the Divine Light of God. The fire (spirit) clinging to the wick (physical), facilitates existence in this Dimension.

When do we use candles? In ancient days oil lamps were used as we use candles made of wax today. The menorah (candelabra) in the Temple used oil. In more recent history, candles are used to kindle the flame. We start the beginning of a Holy Day or Festival with the kindling of the flame, the lighting of candles. We also mark life-cycle events by lighting candles.

The highest of all Holy Days is Shabbat. We begin and end

Shabbat with the "bringing of the Light." Shabbat begins at sundown on Friday evening (see the section on Shabbat for the explanation of the Jewish calendar day). It is a tradition to kindle the Lights of Shabbat in our home and in synagogues on Friday evening. Once the Shabbat candles have been kindled, Shabbat has begun, even if it is before sundown. The candles are left to burn all the way down until they go out on their own. We do not extinguish them, for they represent the Divine Light illumining the world on Shabbat. It is traditional for two candles to be kindled, but some families light more than two. Some families have a candle for each member of the family. Their individual candle is lighted on Shabbat, that they receive the Divine Light of Shabbat. It is a nice tradition that the children, the mother and father each have a special candleholder or oil lamp that is lighted on Shabbat. As each child leaves home they take their lamp with them that they continue to observe Shabbat in their new home.

Another reason we kindle a flame on Shabbat is so the flame of love burning within our hearts is brought to the "outside" that we may unite our love with the Shechinah, the feminine aspect of God's Presence that comes to dwell within us on the Sabbath.

The light from the Sabbath candles is not used for any purpose (such as working) other than to illumine the night with the sweet, soft light of Shabbat. It adds to the sensuality of the Sabbath. Shabbat is our time to lay down the work of the week, and to rekindle the love flowing within us, between us and God, and between us and others. It is a day to take time to look more deeply into the eyes of those we love and share the Divine Light we see glowing there in the windows of their Souls. The light and the shadows of the Shabbat candles as they burn low reminds us to just BE for 24 hours as the light illumines the darkness, engulfing our home in the glow of our love.

We also begin the Festivals of *Passover*, *Shavuot* (Feast of Weeks), and *Sukkot* (Feast of Tabernacles), *Rosh Hashanah* (New Year) and *Yom Kippur* (Day of Atonement) by kindling the Light. On Yom Kippur we also light a candle to honor those who have died. This *yahrzeit* (year's time) candle will burn for the entire 24-hour period of Yom Kippur. At Passover we use a candle to search for leavening in our homes. This light represents our Soul searching in our hearts and in our lives, (which is what the house represents) for *hametz* (leavening) that which puffs us up.

The holiday of Hanukkah is the Festival of Light. While many use oil lamps to signify the Miracle of the Oil at this season, most people light candles in a Hanukiah, the nine-light candelabra. As on Shabbat, the candles are allowed to burn down entirely, their dancing light adding to the joy of the season. For more on these celebrations see Chapter 3.

We show our recognition of others as Divine sparks of the Light of God in this dimension by lighting a candle in honor of them at life-cycle rituals from birthing to dying. The candle represents the transitions our Souls make on the sacred journeys of our lives.

On the eighth day after the birth of a baby we observe a ritual which gives a baby his or her Hebrew name and when boys are circumcised. At the baby naming there is a spiritual tradition of lighting candles. Friends and family gather for the ceremony, during which the parents commit their pathway to raising the child to be who s/he has been created to be. We are reminded of the Covenant made at Sinai to be God's people, remembering all of the Sacred Ways given to us and we include this child in that Covenant. We announce the child to be called by the name of _____ in Israel. Many Rabbis continue the spiritual ritual of welcoming the baby into the Tribe and family by having each guest light a candle and give the baby a blessing from their heart; a message from their Soul that they want the baby's Soul to know upon beginning the sacred journey of Life. By the end of the ceremony there are usually many candles burning brightly. Their flames dance and contribute to the celebration and joy of receiving this child as a gift of life and a promise of the future.

A child's unique journey is also honored by candles used in rituals at the time of their coming of age, (Bar or Bat Mitzvah) and at their wedding. At the end of life a candle will be kindled that will burn for seven days in honor of their Soul. Every year on the date of their death their loved ones will kindle a yahrzeit candle that will burn for twenty-four hours to honor their Soul.

At the coming of age ritual a child assumes his or her place as a member of the prayer community of Israel. As such s/he reads a portion of the Torah to the congregation and speaks of its meaning to him or her. The *Bar* or *Bat Mitzvah* (Son or Daughter of the Covenant) may also light thirteen (twelve in the case of girls who have their Bat Mitzvah at age twelve) candles, each representing a year of life. With the lighting of each candle the young person honors someone special who then comes forward and speaks about the meaning of this sacred event.

Some brides and grooms choose to light a candle to honor their separate selves, their uniqueness, hopes, visions and dreams. Each kindles their own unique candle. They each then use their own candle to kindle the flame of a third candle that represents their marriage and all they envision that marriage to be. All three candles, their personal candles and their marriage candle, continue to burn throughout the wedding, for only by being wholly who each one is, allowing each other's light to shine brightly, can they contribute with integrity to a marriage.

After a lifetime has all too quickly flown by, we continue to honor our loved ones by kindling a candle to burn in the home for the first full week. Traditionally, everything we do for one who has died is done for the purpose of honoring that person. We bury the body within 24 hours. When we return home from the cemetery we light a large *shiva* candle that will burn for seven days (*shiva* means seven), which is the length of the first period of mourning. This period is called *Shiva*. This flame honors the Soul of the person and is not extinguished for the entire first week.

Each year on the anniversary of their death we honor the love that person brought to our lives and the mitzvot they performed in the world by kindling a 24-hour candle. The day of our loved one's death is considered to be more honorable than the day of their birth. Why? Because on the day of their birth all the love and mitzvot, all the gifts they have to offer to the world are only potential. However, on the day of their death, all they brought to the world has been actualized, and the world has become a different place for their having been there.

The Hebrew rituals that mark the transition of the Soul out of the body and back into the Source of All Life are filled with light. This reminds us of the Eternal nature of our Spirit, represented by the light. Even though there is darkness in the mystery of death, we believe in the eternal bonds of love that transcend the veil of death, linking us together forever with our loved ones.

And so, we remember with candles. We remember their light, which continues to glow brightly in our lives in what they shared with us and who we have become because of them.

What are some of the ways your church or faith tradition uses candles? How do you use candles in your private worship? Maybe you would like to the use candles more often into your own spiritual practices.

Candles are a beautiful way to bring a soft, gentle light into your prayer/meditation room. Try choosing candles of different scents to clear, to cleanse, and to purify the room. The glow of a candle can elevate your spirit. Use candles of particular colors for different types of prayer/meditation, or for different seasons. Make the kindling of the flame a sacred action by saying a blessing beforehand. The blessing of the Havdalah candle at the beginning of this section is appropriate. Meditate upon its meaning.

The Psalmist declares, "They word is a lamp unto my feet and a light unto my path." (Ps. 119:105). For this reason, Torah, in the sense of all of God's wisdom, instruction and teaching is depicted as a light.

Mystics have used a flame as a visual meditation tool for centuries. To use a flame for visual meditation, look at the flame until you no longer see the flame, but see <u>into</u> the flame. See the wick, the blue, the white, and the glow of light surrounding the flame. Allow the flame to impart to you the *sod,* the secrets it is holding for you to know about your Soul.

The following guided meditation can help you envision the flame of your own Soul. It can help you connect and communicate with your Eternal Soul.

Candle Meditation

- Sit in the position in which you feel most comfortable when meditating.
- Close your eyes, and deeply breathe in four breaths, inhaling Spirit each time and exhaling your love to God.
- You are entering a room of many candles. The light is softy glowing.
- Each one of these flames is a human Soul.
- Look at the different candles and flames. How do they differ?
- One flame will catch your eye. It is the flame that represents the

Light of your Soul. How does it look?

- What are its characteristics? How do they symbolize your Soul?
- Now your candle and flame is the only one you see. Look into its light and see the beautiful light of your Soul.
- Open your spiritual ears to hear the messages of your Soul.
- What is it saying to you?
- What does your Soul desire to do in this lifetime?
- What does your Soul desire to do now to move forward on your Spiritual Pathway?
- What is your answer to your Soul?
- Name one thing you will do, your first step, to fulfill your Soul's desire.
- Now you are back with all the other candles and flames.
- There is a bright white light beginning to fill the room.
- It is the Divine Light. The flames are each ascending up to the Divine Light. It glistens and radiates a warm, crystalline light that you are drawn to.
- When you are ready, move with your Soul's flame into the Divine Light and feel its warmth bath you in love.
- Know that this is the home of your Soul. This is the place from which you came and will return to when your destiny has been fulfilled.
- Enjoy The Divine Presence as long as you like.
- When you are ready, put the flame of your candle into your open heart, knowing your heart is a safe and sacred place. Know that the light of which you are a part dwells there within your heart, illuminating your life.
- Let the flame of your candle warm your heart with love and give light to your path.
- Now, return to this time and this place. Take four deep breaths, paying attention to how your breath feels in your body.

- When you are ready, open your eyes and see all that is around you in the illumination of the flame you carry in your heart. Embrace that which you see with your love.

You may want to tape record the Candle Meditation so you can play it back and fully enter the meditation.

The candle symbolism: Divine Light, Presence of God, Soul, Spirit, Enlightenment, Transcendence, Divine Love, Redemption, Transition, Eternity, Faith, Torah, Remembrance.

Angels
Messengers of God

> And he (Jacob) dreamed, and, behold, a ladder set up on the Earth, and the top of it reached to Heaven: and behold the angels of God were ascending and descending on it.
>
> GENESIS 28:12

The concept of angels comes from the ancient and mystical traditions of Abraham. Abraham was visited by the angels many times. He was visited by three angels bearing messages about the birth of his son, Isaac, and the destruction of the cities of Sodom and Gomorrah (Genesis 18). Abraham was also paid a timely visit by the angel of the Lord at his greatest moment of testing; the binding of his son Isaac on Mount Moriah (Genesis: 22:11). Continuing in the tradition of his grandfather, Abraham, Jacob encountered angels in a dream he had as he was leaving the land of his father, Abraham. In the dream he saw angels, ascending and descending through the dimensions (symbolized by a ladder). Angels are the Divine Messengers of God, moving between the

Dimensions, bringing the Divine Flow of Plenty down to this World, and carrying the prayers and messages from this World to the Higher Dimensions.

The Hebrew word *malach* (*malachim,* plural) literally means, "messenger" and is translated into English as "angel". The angels are the energies from other dimensions, which bring messages to us. They also carry messages from us to the Presence of the Holy One. This is why the angels in Jacob's dream were going both up and down the ladder. Angels move from one Dimension or World to all of the others to carry out their missions.

When the angels appear in this World they can disguise themselves as human beings and appear quite natural and normal. Other times they can appear with an other worldliness which can be frightening and awe inspiring. That is why their first words to the person they are visiting are often, "Fear not...."

The angels are living creatures who function in the higher Dimensions as we function in this World of physicality. They are not human beings, but a different kind of being created for a specific purpose with specific characteristics. The angels are created beings from a higher realm whose purpose is to carry messages both "down" to this plane and "up" to the "Throne of God". Each angel can carry only one message at a time. They can appear as Beings of Light, or in natural human form as in the visitation of the three angels to Abraham.

> "And the Holy One appeared to him (Abraham) by the terebinths of Mamre, as he sat in the tent door in the heat of the day: and he raised his eyes and looked, and lo, three men stood by him; ... And they said to him, Where is Sara you wife? And he said, Behold, in the tent. And he (the angel) said, I will

certainly return to you at this season; and lo Sara, your wife shall have a son... ."

GENESIS 18:1, 2, 9, 10

Three angels appear to Abraham and Sarah. They deliver to them the message of Isaac's birth. They also revealed to God's servant, Abraham, the information that they were traveling on to the two cities of Sodom and Gomorrah. They had messages to the inhabitants of these cities to flee, for the cities would be destroyed.

"And there came two angels to Sodom at evening, and Lot sat in the gate of Sodom and Lot seeing them rose up to meet them ..."

GENESIS 19:1

There are now only two angels, because the one angel already delivered his message to Abraham and Sarah. The two angels bearing messages to the two cities continue with their mission. Angels bear a direct and solitary message to humans.

The Higher Realm that angels are created Beings from is called the World of *Yetzirah*, the World of Formation. It is the realm of pure emotion and feeling. Because angels are beings of pure emotion, they connect to us, and connect us to other realms by way of emotions or impulses. Each angel carries its own character, qualities and content. The way one angel differs from the other is not by physical form, but, because they are from the World of Emotion, they differ by the essence of the emotion they carry. One angel may be of love, another fear, another joy, or anger, or any emotions or shade of emotion to Infinity. Unlike human beings whose emotions can change from moment to moment, an angel is the essence of a particular emotion and does not vary from that state.

When there is a group of angels expressing a larger totality of emotion, they are referred to as a "camp of angels," or "mansions". A "camp of angels of love" expresses the spectrum of types of love and intensity, each angel contributing its own unique and singular form of that emotion. Because emotions are actually varying degrees of an Infinite continuum, the angels of a camp can be anything from an angel carrying much light, as a deeply, devotional love angel, to the other end of the spectrum, an angel carrying a lower degree of light, an angel which expresses paralyzing fear. There is no moral judgment of either angel; they are simply creations, created for a specific purpose, expressing a single emotional essence.

> "An angel, however is not merely a fragment of existence doing nothing more than manifesting an emotion; it is a whole and integral being, conscious of itself and its surroundings and able to act and create and do things within the framework of the world of formation (feelings). The nature of the angel is to be, to a degree, as its name in Hebrew signifies, a messenger, to constitute a permanent contact between our world of action and the higher worlds. The angel is the one who effects transfers of the vital plenty between worlds."
>
> THIRTEEN PETALLED ROSE, PG. 9

The ancient teachings recognize two types of angels according to their creation. First, there are angels who are an integral part of the Eternal Being, created at the Beginning. It is through these angels that the transfer and flow of the Divine Plenty comes through the dimensions. It is through these angels that Divine Grace flows in waves, arising and descending through the worlds.

While there are an infinite number of these angels, the more widely known are the archangels. The archangels differ from the angels of emotion in that they are beings created in the World of B'riyah, the World of pure intellect, which is a higher Dimension than the World of Emotion. They carry higher light and surround the "Throne of God" or inhabit the "Throne Room". This is not to be taken literally, but symbolically as the closest Dimension to the Source of All Life.

Five of the archangels well known within Jewish and Christian texts will be discussed here: MichaEl, RaphaEl, GavriEl, RaziEl, and UriEl. You will notice that the name for God, El, is at the end of each of the archangels' names. The names of archangels are all Hebrew and carry the meaning of the characteristics of the angel. Their names name their essence.

MichaEl is probably one of the most widely known and beloved of the archangels. The name MichaEl means, "Who is like unto God?" MichaEl is one of the most powerful angels in God's "cabinet" of angels. He is the "Angel of Awe". When considering the question that this archangel's name poses to the human being "Who is like unto God?" the human comes into an experience of the "awe" of God. The experience of awe is a characteristic of Archangel MichaEl's presence. MichaEl is also the guardian angel of Israel. He is the Angel of Mercy (Compassion). In the moment of awe of The Holy One, we experience mercy.

GavriEl is another archangel who is well known. Her name means, "Strength of God." She is the Angel of Courage. When we hear the sound of the Shofar I believe it is GavriEl who calls our hearts to awaken and to take courage, fear not!

Another archangel is RaphaEl. Most people know him as the archangel of healing, as his name indicates, "Healer of God."

RaphaEl is also the Angel of Love. He leads hosts and legions of angels in this "camp." It is through love that healing takes place. It is through love that we heal our world.

The next two archangels are not as well publicized, but are very powerful messengers of light. Their nature is part of the reason they are a little obscure. The first is RaziEl. His name means, "Divine Mysteries of God." He is the keeper of the Divine Mysteries. Have you ever had a moment when a profound truth suddenly "came" to you – you understood a concept or truth that was totally hidden from you previously? This is the work of RaziEl. When you experience an event in your life that doesn't make sense you can seek God's wisdom about it by asking God's messenger RaziEl for assistance to bring the spiritual meaning to you. When you are trying to understand a spiritual concept that is beyond your comprehension you can ask Archangel RaziEl to give you understanding, expand your consciousness, and give you the message of the concept in language that you will understand. He can do this for he is the keeper of the Divine Secrets of *Yah* (ancient name for God).

The last of the archangels we will discuss is UriEl. His name means, "My Light is God." He is the Angel of Illumination. UriEl's presence brings the Effulgence of The Holy One into and through us to the degree we are open and able to receive. UriEl is an open channel flooding us with God's light in whatever measure, intensity or magnification of flow our situation calls for at the time. UriEl brings the Light of Truth.

At the end of this section is a meditation for setting the archangels around you every day. The angels are always near you, however, when you work with the angels and open your consciousness to their presence you will feel their immense love and receive their messages for your life.

The second type of angel recognized by the ancient traditions is the angel who is created anew. These angels can be created by human actions, thoughts and feelings. We create these angels by directing our emotions and thoughts toward other people. The emotions and intentions with which we do a loving deed of kindness or mitzvah creates an angel which is the messenger of the emotional energy we emit. That angel acts as a bridge linking us (the source of the emotion) with the other person, the object of the action, feelings and thoughts. We become linked together by the angel we create with our feelings. The love energy we put out carries our energy "signature" which is as unique as our fingerprint is in the physical world.

Have you ever done something really nice for someone and had them say to you, "Oh you're an angel" ? Sometimes our words speak more truth than we consciously know. What that phrase means is that the love carried in that action produced an angel that links the two of you and continually ministers that love between you two. You are not actually an angel, but you have created an angel that the other person is experiencing as part of you! The book of Song of Solomon (Song of Songs) tells us that "love is strong as death." This wisdom is tells us that our love forever links us with our loved ones even to the other side after their death because our love is the bridge that transcends the dimensions. The angels created by our love for each other serve to link us, to bridge the dimensions between us.

However, a word of caution is required when we are speaking of angels created by our emotions toward others. If we send out emotions of anger, fear, or hatred, the angels created by those emotions also link us to the object of our emotional impulse. It is easy to understand why "what goes around comes around." More accurately, we are building a network of links between ourselves, others and God by our thoughts, actions and feelings which we attach to them. These energies do not need to "go around" they are always in place with our energy signature on them. They will continue to link us – or bind us in that energy until we choose to release that angel by choosing a different way of responding; choosing to respond from our love. It may take some forgiveness, or letting go of our issues, but, it is worth the effort, for this frees our energy. Sometimes we may feel that we can't release our feelings; however, heaven can help us do so if we so choose. We can lift up our feelings to the angels and ask for their help to surrender and release those feelings, and then open our hearts before God in Truth. By doing this we set ourselves free, we set the other person free and we create a new angel. We create a new angel from the old one by raising the vibrational energy, the amount of light of the original angel to the new level that carries a message of Higher Light and of love to that person. It is not always easy spiritual work, but it is much easier than carrying within us the negative feelings that truly hurt us. Creating angels in this dimension is a powerful aspect of the human experience.

With the empowerment of the gift of creating angels through our feelings comes the responsibility to act from our enlightenment. We must use our highest self to create the world we desire around us – one of light, peace, joy and love. The effects of our words and deeds go beyond this material world to spirit worlds beyond us. As humans we are empowered to direct holiness into this world and beyond, and to initiate significant transformation.

Have you ever felt an overwhelming love for God, or sent a prayer of compassion for someone's healing? At that moment, angels were created who are with you and your loved one still.

What angels do you desire to hold within yourself and between you and others?

There are many stories in the Hebrew and Christian scriptures about the presence and ministry of angels. We already explored the visitation of Abraham by three angels and later by the Angel of the Lord on Mount Moriah. There is also the story of a famous wrestling match of the "Mauling Malakh" vs. "Jacob the Jew" later known as "Jacob the Lame." In the Book of Job we read about Job's testing through angelic intervention.

The scenario involves the well-known angel, HaSatan (Satan), who played havoc in Job's life. The scene is the "courts of Heaven". God asks Satan if he has noticed His faithful servant Job. Satan complains that Job is only faithful because of all that God has given him. So God gives permission to HaSatan to visit Job's life with adversity, but warns HaSatan that he may not touch Job's body. Without knowing why, Job finds he is stripped of family, possessions, health, friends and all that was dear to him. It is important to notice in this story that Satan is not a force outside of the will of God, for God set the boundaries of ways that Satan could touch Job. Satan is limited by God's will.

Job knows nothing of the cause of his calamities, while in the Higher Realms there is an ongoing dialogue – even a wager between God and Satan as to the loyalty to God that Job would cling to even in dire adversity.

The name HaSatan means "the adversary". Satan is, as the name implies, simply another member of God's cabinet of angels whose job it is to test humanity through adversity. How we respond to Satan or adversity reveals our "learning edge" or that point where we are gaining new spiritual growth. Satan and adversity can be used to strengthen our resolve when we need great energy to manifest something powerful in our lives. What we are given the opportunity to learn in every situation of adversity is how to open our hearts in love to God in all things, leaning not to our own understanding, but looking ever upward and inward for God's guidance, presence and wisdom. It is not a matter of blind faith, but of our willingness to trust God.

The story of Job teaches us that in our own understanding we see a limited portion of the story of our lives, as did Job. However, the rest of the story is within God. Even in the most puzzling times in our spiritual walk, God empowers us by inviting us to ask for wisdom. While Job's friends all try to understand the wisdom in the situation, in the end, the only answer is the awesomeness and yet the oneness of God.

It is all God, and yet there is awe in the realization that we are part of The One. We are The Many emanated by The One, yet moving in enlightenment back into The One. God asks Job, "Where were you when I laid the foundations of the earth?" Ask yourself this question. One answer is that you were in God. The moment of awe gives birth to true humility. You are no less than a fraction of The Infinite, of The One who powers the Universe and keeps the planets in their orbits. You are no less than an emanation of The One Beyond all beyond; and yet, this is The One as close as your very breath. As the Breath of Life leaves God's mouth it enters yours; and like a wave it returns again to The Source. Your existence is awe-inspiring. It is all God. It is all Grace.

The outcome of the story is that Job is restored twice over what he started out with. His children were restored to him (mystically speaking their souls were reborn to him as his children). Symbolically, after the moment of awe we each double our consciousness. At the end of the story Job included his daughters equally with his sons in the inheritance of his wealth. This is an expansion of consciousness of the Divine inherent in each one of us, for we are all awesomely one. The adversary, HaSatan, angel of God, is the villain of the story who antithetically teaches this principle of life.

In the New Testament scriptures both Joseph and Mary, parents of Jesus, were visited by angels with specific messages (Matthew 1). Zachariah, husband of Elizabeth, both *Cohanim*, descendants of Aaron the High Priest, the parents of John the Baptist was also notified about the birth of a special Soul given as their son. (Luke 1). These people of faith were not above the human experience, but experienced life with all of the human frailties that we do today. Angels continue to communicate messages to humans today; especially to those who are listening for Divine Guidance.

Have you had experiences or encounters with angels? Sometimes our "spiritual ears" are opened and we can hear them "sing" or hear celestial music, which has notes far beyond the harmonies of the physical world. It is quite usual for an angel to deliver a message without taking physical form. At that time you may sense the "presence" of an angel. There are times we experience the messages of other dimensions quite naturally in this dimension. Opening yourself to the angel's ministry of the Divine Plenty is part of the work of the ministering spirits, angels, the Holy Spirit all sent by The Holy One to create a more Holy Place here in our world through you.

The Traditions teach us that each person has a guardian angel. It is said that this angel looks exactly like you in spiritual form; it carries your "energy DNA." Psalms 91:11 refers to your guardian angels and their God-given task:

> "The Holy One shall give the angels charges concerning you, that they guard your path."

> PSALM 91:11

How do you work with your guardian angel? How do you communicate with these messengers of God? You can do following meditation each morning to make heighten your awareness of the angels around you who are there to help you and assist you on your Sacred Pathway.

Angel Meditation

- Sit straight but relaxed with your feet on the floor or in your usual meditation position.
- Breathe, deeply three times: one to move from Assiyah, (physical) into Yetsirah (Feeling), two to move from Yetsirah (Feelings) into B'riyah (Thought) and three to move from B'riyah (Thought) into Atzilut (Being)
- Move the Energy flowing within you – outwardly to greet the Energy (White Light) flowing into your Being through your open Keter (Crown Sephirah) at the top of your head.
- Ask the Archangels to be with you – invite them into your dwelling place, your Being.
- Ask the Archangels to guard your footsteps and pathway, Psalm 91:11 – "The Holy One shall give the angels charges concerning you, that they guard your path."
- Ask the Angels to bring God's messages to you.
- Ask the Angels to work in partnership with you to bring God's Divine Light and Holy Presence into this world
- Set the Archangels around you with the following mystical meditation from the ancient practices:
- Open your consciousness to:
    Michael, Angel of Mercy, before you
    Raziel, Angel of Divine Mystery, behind you
    Gavriel, Angel of Strength and Courage, to the left of you
    Raphael, Angel of God's Healing Love, to the right of you

Uriel, Angel of Light, above you

- Sit in silence and allow yourself to experience their Presence.
- Thank them for their loving care of you, and...
- When you are ready, return to the Presence of this Dimension, to this room, and to all that is around you.

The angels' symbolism: messengers of God.

The Menorah
God's Presence in the Light

And you shall make a menorah (candlestick) of pure gold: of beaten work shall the candlestick be made: its shaft, and its branches, its bowls, its bulbs, and its flowers, shall be of the same. And six branches shall come out of its sides; three branches of the candlestick out of the one side, and three branches of the candlestick out of the other side: three cups made like almonds, with a bulb and a flower in one branch; and three cups made like almonds in the other branch, with a bulb and a flower: so in the six branches that come out of the candlestick. And in the candlestick shall be four bowls made like almonds, with their bulbs and flowers. And there shall be a bulb under two branches of the same piece, and a bulb under two branches of the same piece, and a bulb under two branches of the same piece, according to the six branches that proceed out of the candlestick. Their bulbs and their branches shall be made of the same piece: all shall be one beaten work of pure gold. And you shall make its seven lamps: and they shall light its lamps, that they may give light over against it. And its tongs, and its ashpans, shall be of pure gold. Of a talent of pure gold, shall he make it, with all these vessels. And

look that you make them after their pattern, which was shown
you in the mountain.

EXODUS 25:30-40

The *menorah*, candelabra, that is described here in Exodus shed a
light in the Holy Place of the Tabernacle and later in the Temple
in Jerusalem that did more than simply provide light to a place
without windows. It illumined the walls of colorful curtains, and
the vessels of gold with a glow of the Presence of the Holy One.
It was this menorah that miraculously gave its sacred Light from
the one day's vial of consecrated oil, in the Hanukkah story. (See
Holidays and Hanukkah). It was this menorah that became the
main symbol of the Hebrew people. Why the menorah?

The menorah symbolizes a precious promise and mission of
the people of the Covenant:

> "... I The Holy One have called you in righteousness, and will
> hold your hand, and will keep you and give you for a covenant
> of the people, for a light of the nations; to open the blind
> eyes, to bring out the prisoners from the prison, and them who
> sit in darkness out of the prison house."

ISAIAH 41:6

God's first act of creation in Genesis was to create light. From that
light was manifest everything that exists. From that Divine Light
emanated the Dimensions, created beings in those Dimensions,
and the form and matter of this Dimension. Light is our symbol
of God's emanation of Creation in love. We walk by this light. It
is by this light that our eyes are opened from their blindness and
we see truth; the truth that we recognize ourselves and others as
beings of the light. By bringing the light of Spirit to Earth through

our actions, we bring enlightenment to the planet. We bring this light that we may live in harmony within ourselves, between ourselves and with all of Creation. By this light we are set free from the darkness and imprisonment of fear, judgment and hatred of ourselves and of others. We have not yet reached the fullness of Enlightenment yet. It remains our mission to do so. Therefore, we hold the menorah before us to remind us of how precious the light of the Source of Life is to us. We hold the menorah before us that we may become ever more transparent vessels through which the light may flow to others. As we take the hand of the Being of Light (person) standing next to us, we link ourselves together to form the Greater Vessel through which the Divine Light of God may flow, ever increasingly, to this world. This is the Menorah. Yet, there is more meaning to the mystical Menorah.

The Divine Light is a main theme throughout the mystical teachings. The menorah is actually a mystical tool and symbol. Did you notice how complex the instructions given in Exodus seem to be? How could Moses possibly imagine how to form it? How would it look? The last sentence of the passage is the answer to this question. Moses received the vision of how this menorah would look during his meditations on Mount Sinai. He saw the essence of the menorah as it came through the Dimensions to take its physical form. Its name, *men-orah*, can be understood to mean "from the light." The shape of the menorah is a representation of the Four Worlds and the Tree of Life, the Sephirot.

Tree of Life Menorah

The spaces between the arms represent the Four Worlds of: *Atzilut*/Emanation, *B'riyah*/Intellect, *Yetzirah*/Emotion, and *Assiyah*/Action (physical world). These arms are each made from one continuous piece, as are the Dimensions. Each of the seven branches and the center column represent one of the Sephirot on the Tree of Life. The Sephirot are the "power centers" of the attributes of God. The Divine attributes or energies are around and within everything that exists. The oil flowing through the menorah providing fuel for the light symbolizes the Spirit of God flowing through each human Soul, bringing light into the world.

The menorah is a meditative picture of the building blocks of existence. When its light is kindled the meditator can gaze upon it to enter a world of consciousness beyond and within other worlds. When you experience this consciousness, you can also open yourself to knowing the menorah within your heart; the light that is within "you." Taken in this context, the words of the Rabbi of Nazareth take on a new meaning:

> "You are the Light of the world."
>
> MATTHEW 5:14

> "I am the Light of the world."
>
> JOHN 8:12

We all bear the light of The Holy One. This inner light is referred to in the Hebrew heritage as the Divine Spark. While the Divine Spark is Infinite, we bear it in a finite body. It becomes the Greater Light once more as we unite it in harmony and peace within ourselves and between ourselves and nature. This is the work of unifying the world, bringing "the many" back to "The One" from which it came. When this work is complete, when we increase the light symbolized by the menorah until all darkness in this world is dispelled, then this Dimension, and all of nature will shift into a higher level of existence. It will be the time of the Enlightenment.

Psalm 67 is known as the Menorah Psalm, for there is a tradition that King David had this Psalm engraved on his shield, the verses written in the form of a menorah. It has been used by mystics as a meditation piece and as a formulation for a prayer of protection on amulets. It adorns many prayer books, inviting the reader to follow the arms of the menorah made of the verses of this Psalm.

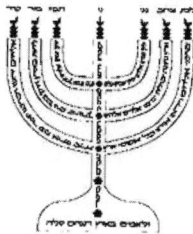

לַמְנַצֵּחַ בִּנְגִינֹת מִזְמוֹר שִׁיר: אֱלֹהִים יְחָנֵּנוּ וִיבָרְכֵנוּ יָאֵר פָּנָיו
אִתָּנוּ סֶלָה: לָדַעַת בָּאָרֶץ דַּרְכֶּךָ בְּכָל־גּוֹיִם יְשׁוּעָתֶךָ: יוֹדוּךָ
עַמִּים אֱלֹהִים יוֹדוּךָ עַמִּים כֻּלָּם: יִשְׂמְחוּ וִירַנְּנוּ לְאֻמִּים כִּי
תִשְׁפֹּט עַמִּים מִישֹׁר וּלְאֻמִּים בָּאָרֶץ תַּנְחֵם סֶלָה: יוֹדוּךָ
עַמִּים אֱלֹהִים יוֹדוּךָ עַמִּים כֻּלָּם: אֶרֶץ נָתְנָה יְבוּלָהּ
יְבָרְכֵנוּ אֱלֹהִים אֱלֹהֵינוּ: יְבָרְכֵנוּ אֱלֹהִים וְיִירְאוּ אוֹתוֹ כָּל־
אַפְסֵי־אָרֶץ:

Psalm 67 Menorah

Another form of menorah is the nine-branched Hanukiah. It carries eight branches, one for each of the eight days that the oil miraculously lasted in the Temple in the story of the Maccabees. (See the section on Hanukkah). The ninth light is the *Shammash*, the helper candle. This light is kindled first, and then the other lights are kindled from its flame, symbolizing the spiritual concept of the Divine Light of the Holy Spirit flowing to and through each of us from the Source of Light out into the World. The Temple was rededicated in those times and the light of the menorah returned to illuminate the Holy Place.

117

Today, with the return of our people to Israel after 2000 years of exile, the symbol of the menorah takes on special significance. The State of Israel uses the menorah as a national symbol. It is stylized in many forms and used on money, stamps, federal signs and keepsakes for those traveling to Israel. There is a large sculpted menorah outside of the Knesset (Parliament House) building, which depicts the history of Israel. Its flames represent the light of hope, *HaTikveh*, which is the title of the national anthem of Israel. This hope is that the new State of Israel brings to every Jewish heart the assurance of the continuance of our Hebrew heritage in peace and safety in the land of our ancestors.

The Menorah is our symbol of hope, our symbol of the Divine Light shining through all of us, illumining our pathway back to God. We carry the menorah in our heart. This too, is your heritage, your light. Like the light of the menorah, let your light shine and flow freely to others that our world might be a brighter place to live.

The menorah symbolism: Divine Light, Presence of God, the Tree of Life, Sephirot and the Four Worlds meditation piece, Enlightenment, Hope, Holy Spirit, State of Israel.

The Star of David
Where Heaven and Earth Touch

The menorah remains the oldest symbol for the Hebrew people; however, probably the most popular and widely recognized symbol is the Star of David. The Hebrew name for the Star of David is *"Magen David,"* which literally means, "Shield of David." This star was used as David's personal symbol of identity on his warrior's shield.

Use of the six-pointed star, or hexagram, is rooted in the mystical traditions. It was most often found in Jewish antiquity within the ancient practices. It has been associated with Rabbi Akiva and his student, Bar Kokhba, ("son of the star"), who was the general who led the rebellion against Rome in 135 CE. The Magen David continues to be used today for spiritual and symbolic purposes.

This symbol is also known in the oral traditions as the "Seal of Solomon". (*Gittin* 68a, Talmud). King Solomon was the son of David and Bathsheba. He reigned after his father David, expanding the borders of Israel to encompass the largest territory in history (beyond the boundaries of Israel today) by means of making treaties. He also increased the wealth of Israel to its height and was known for his God given wisdom. Originally, the "Seal of Solomon" was a ring with the Star of David and the Sacred Name for God on it which he used in spiritual practices. Over time, copies of the emblem on his ring dropped the Sacred Name and the replaced the hexagram (six-pointed star) with a pentagram (five-pointed star). This symbol became known as the Seal of Solomon.

While the six-pointed star has been used in many cultures since ancient times, the Star of David is particular in that it has two intertwined triangles. It has often been stylized in art; however, to maintain its authenticity as a Star of David the triangles must be intertwined.

The hexagram has been used in many ancient, mystical traditions. The intertwined and inverted triangles represent numerous ideas. In Jewish mystical thought the upper triangle represents the Divine Energy coming from above while the lower triangle represents the Divine Energy of this dimension mingled with the Divine Energy of the Higher Realms; Heaven and Earth embracing. The triangle pointing down is likened to the three Sephirot, Divine Emanations, *Keter*/Crown, *Hochmah*/Wisdom and *Binah*/Understanding, flowing from God interlocking with these same three Sephirot reaching up from Creation. The two triangles also represent male and female energy coming together to make wholeness. It symbolizes the kiss of Heaven and Earth.

The six points of the star represent the six directions or points of the Earth from which Energy flows to us and away from us; North, South, East, West, up and down. On Sukkot we shake the *lulav* in these six directions (see the section on the Pilgrimage Holidays, Sukkot) entreating God's blessing in the coming year.

The six points have also been associated with the six attributes of the Messiah listed in Isaiah 11:2:

> And there shall come forth a rod out of the stem of Yishay, and a branch shall grow out of his roots: and the spirit of The Holy One shall rest upon him, the spirit of wisdom and understanding, the spirit of counsel and might, the spirit of knowledge and the awe of the Eternal One; and his delight shall be in awe of The Infinite One.
>
> ISAIAH 11:1,2

This list of six attributes is understood to be referring to the first six Sephirot of the Kabbalistic Tree of Life. The six-pointed Star of David has become symbolic of the Messiah since it is symbolic of the Davidic line, the lineage of the Messiah.

Hebrew mystics use the six-pointed star for amulets and formulations. One such symbol places one of the letters of the Divine Name of God, Yud, Hey, Vav, Hey in each of the six triangles formed by the points of the star. These letters each have an essence that is in harmony with the triangle in which it is placed. This symbol can be used as a visual meditation, as well.

The Star of David has also been used by anti-Semitic governments to identify persons of Jewish lineage. Different governments at different times in history have enacted laws stating that every Jew must wear a hat or armband with the Star of David on it as an identifier. While this has been imposed as a badge of shame, it was worn as a badge of courage and pride by thousands of Jews throughout those difficult times. There have even been some Gentiles of great courage and faith (such as in Denmark during the Nazi era) who have donned the Star of David in solidarity with their Jewish neighbors.

The State of Israel has chosen the Star of David as its symbol on the Israeli flag. The two blue stripes, one across the top and the other across the bottom of the flag, are symbolic of the blue thread represented in the stripe on the Tallit, prayer shawl. The Star of David is now flown proudly on the Israeli flag as a reminder of the faith and trust our people have maintained in The Holy One for millennia. It is a symbol of the fulfillment of the prophecy, "No weapon formed against you shall prosper," (Isaiah 54:17). In truth, the most heinous plots of the last century to eradicate the Covenant People, the Hebrews, did not prosper. The prophets' words and God's promises of encouragement over the centuries give us hope for peace in the future. Each day that the Israeli flag waves the Star of David over the Holy Land of Israel, God's promise of a day of Peace and Light, the day of Enlightenment comes closer.

King David is the foremost ancestor in the line of the Messiah. The Star of David's interlocking trinities are a symbol for the place where Heaven and Earth meet. The Star of David is a symbol and a heritage you carry from ancient days. If you choose to wear it, do so with courage, pride, faith and trust in The Holy One, the God of your Ancestors. As you wear the symbol of the Magen David, the Shield of David, may you find within it God's Divine Protection in your life and the power and meaning of intimacy with The Holy One of Israel.

The Star of David Symbolism: Protection, Davidic Line, Messiah, State of Israel, Jewish identity, the Kiss of Heaven and Earth, Tree of Life, Sephirot, six directions of the world, the interrelated oneness of the dimensions.

3
Spiritual Growth through Sacred Time

The Sacred Calendar

Can there be any doubt that Jesus celebrated, attended and observed the Festivals and Holy Days as part of his own Hebrew heritage? There are many scriptures describing events that happened around the time of the holidays of the Jews that there is little to question. In this chapter we will explore the Holy Days of the Hebrew calendar and also note their presence in the New Testament scriptures.

We keep and celebrate these Holy Days and Festivals because we are instructed to do so by God, "generation to generation, for all time." In its own unique way, each festival and Holy Day move us forward in our spiritual growth and personal revelation year upon year.

Can you celebrate and enjoy these Holy Days as a Christian?

The festivals and Holy Days described in this chapter have been given to the Children of Israel by God and they are part of your inheritance as a Christian. They can be meaningful for your spiritual and personal growth. Many traditions and practices have grown up around them in 4000 years, but the spiritual applications of these holidays are timeless.

Hebrew traditions are not static, but grow, develop and change according to the new light given to each generation. The challenge given to us is "To make the old new and make the new Holy." It is up to you to continue, refine and renew traditions that give deep meaning to these holidays and a place in your life and your sacred calendar.

In this section we will explore Shabbat, the highest of all Holy Days. (The Hebrew word Shabbat, or Sabbath, is also used for any day when work is prohibited.) Also included in this chapter are the Three Pilgrimage Festivals: Passover (Pesah), Feast of Tabernacles (Succot) and the Feast of Weeks (Shavuot). They are called "Pilgrimage Festivals" because the people traveled to Jerusalem to celebrate each of these festivals at the Temple. The two Holy Days included in this chapter are Rosh HaShanah (New Year's) and Yom Kippur (Day of Atonement). We will also study the historical holiday of Hanukkah (Feast of Dedication). There is hardly a month in the Hebrew calendar that is without a holiday.

The holidays give a sense of rhythm and flow to the year. Every year when we celebrate these events they have a unique meaning in our lives according to the focus of our spiritual growth and development at that season in our lives. As you venture further into this chapter, imagine yourself celebrating these holidays. How would they help you to grow in spiritual maturity and in your relationship with the God of Israel?

Shabbat
The Queen of Days

"Remember Shabbat, and keep it holy. Six days shall you labor
and do all you work: but the seventh day is a Sabbath to The
Holy One your God: in it you shall not do any work, you,
nor your son, nor you daughter, your manservant, nor you
maidservant, nor you cattle, nor the stranger that is within
your gates: for in six days the Creator made Heaven and Earth,
the sea, and all that is in them, and rested on the seventh day:
therefore The Holy One blessed Shabbat, and hallowed it"

EXODUS 20:8-11

"If you restrain your foot because of Shabbat, from pursuing
your business on my holy day; and call Shabbat a delight (oneg),
the holy day of the Eternal One honorable; and shall honor it,
not doing your own ways, nor pursuing your own business, nor
speaking of meaningless matters, then shall you delight yourself
in The Holy One and I will cause you to ride upon the high
places of the Earth, and feed you with the heritage of Jacob,
your father: for the mouth of The Holy One has spoken it."

ISAIAH 58: 13,14

When I was in Israel for the first time, nearly twenty years ago,
Shabbat was approaching and I was excitedly getting ready for the
most auspicious day of the week; but who could be prepared for
Shabbat in Jerusalem! I knew the shops would close early and the
school children would be getting out at noon. Our hostess was
inviting guests over for Shabbat dinner. I could not have known
the full impact that Shabbat in the Holy Land would have on my
spirit.

Friday we hurried to the stores to get the food for that evening's feast; fresh fruits and vegetables that have a taste like no other you have ever eaten, a variety of nuts and fresh spices, fish, chicken, a special dessert treat and of course, fresh baked *Challah* (braided egg bread) still warm from the ovens. The energy in the air was one of bustle, noise and excitement that seemed to whisper, "Hurry, Shabbat is coming!" Soon we began to see the children coming home from school and soldiers hitchhiking rides on the side of the road holding up signs: "*Ima* (Mother) awaits!" As the afternoon wore on and our preparations began to be complete, time seemed to slow. As the sun threw long shadows, we heard the distant sound of a Shofar, calling our people to the last preparations of Shabbat. At last, our guests arrived. Everyone was merry, hugging and kissing in greetings at the door, and bringing treats to our Shabbat feast.

As the sun began to sink low in the West, Jerusalem began to hush into a stillness that was like the entire city was holding its breath. The long rays of the setting sun cast pink and gold colors that illuminated the Jerusalem stone of the buildings both ancient and new. Jerusalem was glowing! Ah, now I understood the yearning in the song Jerusalem of Gold. The cooling breeze of evening brought a welcome relief from the summer sun.

It was time to light the Sabbath candles. The simple white candles against the gleaming white Shabbat tablecloth brought to my mind the simplicity and elegance of this day of rest. We kindled the lights, circling our hands above the candles three times, welcoming the Sabbath Bride, the Shechinah, into our home and into our hearts. Then, together, we sang the blessing over the candles. Suddenly, there were no differing accents of those gathered from different countries. There was but one language, our *lashone hakodesh*, the "Holy Language" of Hebrew.

When we finished the blessing we each lifted up a prayer of the heart, knowing that it carried intense holiness, for we had just done a very holy act – lighting the Sabbath candles. We welcomed Shabbat into our Souls as we opened our eyes, the "windows of our Soul" to see the glow of the candles. We then turned to one another whispering "*Gut Shabbos, Shabbat Shalom,* Good Sabbath, and Sabbath Peace."

Our hostess passed out small cups of wine and picked up her *Kiddush* Cup, (a consecrated cup for use on Shabbat and at life-cycle rituals). It is considered our Cup of Joy. We began chanting the Kiddush, a blessing celebrating Shabbat, our day consecrated to God according to our Covenant. The Israeli wine tasted sweet – as sweet as the Sabbath day ahead.

The next ritual involved the washing of our hands – of course not in the manner of an ordinary washing of hands before a meal, but as a ritual washing. We each took a turn at the kitchen sink, filled a two-handled pitcher used to pour water over our hands three times and said the blessing which states we are "lifting up" our hands (in holy service). As towel for drying the hands was handed to the person finished washing, and we each returned to the Shabbat table in silence, not to be broken until after the blessing was said over the Challah, the two soft braided egg bread loaves waiting under their white covering.

When we were all gathered at the table again we were ready for the blessing over the bread, which is called *Hamotzi.* There were two shiny fresh baked loaves on the table under a white cloth cover, which represented the manna. The white cover was the color of the manna, while the two loaves symbolized the double portion gathered on Friday so the people did not have to gather (work) manna on Shabbat, Saturday. Our Hostess removed the cover from the plump loaves of fragrant bread, while a traditional, "oooh, aaah!" went up to show our approval and our awaiting appetites. We said the short blessing, Hamotzi, which speaks of our partnership with God. Saying a blessing does not sanctify the food, but sanctifies the act of eating, raising it from an ordinary act to a sacred act for the purpose of bringing energy to our bodies that we might do loving deeds of kindness. At the "Amen", our hostess salted the bread (symbolic of the salt used in the Temple for preservation of the covenant) and we each received a section and tasted the earthy sweetness of the freshly baked bread. The meal was now ready to begin.

At the end of the evening when I went to my bedroom, I looked out of the open window at Jerusalem in Shabbat. There were no cars or buses traveling in the streets. All was still in the cool night darkness. The breeze across Jerusalem seemed to be sighing, "Ahhhhhh", breathing out the cares of the week, leaning back against the heart of God in rest. This is Shabbat in Jerusalem. This is, as our sages tell us, our taste of *Olam Habah,* the World to Come.

In Israel Shabbat **happens**. Outside of Israel we must **make** Shabbat. Generation to generation, we take this day to renew our covenant with God. This is why the followers and disciples of Jesus met on Sunday, the first day of the week. They were busy Shabbat-ing on Saturday, the Sabbath.

What is the highest holy day of our traditions? Many people may answer that it is Yom Kippur or Rosh Hashanah, the "High Holy Days." While these holidays are called the Days of Awe, they are not the highest day we celebrate. Shabbat is. It is called the Queen of Days. It is thought of as our special day apart with The Holy One according to our covenant.

When pondering the importance of Shabbat, one of my younger students once remarked, "Oh! That must be why we have it every week. So we can practice!"

Sad, but true, many of us work long hours during the week and then work at home doing what must be done during our weekend time off. There always seems to be "one more thing" to do before we allow ourselves to take time off. On all levels of our Being, we desperately need Shabbat to bring balance to our lives.

Shabbat is a time to move from the "doing" of the week to the "Being" of the Sabbath. The Hebrew word, *Shabbat*, is derived from the word for "to rest" or "to cease." We cease from all our creating (work) and light the Shabbat candles and take the next 24 hours to just Be. God created for "six days" but on the seventh day God "rested" from creating anything new. During this seventh period everything God had created could become integrated together, creating wholeness – the Whole of Creation. In much the same way, when you take one day to rest your body, your mind, emotions and spirit you are able to integrate the events of the past week, bringing you into wholeness for the coming week of life.

When we bless each other with words of "Shabbat Shalom" we are referring to this sense of integrated wholeness. The word *Shalom* comes from the root "*shalem*" which means wholeness. If I borrowed money from you, and then paid the last bit of it back, then you could wipe your hands together and say, "shalem" for "it is whole", the debt is restored, completely paid back. And so when we bless each other with words of Shalom we are asking for the person to gain wholeness through the integration of all the worlds within them; spirit, mind, emotions and body in right order and in appropriate amounts. This is a beautiful state of being which is peace. You should have Shabbat Peace this week!

We begin Shabbat on Friday night. The Hebrew day begins at sundown the night before, because in the first chapter of Genesis it says that God called the Light Day and the darkness was called Night. "And there was evening and there was morning, one day." Because night is mentioned first, it begins the "day". So a day starts on the night before. This order is much the same as the way Christmas celebrations begin on Christmas Eve, continue Christmas Day, but, they are usually over by Christmas night.

The night before your next Sabbath, at sundown take off your watch and do nothing by the clock for the next 24-hour period. You don't need your watch to tell you when Shabbat is over, for the sun will tell you by its going down. Try to keep from doing any work, chores, everyday shopping, anything that you do for "maintenance" during the work week. Try engaging only in restfulness activities which elevate your Soul. Do things that are different from what you normally do in the everyday work week.

On the spiritual level, Shabbat is a time for renewal. It is the time to reconnect with our own inner being, who we really are rather than who we are in the many roles we play in our lives. We are able to center ourselves in the uniqueness of who we are and focus on what we are here for, spiritually. It gives us 24 hours to connect with God, in our own individual way, and to stay in that place of intimacy a little longer, drinking in the Presence of God unhurriedly. It is a time to be filled with the Shechinah, the feminine aspect of God's Presence, which is said to come and dwell with us in unity on Shabbat. It is like having an "extra Soul," a Sabbath Soul.

On the mental level it is a time to cease working on problems or worrying about anything. It is time for your mind to rest from the fact gathering and problem solving of the week. It is a time for your mind to integrate and process the experiences of the week on an unconscious level. This can only happen when there is a quiet space in your mind for it to happen. The "piece" gathering of the week is over. Shabbat is that time of when the pieces naturally fall together in your mind so that the patterns of your life can emerge.

These patterns cannot be seen in the busy-ness of the workday. It is only during times of reflection that our minds are quiet enough for the patterns to become evident. These are the patterns that give us information for guidance in the coming week. Shabbat is a time for these thoughts to become part of our subconscious and sometimes even emerge into our consciousness.

Shabbat is a time for revitalizing our relationships. It gives us time to be with each other, look a little deeper into the eyes of our loved one and appreciate who we see there. (Not for the sake of what they are doing, but for the fact of their Being.) It is a time to eat together, laugh, sing, pray, learn, play and dance the dance of life together. When we reconnect with our loved ones and re-energize our relationships we add a depth of meaning to our lives and to the way we express ourselves. Watching a breathtaking sunset is a spiritual and awe-inspiring experience. Sharing that experience with another is a bonding experience that brings us into an intense consciousness of The One-ness of all Life and a oneness with another. Allowing our emotions to have a Shabbat brings a sense of contentedness to our lives.

On the physical plane, Shabbat is a time for resting the body, letting it "catch up" on its energy levels and experiencing delightful treats; a day of tasty meals – not eaten in haste, going to spiritually uplifting services, quietly lying in the sun, or reading materials for the pleasure of it. Engage in any activities that lead you to higher concepts of God. It is a great time for a leisurely walk, a swim, watching a video, doing things together with your family and loved ones. It is a day to do things differently than you do during the work week.

In the Eastern European Jewish experience few had the money for meat during the week. Therefore, it was a special treat to have chicken on Shabbat. This became a traditional food for the Friday evening meal. One course after the other would be brought to the table; the participants in the meal sang *zimerot,* songs, between courses. It is a time for special treats to be served.

Shabbat is a sensual Holy Day from the glow of the Shabbat candles, the sweetness of the wine, the earthy taste and smell of the Challah, to the special dessert always served on Shabbat. This dessert can be anything that delights you. The special dessert is called the oneg which means "delight." It symbolizes our effort to fulfill the words of Isaiah 58:13, 14, which teaches us that God blesses those who "call the Sabbath a delight – oneg."

"If you restrain your foot because of the Sabbath, from pursuing your business on my holy day; and call the Sabbath a delight, the holy day of the Creator honorable; and shall honor it, not doing you own ways, nor pursuing your own business, nor speaking of empty matters, then shall you (show me that you) delight yourself in The Holy One and I will cause you to ride upon my high places of the earth, and feed you with the heritage of Jacob your father: for the mouth of The Holy One has spoken it."

ISAIAH 58:13, 14

We show our delight by making all our actions delightful, not pursuing the business of work, but showing God our faithfulness to the Sacred Ways of Shabbat.

Shabbat is not a common practice here in the US as it is in Israel. We have to make Shabbat here in America for our society does not stop on Friday just because the Sabbath is approaching. Many families develop family traditions to add to the traditions from ancient times. For instance, when lighting Shabbat candles some people light a candle for each member of their family. Some families light two candles to represent the extra Sabbath Soul that enjoins itself in holy Union to the one observing Shabbat.

In one of my congregations there was a family who would order pizza on Friday night, because it was a special treat to their family. The children in the family looked forward to Shabbat every week, for it began a day of family enjoyment together.

We are told not to work on Shabbat. But how do we know what is considered "work?" The sages of the Talmud considered there to be 39 activities that were used in the building of the Tabernacle. These activities laid the foundation for what was considered work. From these 39 activities there are extractions that expand upon the idea of the action, bringing it into modern terms. Some people choose to follow these to a strenuous degree. An example is the prohibition of building a fire. If you are building a fire you must chop wood for the fire. The idea of not building a fire is expanded to ideas prohibiting the use of electricity on Shabbat or riding in the car (the spark plugs produce a spark of fire).

However, the spiritual idea about the prohibition of working on the Sabbath goes much deeper to help us understand the human experience and the higher ways to which we are called. The prohibition of building a fire on Shabbat can be understood to mean "Do not kindle your anger on Shabbat." Becoming angry destroys the peace of Shabbat. So, what do we do when something happens on Shabbat that give rise to our anger? Out of our great love for The Holy One we seek ways to come to the anger and not destroy though it. We learn how to become mindful of what we are doing and feeling. We have the time on Shabbat to look at why we are angry and hear the real message of defense of something very important to us that is behind our anger. We can choose to let it go until after Shabbat when we will have rested senses and a keener sense of justice from which to deal with the issue. We

can choose effective means of self-expression rather than by acting
out our drama through anger. After learning about this concept
in synagogue, two young boys in the congregation decided to
make a Shabbat rule – no fighting on Shabbat. They truly enjoyed
catching each other and reminding each other, "No fighting on
Shabbat!" Of course, none of us are always successful at behaving
according to these ideals, so we need a lot of practice. As my six-
year-old student said, "That's why we have Shabbat every week!"
Truly, Shabbat is a taste of how it can be on Earth and how it will
be as we evolve and become mature and ready for the Messianic
Age, the time of Peace on Earth.

The Hebrew mystics in sixteenth-century Safed, Israel, began a
tradition of greeting the "Sabbath Queen" or "Sabbath Bride" with
an especially joyous Friday night service. They danced and sang
and celebrated the coming of Shabbat as the wedding guests and
the bridegroom would joyously meet the Bride when she enters.
They understood certain scriptures to describe the Sabbath as a
time of holy union between the feminine aspect of God's Presence,
the Shechinah, dwelling on earth with the masculine energy of
God in the Higher Dimensions. It is through unifying all aspects
of The Holy One that the time of the Messiah will come. In like
manner, Shabbat is a time for couples to enjoy conjugal bliss in
union, for which they receive a double blessing. The union of that
which is above with that which is below symbolizes the fulfillment
of the Messianic Age, the World to Come. "The Sabbath day, the
Day of the Soul, is made for love." (Yifrach biYamav Tzaddik, pg.
56a)

There is a ritual at the close of Shabbat on Saturday evening
that recalls the idea and the hope of the World to Come. This
ritual called *Havdalah* (the Division), "divides" the Sabbath from
the rest of the work week to come. It also helps us transition

from the 24 hours of "Being" (Shabbat) into the next week of "Doing." We use a cup of wine, some sweet-smelling spices, and a candle that usually has six wicks braided together. This Havdalah candle represents the days of the week, and the Light of the flame represents Shabbat. Through the blessing of each element, the wine, the spices and the candle, we awaken each of our five senses to the world again. The sweetness of the wine awakens our sense of taste to the sweetness of life. We awaken our sense of smell with the spices as their fragrance fills us with ruah, breath for the body and inspiration for the Soul. We awaken our sense of sight with the flame of the candle, illumining our path for the coming week. We awaken our sense of touch by holding our hands before the light of the Havdalah candle and feeling the warmth of the flame, the warmth of God's love. Finally, we awaken our sense of hearing as we immerse the flame of the candle in the cup of wine, our cup of joy for the coming week. Each crackle and hiss we hear as the flame is immersed is a blessing coming to us in the new week. When the flame is extinguished, we stand in the darkness of the mystery of the new week and sing the hymn Eliyahu HaNavi, Elijah the Prophet. The words ask Elijah to come quickly to us and come with the Mashiach, son of David. Even though this would be a second coming of Mashiach for you, the song would still be meaningful and powerful for you to sing.

The Sabbath is our foretaste of the World to Come; but we keep fresh the hope that soon we will know a world at Peace. After our song, we begin the new week by wishing one another "*Shavuah Tov*", "(May you have) a good week!" and we exchange blessings to each other for a week of health, peace and blessings of light.

It is powerful to begin each new week by marking its beginning and then counting down to the next Shabbat with our friends and families. It sets up a rhythm to life and makes us mindful of the cycles of day/night, week/month, year and season. It gives us a fresh start each week to accomplish that to which we aspire. It brings meaning to community as we journey through cycles of work and rest, doing and being, and integrating our lives naturally together.

Do you have a "Sabbath Day," a day in which you renew yourself, your relationships, give your mind time to integrate the weeks experiences and let your body have a break? The traditions of Shabbat were celebrated by the early followers of Jesus, as well as Jesus himself. Would you like to create a celebrative "Erev Shabbat," Friday evening service, to receive the Sabbath in your community? What traditions have developed in your family around your "day off?" Is it truly a day off or just a day filled with different work at home? Try taking one day to truly rest and do not do any work, nor join others in their work. It may have an impact on your family life! I have seen it happen in families that when one member begins to celebrate Shabbat, the others soon follow suite, finding their time in Shabbat sacred, as well.

Shabbat is a Sacred Way that God has told us to keep, remember and to do. Our society rewards hard work and promotes the work ethic. However, Shabbat is an essential day off to rest and relax, and to get back in touch with ourselves, God and each other. It is not a day off to clean the house, do the yard, to service the car, run errands, shop for groceries or other workday tasks. It is a <u>DAY OFF</u>!

Do you feel guilty taking a day off and letting others know you are not available to work that day because it is your Sabbath? How much more guilty would we feel to say, "Sorry, God, I was just too busy to spend time with you." When you think about it, isn't it kind of crazy NOT to take a day off to truly rest and refresh ourselves every week as we are commanded? When I first began to observe Shabbat in my life I heard myself saying, "I can't afford the time!" But, as I have become observant of the practice, I now know I can't afford the time **not** to take Shabbat. I feel I have been cheated if I don't get my Sabbath Day. My week has no beginning and no end. There is no sense of the upward spiral of my life. Shabbat is God's gift to us. It is a special gift given to you through your Hebrew heritage. Celebrate it and enjoy it! Call Shabbat an *oneg*, a delight, in your life!

Festivals of Passage
Pesah, Shavuot, Sukkot

The 23rd chapter of Leviticus lists when and how to celebrate three Feast Days and two Holy Days. The three feast days are Passover, Shavuot, also known as the Feast of Weeks, (Pentecost in the Church), and Sukkot, also known as the Feast of Tabernacles of Booths. Together, the three Festivals are called, *Shelosh Regalim*, the Three Pilgrimage Festivals. They were considered "traveling festivals" because the people were instructed to go to the Temple to bring their tithes, gifts and offerings, and to offer up their sacrifices. In Biblical times everyone gathered in Jerusalem for these three Festivals every year.

The two Holy Days are Rosh HaShanah (New Years) and Yom Kippur (Day of Atonement). These festivals and Holy Days may be foreign to your sacred calendar and spiritual experiences, however, they were rungs on the ladder of spiritual growth in the lives of the early followers of Jesus, and they were meaningful to Jesus himself. They also belong to you part of your Hebrew heritage of God ordained sacred days.

Pesah / **Passover**
Four Promises of Deliverance

These are the feasts of The Holy One, sacred gatherings, which
you shall proclaim in their seasons. On the fourteenth day of
the first month towards evening is The Holy One's Passover.
And on the fifteenth day of the same month is the feast of
unleavened bread to The Holy One: seven days you must
eat unleavened bread. On the first day you shall have a holy
gathering: you shall do no servile work ... on the seventh day is
a holy gathering: you shall do no servile work.

LEVITICUS 23: 4-8

In Egypt we learned how to be slaves.
In the Wilderness of Sinai,
we learned how to be
the Servants of God.

Why were we slaves in Egypt so long? There we learned how to
serve, that we might serve our God in joy and in holiness. The
story of the Exodus of the Children of Israel from slavery in Egypt
is a well known story found in the book of Exodus, chapters 1
through 15. From that point forward the rest of the Torah reveals
our ancestors' experiences while they were in the wilderness on
the Sinai Peninsula for forty years, before Joshua lead them into
Canaan, the land of Abraham.

While the Children of Israel were in the wilderness of Sinai
a profound event took place. The group that left Egypt together
came into a covenant with the God who made a covenant with
Abraham. This covenant was passed on to his son Isaac, then on to
Jacob, and continued to the Twelve Tribes of Israel. The meeting

between God and the people standing at Mount Sinai was the first time the covenant was made, not with just one family, but with a group of people. Not everyone coming out of the slavery of Egypt was a Hebrew. The group comprised the Hebrew people led by Moses and those who wanted to go with them, possibly including many slaves from other nations. This was the group of people who met with The Holy One at Mount Sinai. God offered a covenant to them, the extension of the covenant made with Abraham, saying, "Now, therefore, if hearing you will listen to My Voice, and keep My Covenant, then you shall be My own special treasure from among all peoples: for all the earth is mine: and you shall be to me a kingdom of priests, a holy nation" (Exodus 19:5, 6). They came to Mount Sinai as a group leaving the slavery of Egypt, but as they each accepted the covenant, they became together, a newly born nation; the nation of Israel. This offering of a covenant must be answered by their free will; but only a person who is free, not a slave, can make a choice. If God was to offer a choice to the Hebrews, to become a nation, they must be free men and women. And so, the Exodus from Egypt was not only about being free to come before El Shaddai, the God on the mountain but, also to be free to make their choice to accept the covenant.

The word for Egypt in Hebrew is *Mitzrayim*. It is a play on words that also means "from the narrow places." When the Children of Israel were delivered from Egypt, they were delivered from the "narrow, places in their lives" and born anew through the birthing waters of the Red Sea crossing.

God instructed them to remember this powerful event every year by celebrating it at the exact time that it happened, generation to generation. That means we are included in these instructions. God is speaking directly to us now each year. We do this by recreating our journey into freedom by ritualizing the events of the story. In that way we go back in Sacred Time and Sacred Space to individually be delivered from "the narrow places" of our lives. We are to take time to look at our lives and see what "holds us in bondage." Through the *Seder*, the ritual Passover Meal, we identify where our lives are being constricted and what is preventing us from "following our God into the wilderness to worship there." We experience deliverance in our lives and become free to follow our Soul's highest purpose of meeting with God.

Leviticus tells us to celebrate Passover on the fourteenth day of the first month. The first month in the Hebrew calendar is Nisan, which usually falls in April. We are told to gather at evening, to eat only unleavened bread (as opposed to leavened bread) for seven days and to do no servile work. It is a holy day of convocation unto The Holy One who brought us out of Egypt, out of our bondage. The night before the fourteenth day of Nisan is when we celebrate the Passover Seder.

But, before we can have our Passover Meal, we must clean our homes of all *hametz*, leavening, to insure that we eat only unleavened bread for seven days and there is no hametz, even crumbs, in our homes.

The home symbolizes the dwelling place of our Soul. This ritual teaches us to search our lives as our dwelling place, the place we live, for the "leavening," that which "puffs us up," or "sours" our life. Leavening is anything that causes us to be empty and hollow inside. We are to search throughout the house for the leavened bread crumbs with a candle, symbolizing the Soul as the candle of The Holy One, searching the inward parts, Proverbs 20:27. We are to search our hearts with the light of Divine Truth. It is an old tradition to use a feather to remove the breadcrumbs we find in our search to sweep the crumbs into a wooden spoon, which we then throw into the fire in the hearth. In analogy, we use a feather to search our hearts for leavening, for the heart is a tender place. We are to compassion (feather) with truth (spoon) in the search. We then cast off the "leavening" into the fire. We let go of it and set our intention not to partake in that attitude or activity again. This ritual is called *B'dikat Hametz*, the Search for the Leavening.

A spiritual application of the B'dikat Hametz can be done by writing down all of those things which we consider to be hametz (that which puffs us up or sours our lives) on a piece of paper. Then we burn the paper in a fireplace or a fireproof container, symbolizing getting rid of the hametz. This can be a meaningful, spiritual preparation for the family and for those gathering at the *Seder*.

The Seder, which means "Order" in Hebrew, and refers to the order of the dinner, includes elements symbolic of the Exodus story. The entire story is re-told, songs are sung, and questions are asked and answered as the dinner progresses. Some people do Hebrew dances handed down since the time of Egypt at the Seder. The Seder may last late into the night, or even all night for those following the tradition of the first Passover. We say a blessing over the eating of *matzah*, unleavened bread. We eat matzah crackers for the entire week, having rid our homes of all leavening agents and products with leavening in them.

A special platter is used at the Seder that is creatively decorated and holds foods used to represent key elements of the Passover story. There is parsley, representative of spring, new life, and hope. We dip the parsley in salt water, which represents the tears of slavery in our lives and take a bite of it. As we taste the salt water and the parsley we remember that even amidst our tears there springs the hope of our redemption.

We also share in the *haroset*, a sweet mixture of apples, nuts, raisins, cinnamon, honey and wine that represents the mortar and bricks that the slaves had to use to build the buildings of Pharaoh.

There is a roasted egg on the Seder plate to symbolize the cycles of life, rebirth and resurrection. There is *maror*, horseradish, for the bitterness of slavery. Finally, there is the Shankbone of a lamb representing the *Pascal Lamb*, the sacrifice which was eaten and whose blood was placed on the doorpost of the house. The mystics (many of whom were and are vegetarians) use a beet to represent the sacrifice. The juice of the cut beet stains red reminding us of the blood on the doorposts of the house. The shape and size of the beet reminds us of the human heart. It reminds us to open our hearts to God, to trust and walk with The Holy One intimately in our lives. It reminds us that it is in the heart that we are able to give up our stubborn ways, our self will and out of love for The Divine follow God's Sacred Ways. The cutting of the beet reminds us that it is in the heart that the Covenant is cut (made) and through the love of our hearts that it is kept.

There are four cups of wine lifted up in the Seder, each symbolizing part of the redemptive story. However, there is also a fifth cup, the Cup of Elijah. We raise this cup and we open the door to the room symbolically to look for Elijah the Prophet and invite him to come in. There is an empty chair at the table in preparation for our hope – that maybe this year he will come to announce the coming of the Messiah! It is believed that Elijah will come back as one who comes to announce that New Dawn. Could this be the cup that Jesus raised with his disciples, instituting the ritual of Communion?

The theme of the coming of Messiah or the Messianic Age is part of the Passover Meal. A chair is left empty at the table in preparedness for Elijah, should this be the year he comes. A special cup called Elijah's Cup is used as an fifth cup symbolizing this time of the redemption of the world. Some people practice the tradition of passing the empty Elijah's Cup around the table, each person adding a little of the wine (symbol of joy) from their own Seder cup to help fill Elijah's Cup. In that way when the cup goes all the way around the table it is fill from the contributions of each person, for we all have our part in bringing the Messiah by our prayers and deeds to repair the world. Then we sing "Eliyahu HaNavi," "Elijah the Prophet", a hymn about the coming of Elijah. It is the same song we sing at the close of Shabbat, during Havdalah.

It is most likely during this part of the Seder that Jesus instructed his disciples to remember him, when doing this ritual every year, knowing that as Jews they would keep the Passover as it is one of the Sacred Ways of The Holy One (Mark 14).

Passover comes at the first cycle of the full moon after the spring equinox. It is a time of new birth, the beginning of the growing season. It is during the first month of the calendar year, which indicates new beginnings. It is a Festival that focuses on the deliverance and redemption of the World of B'riyah, the World of Intellect, our minds and thoughts, and the World of Yetzirah, Emotion, and our feelings. In the Exodus story, just as the Pharaoh went back and forth on his intention to let the Hebrews go, our minds go back and forth, telling us things that can prevent us from moving forward in our lives. It is the emotion of fear that feeds our minds thoughts of failure and isolation and it is the emotion of love that inspires our minds to rise to the challenge of the vision of our Spirits. We stand in the fear or love, whichever we choose. It is only when we choose to act from our love and trust in God that we come out of the slavery of our fearful thoughts and walk in freedom. Passover is the festival that delivers us from the slavery of our own minds and hearts. That is where we must first be set free. Passover is the festival that gives us the freedom to follow the Divine Light of God's Ruah HaKodesh, the Holy Spirit.

> And you shall relate to you son (the next generation) on that day, saying, This is done because of that which The Holy One did for me when I came out of Mitzrayim (Egypt)... You shall therefore keep this ordinance in its season from year to year.
>
> EXODUS 13:8, 10

The power of deliverance and redemption at the time of the Exodus in Egypt remains throughout Eternity, that we may tap into that same redemptive power every year in our lives. We pass on the story of our peoplehood and the love extended to us by God, through retelling the story every year to the next generation. Why every year?

Each year of our lives our understanding opens a little more, as we experience and integrate the lessons of our lives and develop spiritually. In the re-telling of the story each year we gain more insight and wisdom into the meaning of Passover for our lives and for the world. Each year our sons and daughters learn and grow and become who they are becoming, identifying as part of the people of Israel through our family story. Each year they are able to integrate this story into their own personal story a little more deeply. Therefore, as we cycle through the years, we are not revisiting the same place Passover after Passover, but the pathway is a spiral; each year lifting us higher in our Sacred Journey together.

When we re-tell the story of the deliverance of our people to our children, it is also an opportunity for us to also tell them stories of our own walk with The Holy One; ways that El Shaddai has delivered us in our lives and guided us to places of freedom.

This serves as a beacon for the young ones to center on when they are in difficult times. This gives them a sense of 4000 years of ancestors in their Hebrew heritage to draw upon for strength. It teaches them the power they have within them to overcome whatever obstacles block their pathway. It serves to teach them The Infinite and the incredible resource they have within them to help them draw upon God in trust. They know they are not alone, for it gives them identity in the peoplehood of our Covenant of Abraham, the Covenant of Sinai.

The Hebrew grammar used in Exodus 13:8, 10 indicates the nature of the Divine directive.

> "And you shall relate to your child on that day, saying, 'This is done because of that which The Holy One did for me when I came out of Egypt.'"
> "You shall, therefore, keep this ordinance in its season from year to year."

The personal pronoun "you" in "And you shall relate..." is in the singular. Although this command is obviously being spoken to many people down through countless ages, both those present and those in generations to come, it is said to each of us as individuals. It is a directive to pass down to the next generation what God has done in our lives, each one personally and individually. The Passover Ritual makes sure that we have the opportunity to do that, every year.

Do you have a way to pass on to your children and their children the experiences you have had with God? Have you ever been to a Seder? It is a powerful experience. It is also a way to spiritually focus in preparation for the Holy Week of Easter. Maybe your church would like to have a Seder together. You could have a

Seder in your home, inviting your friends and family. Discuss what this ritual and experience means in your own spiritual growth.

Maybe you would like to make a Christmas Seder, as Rabbi Zalman Schachter-Shalomi once created for a church. You could re-tell the story of the birth of Jesus, using frankincense and myrrh and some gold pieces for the gifts, milk for Mother Mary (Miriam in Hebrew), and a candle for the guiding light of the star leading the way to Bethlehem. You could tell the next generation experiences you have had with God and with Jesus in your life. You will begin a relationship with your child on a new level of Soul-sharing that is rare and precious. Each Christmas, re-tell the story and one Christmas, your child will tell you the story and tell you something that happened to them with God that year. What better inheritance can you pass on to your children and your children's children that to help them open their own connection and communication with God? This type of personal and communal revelation is what the next Festival which is linked to Passover is about. That Festival is Shavuot, the Festival of the Revelation at Mount Sinai.

Shavuot / **Feast of Weeks**
Covenant on Sinai

"And The Holy One said to Moses, "Go to the people and sanctify them today and tomorrow, and let them wash their clothes and be ready on the third day: for on the third day The Holy One will come down in the sight of all the people upon Mount Sinai."
"And it came to pass on the third day in the morning, that there were thunders and flashes of lightning, and a thick cloud

upon the mountain, and the sound of a Shofar exceeding loud; so that all the people in the camp trembled. And Moses brought the people out of the camp to meet with God; and they stood at the foot of the mountain. And Mount Sinai smoked in every part, because The Holy One descended upon it in fire: and the smoke of it ascended like the smoke of a furnace, and the whole mountain quaked greatly. And then the voice of the Shofar sounded louder and louder; Moses speaks and God answers him by a Voice."

EXODUS 19:10-11, 16-19

Seven weeks shall you number for yourselves ... And you shall keep **Shavuot**, the Feast of Weeks to The Holy One your God with a tribute of a freewill offering of your hand, which you shall give according as The Holy One your God has blessed you: and you shall rejoice before the Holy One of Blessing, your God, you and your son and your daughter and your manservant and your maidservant and the Levite who is within your gates and the stranger and the fatherless and the widow who are among you in the place which The Holy One your God has chosen as the residence of the Holy Name, **HaShem**.

DEUTERONOMY 16: 9 – 11

In the third month after the Children of Israel were gone out of the land of Egypt, the same day they came into the wilderness of Sinai. And Moses went up to God and The Holy One called to him out of the mountain saying, Thus shall you say to the house of Jacob, and tell the Children of Israel; You have seen what I did to Egypt and how I bore you on eagles' wings and brought you to myself. Now therefore, if you will listen and hear my Voice, and keep my covenant, then you shall be my own special treasure among all peoples: for all the earth is mine: and you shall be to me a kingdom of priests and a holy nation.

EXODUS 19: 1 – 6

The Festival of *Shavuot* (Weeks) is a beautiful time of revelation, love and devotion between God and Israel. It is the sacred event of covenant making. Interestingly, Shavuot usually falls in the month of June, which is also the month popular for weddings, the making of a covenant between a man and a woman. Shavuot is when God revealed God-Self with unprecedented eminence to an entire group of people at Mount Sinai. It was when the Torah was given in Divine Revelation. Shavuot is the time of sealing the Covenant of God and Israel, and the giving of the Torah, which is our love letter from God.

The Torah is considered by our sages and mystics to be our *Ketubah*, (wedding contract) given to us by God. Every year Shavuot is an opportunity for a new revelation of God's powerful Presence in our lives and a new and deeper illumination of Torah, God's words in our hearts.

It was at Shavuot that God began to reveal a powerful eminence beyond human experience. The people were frightened and urged Moses to go up on the mountain, to hear God's Voice, and to come back and tell them God's words. Moses went up on the mountain and received the Ten Commandments, the beginning of the instruction in the Sacred Ways of harmony and holiness. God offered direct revelation to the people. But only one man had the heart to hear God amidst the frightening chaos, lightening, thunder and quaking of the Earth. God was near. Moses opened his heart. God continues to offer that Presence and the Eternal Dialogue to every open heart today.

The Festival of Shavuot focuses on the World of Being (Spirit), Atzilut. To understand how we must explore the basis for the holiday and how it has been celebrated down through the ages.

Did you know that the Disciples of Jesus celebrated Shavuot? Can you find the account of it in the New Testament writings? We will discuss this later in this chapter.

The scriptures at the beginning of this section on Shavuot teach us some of the main aspects of this traveling festival.

In the first text, we are instructed to count seven weeks (seven of seven, forty-nine days and then the next day, the fiftieth, is Shavuot) to the next festival, the Feast of Weeks, Shavuot, the Festival of Giving of the First Fruits, as the second text instructs us. It was a time when everyone brought the first part of their harvest (whatever that may be) to the Temple to offer it up to God in thanksgiving, recognizing from where the blessings came. The Priests were instructed to offer two loaves of bread. Therefore, there is both the communal and the individual aspect of the offerings. What is the symbolism behind these offerings? How do we apply the spiritual principles set forth in this festival today?

The two loaves of bread represent our partnership with The Holy One, Creator of ALL. When we begin a meal we say a blessing over the bread which when we translate this blessing into English it says, "Blessed are you, O Holy One, our God, Who brings forth bread from the Earth." How does this blessing speak to you of our partnership with God?

What does it mean, "Who brings forth bread from the Earth."? Have you ever seen a field of bread growing? Of course not! But wheat does grow – by God's outflow of Life-Energy. Then we take the wheat and make bread to feed the hungry. This is the partnership. God extends life, grace, existence, and we are to shape it and mold it to that which serves and promotes life. The

Priests would lift up two loaves symbolic of the People Israel as a community dedicated to this task. Then every individual would bring the first part of their harvest to offer in thanksgiving. As the individual offered their portion to God (according to how they are blessed as a portion of the harvest) they would spiritually be placing themselves in the collective whole, claiming their "membership" and putting themselves in the Divine Flow of Plenty by their reciprocity. This was a joyous Festival!

Families would travel from wherever they lived to the Temple (once it was built in Jerusalem by Solomon) to give their offerings. They would travel and camp together. There would be announcements made as they approached Jerusalem telling them they were approaching the Holy Temple. The entire nation entered a time of Thanksgiving together at the very transition between spring and early summer.

Spiritually, while Passover is the time of new life, new energy to grow and bud forth, Shavuot is the season for the beginning of maturity. Fifty days after Passover, at Shavuot, the buds have bloomed and the fruit and grain has begun to mature. It is a time in the human cycle when the newborn has matured through childhood to young adulthood and is reaching out to make bonding relationships with others. It is the time of the bridegroom making covenant with his bride – and the bride receiving her groom in love. This is what the third text relates to us.

Through careful study of the text it is evident that the giving of the Torah and the Revelation at Sinai happened on Shavuot, the year the Children of Israel left Egypt. It too, speaks to us of the partnership between us and God, for the Torah, the Light Bearer, teaches us Wisdom and the Sacred Ways for us to enlighten our world and live in harmony. But it is up to us to "BE Torah" by embracing it and living it through the actions in our lives. Torah can do nothing without our living it out through our actions – every day. It is a "lamp unto our feet, a Light unto our path." Just as we receive God's physical blessings and return a portion in Thanksgiving, so too are we to receive fresh revelation from the Word of God, the Torah, and offer it back to God through living it in our lives.

Just as the Priests offered up two loaves in the Temple to The Holy One representing the partnership of receiving the harvest and making bread to feed and nourish the peoples of the earth, so, too are we to take the Divine Wisdom, light and spiritual principles we receive from Torah and contribute them to the world by our actions to improve our world with peace, that we make it a more Holy Place, revealing the sacred within All. This we offer as a spiritual community. This is Shavuot.

In order to raise our consciousness of the beautiful love between Creator and Created, Emanator and the Emanation, the Kabbalists (mystics) consider Shavuot, as the wedding day of God (the groom) and Israel (the bride). It is a time when the Bride's veil has been lifted, so that The Holy One may come in unto her in Holy Union. It is the time for making a covenant together of indissoluble marriage. It is past the time of the first blushes of love between the newly betrothed (engagement – Passover) and now it is time for the maturity of marriage, the struggles and deep bonding of the everyday husband and wife. To ritualize this idea, on Shavuot some congregations read a poetic *Ketubah* (the wedding contract between the Groom and the Bride). One of the most popular ones dates from the sixteenth century mystics of Safed, Israel. The following is an excerpt from that Ketubah:

Friday, the sixth of Sivan, the day appointed by The Holy One for the revelation of the Torah to His beloved people

... The Invisible One came forth from Sinai, shone from Seir and appeared from Mount Paran unto all the kings of the earth, in the year 2448 (Hebrew calendar) since the creation of the world ... The Bridegroom (God), Ruler of rulers, Prince of princes, Distinguished among the select, Whose mouth is pleasing and all of Whom is delightful, said unto the faithful, lovely and virtuous maiden (the people Israel) who won His favor above all women, who is beautiful as the moon, radiant as the sun, awesome as bannered hosts: Many days will you be Mine and I will be your Redeemer. Behold, I have sent you golden precepts through the giver of the Sacred Ways, Jekuthiel (Moses). Be unto Me, My mate according to the Ways of Moses and Israel, and I will honor, support, and maintain you and be your shelter and refuge in everlasting compassion. And I will set aside for you, in lieu of your virginal faithfulness, the life-giving Torah by which you and your children will live in health and tranquility. The bride (Israel) consented and became His spouse. Thus an eternal covenant, binding them forever, was established between them ... The dowry that this bride brought ... consists of an understanding heart that understands, ears that hearken and eyes that see... I invoke Heaven and Earth as reliable witnesses. May the bridegroom rejoice with the bride whom He has taken as His own, and may the bride rejoice with the Husband of her youth while uttering words of praise.

This centuries-old text uses anthropomorphic language for The Infinite, and is gender specific, to relate the love and desire between Israel and God in a way that makes this relationship personal between each of us and God. It invites us as participants in the paradox of each of us having our own individual and unique relationship with The One while at the same time being part of the bonding covenant made with the peoplehood of Israel across the span of time. The ancient is now, the now becomes Eternal.

Does this metaphor sound familiar to you? Does it remind you of the wedding metaphor of Christ and the Church? These are the roots that nurtured that metaphor to the early Church; those Jews who followed the rabbi from Galilee knew this, for it was part of their culture and spiritual experience. While the Ketubah above was written in the sixteenth century, it was based upon the Kabbalistic ideas of the covenant from the ancient days. This too, is your heritage.

Shavuot is the festival that the disciples were celebrating when they gathered together on the night referred to as Pentecost.

> To them also Jesus showed himself alive ... appearing to them during forty days, (after his death) and talking about the things of the kingdom of God. And while being in their company and eating at the table with them, he commanded them not to leave Jerusalem, but to wait for what the Father had promised ... For John baptized with water, but not many days from now you shall be baptized with the Holy Spirit.
>
> ACTS: 1:3,4,5

> And when the day of Pentecost had fully come, they were all assembled together in one place, when suddenly there came a sound from heaven like the rushing of a violent tempest blast, and it filled the whole house in which they were sitting ... And they were all filled with the Holy Spirit and began to speak in other languages, as the Spirit kept giving them clear and loud expression... But Peter, standing with the eleven raised his voice and addressed them, (the crowds hearing them) "For these men are not drunk, as you imagine, for it is only the third hour (9:00 AM) of the day..."
>
> ACTS 2:1,2,4,14,15

It has been a Jewish spiritual tradition for centuries to stay up all night the night before Shavuot (remember, the day begins the night before) to read from the Torah, (first five books of the Bible), the Prophets, the Writings such as Psalms, Proverbs and especially the Book of Ruth.

Ruth's story exemplifies the person who receives the Covenant through her love, not through the demands of birth. It is the story of love and devotion given out of free will, for Ruth, a Moabite woman, chose to stay with Naomi, her Hebrew mother-in-law even after the death of both of their husbands. She chose to leave the land and gods of her family and follow Naomi back to Canaan to an uncertain destiny. She is the shining example of one following God out of love. While her fate as a poor widow living with another poor widow did not look good, in the end she is rewarded for her faithfulness, for she is the grandmother of King David, the forbearer of the Messiah. Her story is creatively told on this night, studied and questioned for new insights. The story of Ruth takes place during the barley harvest, as does the Festival of Sukkot.

Other poems, stories and spiritual resources for fresh revelation in meditation and prayer are shared by groups gathering together on this night. It is not surprising that on this night, the disciples were gathered together in a high meditative and prayerful consciousness, studying and praying. This opened their consciousness and prepared them to receive this powerful experience and manifestation of the Holy Spirit dancing as tongues of fire upon them by early morning.

In congregations today Shavuot is a time for celebrating the giving of the Torah and the Revelation on Sinai by decorating the synagogue (and homes) with greenery and roses. The *Midrash* (oral tradition stories) tells us that when God became eminent on Mount Sinai the entire mountain burst forth in roses. Before the Torah is read in synagogue, spiritual poems or a "Ketubah" between God and Israel is read. Groups still stay up all night on the Eve of Shavuot to read inspirational literature, share, meditate, study, and pray together. Then they greet the dawn and the time for morning prayers from a higher state of consciousness.

When I lived in Jerusalem I walked to the Temple Mount in the pre-dawn darkness at 4am on Shavuot morn after studying late. In the stillness and quiet of the neighborhood I began to see one person, and then another, then a couple; more and more people joined the procession toward the East. Soon the street was alive with people walking toward Mount Zion in sacred silence. As I walked up the steep path on the south side of the mountain my breath came heavy. However, I took heart to keep going as I noticed the couple just ahead of me. They had white hair and had difficulty walking on level ground, and yet, slowly and surely, they were winding their way up this ancient mountain to join their kinsmen and ancestors to witness the dawn of this auspicious day.

At last I was walking through the archaic stone gates of the Old City. I wound my way through narrow streets I knew by heart in the darkness and stood across the square from the Temple. I chose to stand high on the overlook rather than become a wave in the sea of people pressing to get down into the square in front of the Kotel, the Western Wall. I took up my position looking straight across at the Temple remains, and beyond, across the Kidron Valley to the Mount of Olives. We watched and waited in silence for the first beams of light to brighten the sky in the East. The hour we waited seemed an eternity. However, all in one moment the Dome of the Rock lit up, reflecting the first rays of the new day. The light grew over the Mount of Olives, spilling over the Temple walls. I was mesmerized by the invitation to the light. My eyes remained fully engulfed in the light, the warmth, the blessedness; my Soul was immersed in the Presence of the Divine. Nothing else existed for those few moments; only light. No sound, no breath escaped a mouth. It was the first moments again, like the moments of God's Presence on Mount Sinai. We were in sacred time and space, together and yet each one was alone with God. We were all engaged in saying the Kiddush (blessing over wine) and the Motzi (blessing over bread) as our first actions for this new Shavuot. Whoever had these items shared them with those who did not have any. We were strangers from all over the world, yet family. This is Shavuot in modern-day Jerusalem.

Many congregations use the Shavuot season as a time for Confirmation for mid-teens. While Bar and Bat Mitzvah is a ritual for coming of age to mark the beginning of a twelve year old girl's or thirteen year old boy's inclusion in the prayer community, Confirmation is a time for group commitment, standing together as the next generation of Israel for fifteen and sixteen year olds. It is a time for a young adult to confirm his or her acceptance as a member of the "next generation" to receive the Covenant of Israel and "Be Torah", keeping and guarding the Sacred Ways. Thus, it is celebrated at the Shavuot season; the time of the giving of the Torah at Mount Sinai.

There is also a custom to take the first graders in Torah school, who will be learning to read Hebrew, to the synagogue and help them learn the first letters of the Hebrew Alef Bet. As they learn they are given honey or sweets to teach them the "sweetness of Torah."

> How sweet are your words to my taste, sweeter than honey to my mouth.
>
> PSALM 119:103

And, as always, there are special foods associated with this festival. It is a time to celebrate with dairy dishes such as; blintzes with sour cream, kugel (noodle pudding), and in modern times, yogurt dishes, quiche, cheesecake and ice cream. What is the idea behind this tradition of dairy foods? It is the season we were given the Torah; the words of Torah are <u>mother's milk</u> given from El Shaddai (The Nurturer) to teach us and help us to grow and reach spiritual maturity. Therefore, we remember this with the eating of dairy dishes.

How do you celebrate Pentecost/Shavuot? How would you like to mark and celebrate this festival that calls us into an intimate relationship with The Holy One? Maybe your prayer group or meditation circle will hold a vigil the night before, reading, singing, praying, meditating and talking about the story of Ruth this year.

What is your answer to the groom who is calling you to come and be "A Kingdom of Priests, a Holy Nation." Maybe your study group of friends would like to come together and share how you connected with The Holy One the first time and what that relationship has meant to you in your life. After sharing each one could place a rose (symbolizing the roses that bloomed on Mount Sinai when the Torah was given) in a an empty vase in the center, that by the end of the time of sharing you have a vase filled with a beautiful bouquet of multi-colored roses representing your community and the beauty it carries as the roses of Sinai.

What fresh revelation will you receive this year in your life on Shavuot? Maybe on Shavuot you could write your "Ketubah," your covenant as you experience it with The Holy One. Keep this covenant in a special place, so that you can see it every day.

Enjoy Shavuot, Pentecost, as it is the day of God sharing more Light than ever before with you, year after year. This is your Hebrew inheritance.

Sukkot
Ripening of the Harvest

The fifteenth day of this seventh month shall be the Feast
of Booths for seven days to The Holy One. On the first day
shall be a holy gathering: you shall do no servile work. Seven
days you shall offer an offering made by fire to the Hoy One:
on the eighth day shall be a holy gathering to you; ... it is a
solemn assembly; and you shall do no servile work... Also
on the fifteenth day of the seventh month, when you have
gathered in the fruit of the land you shall keep a feast to
The Holy One seven days: on the first day shall be a Sabbath,
and on the eighth day shall be a Sabbath. And you shall take
for yourselves on the first day the fruit of the tree hadar,
branches of palm trees and the boughs of thick leaved trees
and willows of the brook; and you shall rejoice before The
Holy One your God seven days... I shall be a statute for ever
in your generations... You shall dwell in booths seven days;
all generations may know that I made the children of Israel
to dwell in booths, when I brought them out of the land of
Mitzrayim: I am The Holy One your God.

LEVITICUS 23:33-44

Seven days shall you keep a sacred feast to The Holy One your
God in the place which The Holy One shall choose: because
the Holy One your God shall bless you in all your produce, and
in all the work of your hands, therefore you shall surely rejoice.

DEUT. 16:15

Sukkot, the Feast of Booths or the Feast of Tabernacles, is the fall
festival that connects us with the physical world. It is observed on

the fifteenth of the Hebrew month of *Tishrei*, at the full moon. If Passover is the festival of new life and Shavuot is the festival of the bloom of life, then Sukkot is the festival of full maturity, the time of the ingathering of the harvest.

Passover focuses on the World of Intellect, and the World of Emotions within us. It provides deliverance and redemption from the thoughts and feelings that enslave our minds and hearts and block us from progressing on our Sacred Pathway. Shavuot focuses on the World of Being, Spirit. It is the time of fresh revelation from Spirit. It is a time for making a covenant that builds and renews our relationship with The Holy One. Sukkot then, focuses on the World of Doing. It causes us to be in touch with the physical world around us and enables us to express the other three worlds or our spiritual vision, our thoughts and our feelings in the physical world of action. It is the time for us to "harvest" the fruits of our labors for the year. It is the season to connect to this world, our planet Earth and celebrate the revealed (Divine) in the hidden (physical).

This fall festival of harvest is more than just "Jewish Thanksgiving". It is a time when we are instructed to live in "booths" or little huts for seven days, bringing us close to the elements of the Earth and getting us back in touch with nature. We are also to bring a portion of the harvest in offering to The Holy One. Finally, it is a festival of blessing, for while we thank The Holy One, the Source of All Life, for the bounty, we are also receiving the blessings for next year's bounty as well, – that we may prosper in all we do. Thereby, the Source of All Blessing is blessing us as we place ourselves back into the Divine Flow after receiving the harvest by offering a portion of the harvest back to God, fulfilling the principle of reciprocity.

At Sukkot we are also instructed to wave a palm branch, a

willow branch and a branch of "*hadar*," the fragrant myrtle tree. How and for what purpose do we "dwell" in a *Sukkah* and gather these branches together and ritually wave them?

First let's examine the idea of a booth, or Sukkah from which the festival gets its name Sukkot, (the plural form of the word for "booths"). We are reminded by this ritual that the Children of Israel lived in "booths" or temporary dwelling places in the wilderness after they left Egypt. This symbolizes the transient nature of life. It reminds us that we are in a temporary or temporal state in this world. The mystics say that the Sukkot booths represent our body as the temporary dwelling place of the Soul. Our Soul is "in the wilderness" being guided and provided for by The Holy One, even as the Children of Israel were guided by the Presence of God in the pillar of fire at night and the pillar of cloud by day in the wilderness. They were provided for through the manna that fell miraculously every night for them to gather as food the next morning. Their water was provided by God, their clothes did not wear out, nor did their sandals. The wilderness was a place of grace that taught the new generation to depend and rely upon God's goodness, generosity and faithfulness for everything. Sukkot teaches us these lessons of fulfillment in our freedom (Passover) and blessing in the Covenant (Shavuot), providing us with all good in this temporary dwelling place of the Soul.

The Sukkah also reminds us of the temporary huts that were built by the workers at the time of harvest. These huts provided them with shelter so they could stay in the fields at night and not have to travel back up to their homes during the busy days of harvest.

Today, we build a Sukkah in our yard and/or at the Synagogue. For thousands of years this has been a tradition. It is our season of "Jewish camp out". Granted, not many families in the US actually spend the night in the Sukkah, but it is a powerful experience for those who are in a climate where it is possible. In Israel every home, apartment and dwelling has a Sukkah built on the balcony or in the yard.

The Sukkah must be constructed as a temporary structure. It must have at least three walls that are not a part of a permanent structure. To insure the temporary nature, the "roof" is made by laying branches (usually palms where available) across the top of the frame. The rule of thumb is that you must be able to see the stars at night through the greenery and if it rains that the drops fall through. It is not built with comfort in mind, but to put us close to the energy of the natural world around us. The "walls" are made of various materials. Some people hang canvas from the Sukkah frame. Some people use netting, lattice work or boards. Then, the Sukkah is decorated with all types of fruits, vegetables, flowers, pictures or anything bright and joyous. We dangle apples, oranges, squashes, flowers, herbs, onions, garlic, any fruit or vegetable from the inside of the leafy roof. Some people have the children make windsocks and mobiles to hang. Some Sukkahs sing with the sound of gay wind chimes catching the breeze. In Arizona our congregation would hang clusters of dried red peppers and a beautiful piñata. The Sukkah can be a congregational project or the project of individual families and friends. Building the Sukkah is a fun occasion and wonderful preparation for this Festival in which we are actually **instructed** to be joyous (Deut. 16:15).

Many families traditionally take their meals in the Sukkah. Some use the Sukkah as a special place to do their daily meditations and prayers. When you enter the Sukkah, there is a sense of peace, quiet and solitude. Your feet feel the earth beneath you and the smell of the leafy roof refreshes your senses. Your eyes see the bounty of the harvest and the beauty of the flowers. The breeze gently plays on the wind chimes and brings the hanging decorations to life. The sun speckles the Sukkah with spots of dancing light and at night the full moon illumines the Sukkah with its silvery-soft shadow-light. Life is teeming all around you. The Energy of Mother Earth beckons you to join your energy to her energy in Divine Union. Sukkot reminds us that we are flesh and blood as well as Spirit; we are the Infinite within the Finite. Sukkot reminds us that we and the Earth are One and The One – and Beyond.

Rabbi Isaac ben Luria, a great mystic who lived in Safed, Israel in the sixteenth century, taught his disciples the spiritual practice of inviting a special guest to the Sukkah each night. While it is our tradition to invite someone who is economically challenged into the Sukkah to share our meal, this is a special guest of another kind. This guest is one of the seven great shepherds of our people, Israel. The seven are: Abraham, Isaac, Jacob, Joseph, Moses, Aaron, and David. In modern times women guests, shepherdesses of our people, have been included with these. I invite the following: Sarah and Abraham, Rebecca and Isaac, Rachel, Leah and Jacob, Deborah and Joseph, Miriam and Moses, Esther and Aaron, and Ruth and David. A special prayer is said, inviting all of these guests to dwell in the Sukkah each night. A blessing is also said asking one of these ancient couples to be the guests-of-honor each night. A meditation can also be held to open yourself to any wisdom or message the guest-of-honor Shepherd may want to impart to you. This is done to tap into and remember the wisdom they bring to us throughout our lives. It is to remember that we are all One and our ancestors join us in the work of world enlightenment.

The Sukkah takes on *Sukkat Shalom*, the **Sukkah Peace**. The first night of Sukkot, the candles are kindled signifying the beginning of the festival. Blessings are said in the Sukkah, and the waving of the branches (as instructed in Lev. 23) is done in the Sukkah. Three myrtle twigs, two willow branches and one palm branch are bound together in a holder woven of palm leaves. This is called a *lulav* and is held in the right hand. In the left hand is held an *etrog*, a lemon-like fruit sometimes called a citron, which has a beautiful fragrance. The fruit and branches are brought together with the arms outstretched to draw them toward the heart while a blessing is said. This is done in six directions; each of the four directions of the compass, East, South, West and North and then above and below. What is the meaning of this? Through the doing comes the understanding. It becomes more and more apparent each year as you wave the lulav and etrog, drawing the energy of the directions and dimensions toward your heart.

Spiritually, the key lies in the prayer we say as we wave the branches.

Ana, Yah, hoshiah, nah. "Please, Holy One, deliver us."
Ana, Yah, hatzlicha, nah. "Please, Holy One, prosper us."

The root of the Hebrew word *hatzlicha*, for prosper, is *tzalach*. It means to succeed, do well, prosper, thrive, flourish, to be fit for, to appear, cover, alight (fall) upon. In the book of I Samuel: 16, 13 this word is used and translated: "the spirit of The Holy One came mightily upon David..." By putting all of the meanings of this word together, the connotation is broad, including God giving us heightened abilities and the blessing of the spirit of God upon what we are doing that the work of our hands may not only prosper, but flourish. As we stretch out our arms holding the lulav and etrog and draw them back towards our heart while shaking the branches in the different directions, asking God's blessing and help, we are gathering Divine Energy from the "four directions of the earth" plus Heaven above and the center of Mother Earth below. We connect the Divine Flow of Plenty of God's love from the six directions to our hearts.

The ritual of the shaking of the lulav and etrog may well be in the category of "you had to be there" to gain the full benefit. Throughout the year, during difficulties and times when our faith is tried, we can reconnect to this ritual in memory and bring our thoughts and our feelings back into harmony with our Spirit and our faith. The Spirit within us tells us that just as God cared for the Children of Israel in the wilderness, God is caring for us today. This cannot be understood through our logic or intellect. It is a matter of our faith. Sukkot is a ritual that continues to support us throughout the year, as we use the elements of the lulav in other rituals.

At the end of Sukkot the leaves of the myrtle are stripped off of the branches and used in the sweet and fragrant Havdalah spices. Each Havdalah as we smell the spices and awaken our sense of smell, we remember Sukkot and God's care of us for the coming week; for the sense of smell carries memory and awakens within us that moment of intimacy with The Holy One that we shared under our Sukkat Shalom, *Sukkah* **of Peace.** It helps us remember who we are.

Maybe this is a memory King Solomon wanted to evoke for people entering the Temple when he chose the season of Sukkot for its dedication. It certainly fit in with the mood of the holiday, the heightened joy at creating this "meeting place with God" that carried such beauty for the glory of God. It was on the eighth day of the Hebrew month of Tishri that the seven-day dedication began, after which began the seven-day celebration of Sukkot.

> He (King Solomon) assembled all the elders and leaders of the
> people. They brought the Tent of Meeting, which still survived

from the days of trekking in the wilderness, holding the Ark with the two stone tablets Moses set in it at Sinai ... they brought it from the place on Mount Zion the city of his father David and placed it in the Holy of Holies under the wings of the **Keruvim** (Cherubim)... And every Israelite assembled to celebrate the dedication of the Temple and to hear Solomon say "But is it true that God will dwell on earth? – Here, the most heavenly of heavens cannot contain You; far less this house that I have built! Still Holy One, my God, turn your face to hear the prayer of entreaty, the prayer of praise that your servant prays to You today – so that Your eyes may be open toward this house day and night."

I KINGS 8

Perhaps in wisdom, King Solomon wanted to instill in the hearts of the people that just as the Sukkah is a temporary dwelling place, so too, is this Temple, resplendent and grand, it was still only a finite meeting place with The Infinite. This is why he added to his prayers that even if people face toward the Temple that God would hear and answer their prayers. To this day, we face east when praying in order to face the direction of the Temple.

Did the Rabbi from Galilee and his family and disciples travel to Jerusalem and rejoice in the rituals of Sukkot? As devout men of God, you bet they did! You can read about Jesus' plans for Sukkot, the Feast of Tabernacles, in the Gospel of John chapter 7. In verse 37, at the culmination of the festival Jesus announces, "If any man is thirsty, let him come to Me and drink!" Now, while this is an inspirational call at any time, why does the text make it a point to tell you that it is on the final and most important day of the feast?

There is a ritual that was not mentioned in the Torah, but

is handed down to us in the Oral Traditions (the Talmud). According to the Rabbis, this special festival added to the joy and tumult and was known as the "Rejoicing of the House of Water-Drawing", *Simhat Beit HaSho'evah*. It was a water libation ritual. It was a time of singing, dancing, burning of enormous menorot (plural of menorah). There was the playing of cymbals, trumpets and shofarot and an intense "outpouring" of rejoicing in the streets parading to the Temple. Water (offering of the poor) and wine (offering of the wealthy) were poured out together and on the culminating day, a special prayer for rain was lifted up, that the land may receive God's blessing of having enough water in the coming season to insure the growth of the next year's crops. At the season when water was the center of celebration, Jesus alluded to the waters of wisdom that he was offering; the spring of the Holy Spirit, Ruah HaKodesh, flowing from within for those who were open to it. Each of the three Pilgrimage Festivals held spiritual power. Jesus celebrated them and taught others to connect with their deeper spiritual meanings.

> And it shall come to pass, that every one that is left of all the nations who came against Jerusalem shall go up from year to year to worship the Guide of the Cosmos, The Holy One of Hosts, and to keep Sukkot, (Feast of Tabernacles or Booths). And whoever does not come up of all the families of the earth to Jerusalem to worship The Fountain of Life, The Holy One of Hosts, upon them shall be no rain."
>
> ZECHARIAH 14:16, 17

It is from this prophecy that we associate Sukkot with the times of the Messiah. The lulav and etrog became artistic motifs in ancient

SPIRITUAL GROWTH THROUGH SACRED TIME

Jewish art representing messianic redemption and the hope of rebuilding the Temple.

What new insights do you now have for understanding the symbols and spiritual principles of the prophet Zachariah's message? Does Sukkot hold new meaning for you as a follow of Jesus?

Each year as we journey through the cycle of the Festival holidays we greet them from a new place in our lives. We are not simply doing each holiday again and again, for the cycling is not a circle bringing us to where we began, but it is a spiral, taking us ever higher as we learn and grow from each year's new knowledge, experiences and wisdom. We hear the message of the holiday afresh each season, for we are as a new person each year. You are in a different place in your life this year than you were last year. How will these festivals and all of the holidays be different for you this year? The message each festival carries will be essentially the same, however, we may learn new ways to apply their wisdom and spiritual principles that will shed new light on the pathway we are now traveling. Each year the holidays and festivals speak to us anew as we spiral to ever growing heights and greet next year's celebrations from a higher place.

How would you like to celebrate the Feast of Tabernacles this year? How would you mark this time of fulfillment of the sun (the fall equinox) and the moon (the full moon)? Who do the sun and moon symbolize? (Hint: If the Sun is God, who might the moon be?) You may want to build a Sukkah at your church or your in your yard and have discussions about the symbolism of this Festival within the peaceful arms of the Sukkah. What does the "harvest" symbolize to you? Is there a connection with the end of the growing season and the end of times before the Messianic Age?

Sukkot is our season to experience the Glory of the Earth fulfilled. It is a time of spiritual maturity, and connecting with the Earth, fullness of cycles and rejoicing in the bounty of God's grace. This too, is your Hebrew inheritance. Rejoice in it!

The Days of Awe
Rosh HaShanah and Yom Kippur

In chapter 23 of Leviticus God ordains that there will be two Holy Days, the first and the tenth of the seventh month. The first is a day of blowing the Shofar, which we call Rosh HaShanah. We blow the Shofar to announce the New Year. The tenth day is the Day of Atonement, called Yom Kippur. It is a Holy Day for the people to come into harmony and wholeness within themselves, within the community and between the community of Israel and God. It is, for Israel, the Day of At-One-Ment.

Rosh HaShanah
The Shofar Call of the New Year

And The Holy One spoke to Moses, saying, Speak to the Children of Israel saying, In the seventh month, on the first day of the month, shall you have a Sabbath, a memorial of blowing of horns, a holy gathering. You shall do not servile work.

LEV. 23:23,24,25

Rosh HaShanah literally means the "head of the year". It is the Hebrew New Year. How can this be since it is at the beginning of the seventh month?

The Hebrew calendar actually has <u>four</u> New Years. The first New Year is on *Nissan*, the first month of the Hebrew calendar and the spring month of Passover (Pesah), when the months of the Hebrew calendar begin anew. Nissan is considered the first month of the calendar. However, the date of the <u>year</u> changes, on Rosh HaShanah (New Year) at the beginning of Tishrei, which is actually the seventh month. The other two New Years are *Tu B'Shvat*, the wintertime New Year of the Trees (so you may number the years of a tree, for you are not to gather its fruit until the fourth year in its maturity). Finally, there is the New Year of the Kings, in summer. This was the time Kings were anointed. This enabled an accounting of years according to the "reign of King So-and-So." This New Years has fallen into disused since we no longer anoint Kings or Queens in Israel.

Having several New Years is not as strange as you might think. When you think about it, we have several New Years in the US. There is the calendar New Year on 1 January when the year date changes; then the new academic or school year begins in late August, early September. Many corporations begin their new fiscal year on 30 June or 1 July. These do not seem confusing to us because they have meaning throughout the year for us. So it is with the Hebrew New Years. They each carry meaning to the spiritual aspects of the year in our lives.

Rosh HaShanah is the when the date of the year changes. The Rabbis consider that Rosh HaShanah is the birthday of the world. It is a tradition that the Creation was finished on Rosh HaShanah. We celebrate Creation in all of its Divine glory and in awe. The ten-day period between Rosh HaShanah and Yom Kippur (Day of Atonement) is a time of accounting for our actions and putting our relationships in order as we stand before The Holy One. It is a time for repairing those relationships that have suffered damage during the year and for asking forgiveness from others when we have transgressed against them whether we did so knowingly or not. It is a time for renewal of our minds and hearts. It is a time for revitalizing our relationship with God both individually and as a community. The ten days culminate at Yom Kippur. For these reasons and more, this period is called the "Days of Awe" (*Yomim Noraim*). Rosh HaShanah and Yom Kippur are referred to as the "High Holy Days." They serve to prepare us for the festival that comes five days later, Sukkot (Feast of Booths).

Just as we celebrate the seventh day of Creation, Shabbat, as a special day, a Holy Day set aside for our rest and reconnection with God, we also celebrate the seventh month is a "Sabbath month", filled with celebrations of Creation, and days of rest, that we may have time to reconnect and renew our relationship with God, first within ourselves, then between ourselves. The month seems to have one Holy Day after the next as we celebrate Rosh HaShanah, (New Year), Yom Kippur, (Day of Atonement), Sukkot, (Feast of Tabernacles) and a final festive celebration called *Simchat Torah*, the time of our "Rejoicing with the Torah". This last holiday celebrates the end of the yearly cycle of reading the entire Torah, a section at a time each week. On this holiday the last verses of Deuteronomy are read followed directly by a reading of the first chapters of Genesis. In this way they are "married". By joining the two readings we continue reading the Torah without a break, one week to the next, year by year. It is a joyous celebration with music and dancing with the Torah, even carrying it out into the street in a joyous parade that is reminiscent of the time when David danced before The Holy One as they brought the Ark of the Covenant back to Jerusalem. (See II Samuel 6:12). Tishrei is the seventh month, a Sabbath month with all its celebrations and its spiritual power to renew us body, mind and spirit.

Because Rosh HaShanah falls in the seventh month it also gives us the opportunity to check on our spiritual progress since Passover and Shavuot with the new covenants we made at that time concerning the work of our sacred pathway. It is a season to reflect upon the progress we have made to manifest our visions. We are able to make adjustments and course corrections in the light we receive during the High Holy Days.

At Rosh HaShanah we remember that we are unique in our creation, as is every one around us. We honor this uniqueness in our relationships, strengthening them by learning to ask others for their forgiveness for our wrongdoings and extending forgiveness to others as they ask us for it. This is not always an easy task, for sometimes our spiritual and emotional wounding goes deep. Rosh HaShanah marks the beginning of examining our lives to see where we need to extend life to those who ask "for-give-ness." The word in English can be thought of as "for-giving-life," or the "thumbs up" sign. In ancient Rome in the Coliseum, the crowd would decide the fate of the defeated gladiator with a "thumbs up" indicating "give him life" or "thumbs down" for "give him death." When we for-give others we are giving the "thumbs up" sign, saying, "I am for-giving him/her life." We must learn how to do this, letting go of our resentments and prejudices if we are to go to God on Yom Kippur, ten days later and ask God to forgive us individually and as a community. We must have cleared the slates of rights and wrongs between us, freely extending our compassion to one another before we can go to God to ask for compassion and mercy. We are not asked to forgive the offending action, but the person who committed the action against us. We can leave the judgment of the offense to God. It is our obligation to for-give others and to ask others for for-give-ness for the offenses we have committed against them. Then, as a community, we are able to stand together in unity on Yom Kippur. This is a mid-year process of cleaning house (like Passover) and clearing the air. It does not mean we do not do this on a daily basis during the rest of the year, but it gives us time to focus upon what is going on in our lives and relationships, and to do something about it. When we do this as a community, we are able to tap into the power of the group. If our prayers are powerful as individuals, then so much the more so when we pray together. It gives us the opportunity to heal our community and clear the air of resentments and start anew in harmony.

It was this spiritual principle that Jesus was teaching about when he said, "And whenever you stand praying, if you have anything against any one, forgive him and let it drop – leave it, let it go- in order that your Father Who is in Heaven may also forgive you your [own] failings and shortcomings and let them drop" (Mark 11:25). And on the subject of asking forgiveness he taught, "So if, when you are offering your gift at the altar you there remember that your brother has any grievance against you, leave your gift at the altar and go; first make peace with your brother and be reconciled, then come back and present your gift" (Matthew 5:23,24). It was understood within the Hebrew traditions that in order to receive compassion, we must give compassion to others. Rosh HaShanah is the beginning of the "Days of Awe" when we stand seeking grace before The Holy One. It is this same grace that we are expected to extend to others.

Divine Grace, or *Hesed,* in Hebrew, comes to us at a time when we are most empty. When we come to a place in our lives when it seems we have done all we could or we see no options or alternatives left open to us, then The Holy One of Blessing steps in and extends grace to us. It is then, at our time of "emptiness" when we are clear of our ego and self will that we see the miracles come into our situation that tells us God is somehow there. The One Who powers the Universe – and beyond! – is there knowing what is going on in our life. The spiritual principle at work here is that in order for something to be created, there must be an empty space. Only in an empty space is there Infinite Possibility.

Rosh HaShanah comes at the beginning of the month, which is the time of the new moon. It is a time when the sky is "empty" of the light of the moon. The world is at its darkest. So it is fitting that we celebrate creation at this time of "emptiness." It is fitting that we begin anew our Soul's work in the empty space of the new moon. It is to this work that the voice of the Shofar calls us.

Rosh HaShanah is the holiday of the "blowing of the Shofar." This is one of the most powerful services of the Holy Days. Our sages call the sound of the Shofar blast the "wake up call to the Soul." It awakens us to our higher calling, our spiritual reason to be living. It calls us to awaken to our relationships and to the Voice of Spirit, as the breath (ruah) of the one blowing the Shofar fills the ram's horn, sending vibrations into the room that resonates in our heart. It speaks to us about our experiences of the year and calls us to action; compelling us to fulfill our sacred mission, to move forward toward the beautiful Light of the Divine.

It was a ram who appeared to Abraham and became the sacrifice that "God provided" in Genesis 22. The call of the ram's horn, the shofar, reminds us of this test of Abraham's love for God, even to giving up the life of his son, his only and beloved son, whose life was a miracle from God. Abraham passed the test!

The shofar's call is like a beacon leading us home through the darkness of the sky of the new moon, promising us safe harbor, rest and peace. On Rosh HaShanah we are instructed to blow the shofar. Our rabbis say that the blessing is not in blowing the shofar, but in hearing the shofar. The notes of the shofar are familiar to us, but their message is fresh each year. The understanding is that "hearing" does not refer to simply having our ears pick up the sounds, but that our heart "hears" the message. That our Soul meets with The Holy One in the vibrations of Spirit and we become conscious of The Presence and respond with love and the desire for harmony. Each year the shofar gives a new message of Divine Guidance to those who have ears (open in their Soul) to hear.

When have you heard the shofar call in your life? When has your Soul awakened to the Awe of The One and your heart overflowed with love for that sweet Presence? This is Rosh HaShanah. How and when did you answer it? The answer of your Soul is given on Yom Kippur, the Day of Atonement, ten days later.

On Rosh HaShanah it is traditional to dip slices of apples in honey. Simply put, this symbolizes "sweetness in the coming year." The apple symbolizes desire. On Rosh HaShanah, the birth of Creation, it is our desire to be in Divine Union and harmony with The Holy One, our Creator, and with all of Creation. The apple also represents the human being, for when the apple is cut in a cross section the five seeds at the center form a pentagram, which corresponds symbolically to the human form, five fingers and toes, five senses, and five extremities, two arms, two legs and a head, all five extremities potentially "seeds" of life.

The apple has a sweet fragrance, taste and shape. It is used symbolically for the sweet fragrance of the presence of the Lover in Song of Songs (Song of Solomon) 7:9. Proverbs 25:11 compares the timely spoken word to "apples of gold in mosaics of silver." The apple symbolizes sweetness, beauty and hope for fulfillment and therefore in the Kabbalah it symbolizes the human ability to attain supreme holiness. It is at Rosh HaShanah that we re-commit ourselves to that high calling.

The honey in which we dip the apples symbolizes rebirth and spiritual growth. We use honey to mark this time of the rebirth of Creation and personal growth with sweetness. Psalm 19:8,11 compares the sweetness of honey to the Word of God: "The Torah (Divine Word) of The Holy One is complete (faultless), restoring the Soul... more to be desired than gold, even much fine gold: sweeter also than honey and the honeycomb." Dipping apples in honey is our symbol for the hope of the coming year.

Another tradition held on Rosh HaShanah is to fill your pockets with breadcrumbs, walk to a nearby stream or lake and empty all the crumbs into the water. This tradition is called *Tashlich*, which means "to cast". The breadcrumbs represent our sins of the year. This is done to put into action the verse in Micah 7:19, "And You will cast all their sins into the depths of the sea; you will show truth to Jacob; loyal love to Abraham, as you have sworn to our ancestors from ancient days." The water represents the Word of God, our Torah. It is when we see our actions of wrongdoing in the Light of Torah that we ask forgiveness and bring our actions into harmony with the Divine. Water is transformative. It is out of the waters that Creation grew "And the Spirit of God fluttered over the face of the waters." So it is that just as water is transformative for physical Creation, Torah, is transformative for the Soul, bringing it enlightenment. It is through studying and living Torah (the Light Bearer) that we transform our conscious mind in harmony with the Light in our Souls. We celebrate our transformation and renewal at Rosh HaShanah.

This Holy Day, the day of blowing the Shofar and celebrating Creation is part of your Hebrew heritage. How would you like to celebrate Rosh HaShanah this year? Could your spiritual community use this day to begin a ten day healing process, bringing all relationships into reconciliation and peace? Would you like to "hear" the message of the Shofar awakening your Soul to God's message for your life this year? How do you celebrate the birthday of Creation?

The *Hebrew Heritage* series was created to help you answer some of these questions, for *Rosh HaShanah* is your Holy Day, too.

But remember, **Rosh HaShanah** is only the beginning. The height of the Holy Days of Awe is Yom Kippur, the Day of Atonement. It is a day of coming before God as a community, as *Am Yisrael*, the people of Israel. It is a day for setting the tone for the year to come. It too, is your Hebrew heritage.

Yom Kippur
Sacred Day Of At-One-Ment

"And The Holy One spoke to Moses saying, "Also on the tenth day of this seventh month there shall be a day of atonement: it shall be a holy gathering to you; and you shall give answer to your Souls, and offer an offering made by fire to The Holy One. And you shall do no work on that very same day; for it is a day of atonement to make atonement for you before The Holy One your God ... it shall be a statute for ever throughout your generations ... on the ninth day of the month at evening, from evening to evening shall you celebrate your Sabbath."

LEVITICUS 23:26 – 32

At Yom Kippur, the Day of Atonement, we stand before God, the Covenant Keeper, as a community. It is a time for giving answer to our Soul (Heshbon HaNefesh, accounting of our Soul) in honesty in The Divine Presence. It is a time for renewal. We renew our commitment to the Sacred Ways, we renew our relationship with God, we renew the vision of our spiritual community. In all of this renewal, there is one thread of continuity that is the thread of unity. Yom Kippur is the Day of At-One-ment. We come together as one. We come together before The One. It is the day to feel the Oneness of our community and Universe.

As Shavuot is the festival that links to and fulfills Passover, so too, Yom Kippur links to and fulfills Rosh HaShanah. Yom Kippur is the point of Rosh HaShanah; for maturing in a consciousness of the Oneness of All Life is the fulfillment of the diversity in Creation. Just as we are "face to face" with The Holy One at Sinai on Shavuot, we are "face to face" with The Holy One at the mountain within us on Yom Kippur. This mountain within where we meet with The Holy One is the mound of our misdeeds, misunderstandings, regrets, resentments and sorrows that we have experienced during the year. Yom Kippur is the time to make atonement, a covering, of the dark places of our lives. It is a time for transforming these places with the light of our integrity, understanding and commitment. It is a time to love, a time to extend forgiveness, and to commit ourselves to expressing our love through deeds of kindness.

The Spirit of God covers us on the Day of Atonement like a great tallit (prayer shawl). When we are under this "tallit" for 24 hours we see the fringes at the corners and remember God's Presence. We look at our lives in the light of the Luminous in truth with love, honesty with compassion. When we see the tzitzit (fringes) of our prayer shawl we remember to keep our eyes on The Holy One, not to be led astray by our eyes (what we see) or our hearts (what we feel) but to be led and encouraged by the Spirit of God. We examine ourselves and our lives at this point midway through the year and acknowledge our spiritual pathway up to this point. We open our hearts to do *t'shuvah*. This Hebrew word is usually translated "repentance". However, the root word means to "turn about" or "return." Yom Kippur is our opportunity to bring back into the Divine Light those deeds and areas of our lives that are out of harmony with God higher purpose for us. It is our opportunity to acknowledge our wrongdoing, the places where we "miss the mark" (*Het*, sin) and to return to the Sacred Ways as we now understand them.

We look within areas of our lives that we don't feel or sense the Presence of God, to see if we are the ones who have turned away; for The Holy One IS, and remains, however, we sometimes turn, become distracted, or shield ourselves from direct encounter with The Divine. We do this when we desire our own way, even when we know that way to be wrong, or less than what we really want for our lives. Yom Kippur is our opportunity to turn ourselves around, and may bathe more fully in the countenance of the Holy One once more.

Yom Kippur is our opportunity to "go behind the curtain" as the High Priest went behind the curtain into the Holy of Holies, God's most powerful Presence to do sacrifice and to recognize God by pronouncing the most holy name. We go behind the curtain of our innermost secrets and find The Holy One dwelling there, ready for us to sacrifice the bullock of our Self wills, on the altars of our hearts. We then, turn our eyes to meet with God at the Mercy Seat (covering of the Ark) within the Holy of Holies, our own Soul. There, out of love for our intimate Friend, our Rock we come back into the embrace of Oneness, the Holy Union of our hearts; we return to the Sacred Ways and God's ever-present love. It is we who have turned away. Even in our turning away, God extends life to us and enfolds us in love. This is Yom Kippur.

In order to more intensely experience the spiritual aspects of the Holy Day, some people fast from sundown to sundown. The idea of fasting (abstaining from taking food or water) comes from translating the Hebrew words *v'i-ni-tem et nah-she-tei-chem* as "to afflict your Souls." (Leviticus 23:32). However, the root of the first word, *v'i-ni-tem,* is *ana,* and it means "to answer or testify." Therefore, it would be more correct to translate this phrase as "give answer for your Souls." This is a different message. It speaks of plumbing the Soul to answer for our actions and opinions. It speaks of the testimony of the heart for examination at this season.

Those who like to stay with the tradition of fasting, however, feel that the Soul is better able to focus upon the spiritual work of Yom Kippur better if it is not involved in the physical aspects of bodily function (eating, digesting). It is understood that during intentional prayer and meditation the body receives energy from the spiritual plane and does not require physical food. This may well be what Jesus was referring to when he went up on the mountain to pray and meditate alone and his disciples were concerned that he had no food with him:

> Meanwhile the disciples urged Him saying, Rabbi, eat something. But he assured them I have food to eat of which you know nothing and have no idea. So the disciples said one to another, Has someone brought him something to eat? Jesus said to them, My food is to do the will of Him Who sent me and to accomplish and completely finish **His Work.**
>
> JOHN 4: 31-34

Concerning fasting, some people do not fast, but instead they focus and meditate on the words spoken by the prophet Isaiah:

Is not this rather the fast that I have chosen? To loose the chains of wickedness, to undo the bands of the yoke, and to let the oppressed go free, and to break every yoke? Is it not to share your bread with the hungry and that you bring the poor that are cast out to your house? When you see the naked that you cover him and that you hide not yourself from your own family? Then shall your light break forth like the morning, and your health shall spring forth speedily: and your righteousness shall go before you; the glory of The Holy One shall be your rearguard. Then shall you call and The Holy One will answer you and you shall cry and The Infinite shall say, Here AM I.

ISAIAH 58:6-9

Yom Kippur day is a twenty-four hour period of searching our Souls for any actions thoughts and feelings that are missing the mark of our high calling as a "kingdom of priests, a holy nation." This day for evaluation is often confused with our sense of judgment. While the Torah simply focuses upon atonement, forgiveness and renewal on this special day, the traditional liturgy that has developed over thousands of years paints a metaphoric picture of God opening a "Book of Life" and writing our names in it – or not. The names are inscribed on Rosh HaShanah and "sealed" on Yom Kippur. With this emphasis, many people interpret the Day of Atonement as the Day of Judgment. The prophets encourage us **not** to judge for only The Holy One knows the heart (book of Job) and the sacred journey of our Souls and is therefore in a position to judge. In the tradition of the prophets, the Rabbi from Nazareth taught:

"Do not judge and criticize and condemn others, so that you may not be judged and criticized and condemned yourselves.

> For just as you judge and criticize and condemn others
> you will be judged and criticized and condemned and in
> accordance with the measure you deal out to others it will be
> dealt out again to you."

MATTHEW 7:1, 2

On the Day of Atonement we are to ask forgiveness and forgive. We are to let go of judgments, and thus not be judged. While it appears that Jesus is saying not to judge other people so that we would not be judged **by** them or God or any other external source, we can also learn a deeper, more subtle truth from these words; that the judgment we use on other people is the same judgment we use on ourselves, criticizing ourselves in the same way. If we judge others harshly, we can see with careful introspection that we harshly and unjustly demand perfection of ourselves judging any flaw imagined or real. Our rationale may kick in so fast we may not even realize that we are accusing ourselves in some particular area of our life. However, we create "not good enough" feelings deep within us from these unjust judgments. The deeper Truth is, that as we let go of judging others, then we are letting go of judging ourselves and criticizing ourselves as well. God is the only just judge. God knows our hearts and our sacred journey better than we ourselves.

Try the following exercise this year for ten days, from Rosh HaShanah to Yom Kippur. Set your intention to *not* use the word "good" or "bad" in any sentence. Instead, express in descriptive language how you feel about something. For example, if you are complimenting a friend, letting him/her know how well s/he did while giving a speech, instead of saying, "That was so good ..." say something about what you experienced – "You were so clear about ... I really connected with the part about ..." By setting an

181

intention not to use the word "good", you will notice how often you are "judging" or labeling others and situations in your life – this is good, that is bad. If you use the word "good" and break your intention, correct your sentence with what you want to say and get right back on your intention. Simply recommit to your intention of not judging and not using the word "good" or "bad" for ten days. This is a guilt-free zone; you are to have no judgment or criticism about your own slips. Simply know you are refining one of your learning edges, a place in your life that you would like to become more conscious and enlightened. Little by little you will notice that you feel different about yourself as you refine your ability to discern. This can be part of your personal renewal at Yom Kippur.

By the end of the Yom Kippur day, at the service called *Neilah*, or "The Closing of the Gates" we each feel our strongest sense of kinship with one another and partnership with God. The metaphor of the "Gates of Heaven" closing compels us to do any unfinished business of the heart with each other or God before the culmination and ending of this Sacred Time in Sacred Space. There is an expectancy of spirit as the sun is setting, the long shadows give way to darkness and we hear the last long blast of the Shofar call our Souls to transition. This service completes the transition from confusion, rebellion, and denial to reconciliation, renewal and rejuvenation. We are moved from our feelings of isolation to a sense of connectedness. The Shofar calls us to leave our fears and turn to love; to turn from weariness of life to inspiration. As the long, long blast of the shofar falls silent, echoing against the walls of the synagogue, it also resounds within the walls of our hearts. We breathe out a sigh: a sigh of relief, a sigh of love. Another Yom Kippur has brought us each into a new place of wholeness and peace within The Holy One. We are in Shalom!

After sundown everyone gathers to "break the fast." We

replenish our bodies' food and liquid with delights that seem the tastier for having fasted. We also enjoy a new level of closeness with each other for having spent this auspicious day together. The joy is heightened by the solemnity of the day. The relief is tangible, as each person feels renewed in spirit and free from burdens carried too long.

Rosh HaShanah and Yom Kippur are considered High Holy Days. However, they are still truly preparation days for the third of the three traveling Festival days, Sukkot. After we celebrate the birth of Creation and the renewal of The Oneness of All Life the way is clear for us to celebrate the Divine in all of Creation. We are ready to live in harmony with Creation and with our ancestors in our Sukkah (hut) on the Festival of Sukkot.

Yom Kippur, the day of renewal before God for both the individual and the community, belongs to you, as well. Yom Kippur was observed by the disciples, the Church of ancient days. How could it revitalize your community to celebrate it this year? Perhaps you would like to have a Shofar service and celebrate the day of Creation, as a day of "Calling all Souls".

Prayer groups, the Board and social groups within the Church can gather during the ten days between Rosh HaShanah and Yom Kippur to have a "Forgiveness Circle". Each person goes to others individually to offer apologies and ask forgiveness for anything that may have come between them during the year. One person starts their journey around the circle standing in front of the next person in the circle. When that person has completed asking and receiving forgiveness he/she moves to the next person in the circle and then the next, while the second person in the circle simultaneously starts his/her journey around the circle. As each person engages in the forgiveness circle, the circle becomes smaller and smaller until finally, the circle reappears with everyone having given and received apologies and forgiveness. It is not a ritual to be entered into lightly. It takes real courage to face your neighbor with true openness of heart and honesty. It demands that all fences of pretense, guardedness and defensiveness be taken down. But, the rewards of freedom and openness within the community are well worth the process.

On Yom Kippur maybe your group would like to have a day of celebration of God's grace and faithfulness to forgive. It can also be a day to fast and pray for the larger community of humanity across the globe to come into harmony and shalom. It is an opportunity for your faith community to stand before the Throne of Grace and receive forgiveness for your shortcomings, frailties and errors, and then to receive renewed relationship, Divine Guidance and freedom of heart to enter the sacred days of the Harvest Festival of Sukkot.

Sacred History
Hanukkah & Purim

The two historical holidays of *Hanukkah* (Feast of Dedication or Festival of Lights) and *Purim* (celebration of the story of Queen Esther) have been celebrated since the time when these historical events occurred.

The story of Hanukkah can be found in the books of Maccabees I, II in the Apocrypha. It is about the revolt led by Mattatias, a man of great courage from the priestly tribe and family of the Hasmoneans against the Syrian tyrant Antiochus Epiphanes, the Hellenistic King of Syria, which was part of Alexander's great Empire. The guerilla warfare went on for three years from 169 to 166 BCE.

The Book of Esther tells the story of Purim, which took place in 356 BCE in Persia. The Kingdom of Judah had been captured and taken into exile into Babylon. Babylon was then defeated by the Persians and became part of the vast Persian Empire. The Hebrews were first called Jews (short for Judeans) during this exile. The Persians allowed the "Jews" to return to their land and rebuild the Temple. However, only a remnant returned, for they were quite comfortable in the Babylonian/Persian metropolises, the then New York of the Middle East. Things weren't so bad there, so they thought.

The story of Esther and her Uncle Mordecai tells of intrigue, deception and plots of murder. It also tells of God's deliverance and Divine plan, human courage and the strength of community. The underlying theme in Esther is one of "opposites" as it is one of secrets on the earthly plane and of God's omniscience (all knowing) and deliverance from celestial planes. Although God's name is not mentioned one time in the entire book, it is clearly evident that it is by God's Divine plan that the events fall in place. Purim is an enormously joyous celebration. It is the "Jewish Mardi Gras," celebrated with parades, music, food, singing and dancing in the streets in Israel. It is a time of reading the story and cheering and hissing at heroine and villain of the story read in its entirety in the Synagogue. There are plays and *shpiels* (a variety show or play), carnivals and of course eating special foods baked for Purim all in celebration of this holiday.

Hanukkah
Festival of Lights and Festival of Dedication

Hanukkah falls in the darkest hours of the year when the winter sun has journeyed to its farthest reaches north and then begins its return south again, giving more and more light to the long, dark days of winter. Its theme of light in the darkness serves to remind us to dedicate our hearts in hope of God's miracles of grace.

Hanukkah has many names. The Hebrew word Hanukkah comes from a root meaning to dedicate, consecrate and to educate. When we put these three meanings together we understand that to consecrate our lives to Holy service, we must educate our minds through study, training our minds with higher thoughts, and we must dedicate our hearts to love – love of God, ourselves and others. We dedicate our hearts to be tender and strong compassionate and trusting.

Historically, Hanukkah celebrates a "David and Goliath" type of victory of little Israel against the giant Greco-Syrian tyrant Antiochus. This was the first war fought in order to <u>gain</u> religious freedom, for the Hebrews had been forbidden to practice their Sacred Ways, (eating according to the instructions in Torah, circumcising the young in covenant, celebrating Shabbat or bring sacrifices to the Temple). The Temple had been taken over and used for profane purposes.

In the face of the popular Hellenistic influences of the day and the formidable Greek empire's army, a priest by the name of Mattatias banded together with his sons, Judah being the leader, and fought by striking like a hammer, giving a punch to the enemy and then fleeing back to the cover of hills and mountain regions. The Hebrew word *ma-ccav* means to punch, or perforate. This little band became known as the *Maccabees* from a derivative of this word, *ma-ke-vet*, which means "mallet or hammer" for they struck a blow at their enemy and then were gone.

The Maccabees were relentless in their quest, even facing the elephants that Antiochus' army brought to the battle. These were the armored tanks of the day, certainly frightening to any foot soldier! More and more people joined this small band in the guerilla warfare they were waging.

In the aftermath of the war the Israelites reclaimed the Temple which had been desecrated and defiled. They worked to clear the debris, wash and cleanse the walls, floors, holy vessels, curtains and ornaments. It was a tremendous undertaking to restore the Temple for rededication to The Holy One.

When the day finally arrived to kindle the Light of the Menorah in the Holy Place, only one vial, one day's worth, of the specially prepared and consecrated olive oil could be found. It would take eight days to prepare new oil according to the instructions in Torah. By faith, the Priests poured the contents of the small one day vial of oil into the Menorah, and kindled the wicks. It lifted their hearts as it burned brightly, once again filling the Temple with the luminous brilliance of the Menorah. At once, they began the work of preparing new oil.

On the second day the Priests expected to come in to find the Temple in darkness as the oil should have been depleted. To their amazement, the Temple was still aglow with the soft dancing light of the Menorah! It was a miracle! The oil had not been consumed by the flames; the light still filled the Temple.

The third day their hope grew, yet, their logic told them otherwise – surely, the oil would have run out by now. But, as they entered the Temple, the soft glow of the Menorah illumined the gold and richly colored red, purple, and blue fabrics on the walls, and the room was filled with light. The oil was lasting; the Menorah was casting its beautiful light throughout the dwelling place of The Holy One.

The fourth, the fifth, the sixth, the seventh, and finally the eighth day came and the oil had lasted for the Menorah to burn in honor of the Light of God's Presence. This was the Miracle of the Oil. At last, the new oil was ready. In partnership with God, the Priests had used what oil was available and trusting God began doing what they could to provide new oil for the light. God had filled the Temple with light from one vial, until the Priests fulfilled their sacred duties, preparing new oil. This is the miracle of the light.

It is from this oral tradition story that Hanukkah gets the name the Festival of Lights. For eight days, symbolizing the eight days of preparing the oil, we celebrate Hanukkah, beginning on the 25th of the Hebrew month of Kislev. This is the winter season of the shortest day and darkest night. This holiday teaches us to bring our light no matter how long or convincing the darkness, to be in partnership with The Holy One to illumine the Earth.

On the first night of Hanukkah families say a blessing and then kindle the first lights of a *Hanukiah*, (a menorah used at Hanukkah) which has nine lights on it altogether. The Hanukiah is set near the window so that it can be seen by others and the light can reach out to the world. There are eight lights for the eight days, plus a light called the *Shamash*, or "helper" candle. The Shamash is kindled with a match first and then it is used to kindle the other lights. The first night only one light (plus the Shamash) is kindled. Each night another light is added until on the eighth night all eight lights plus the Shamash, the ninth, is kindled. Each night the dancing flames of the lights burn down, adding a festive glow to the room. At the darkest and coldest season, we experience the effect of the lights of Hanukkah symbolizing how we affect the world as we add our light to the light within others to make this a brighter, warmer and more holy place.

In Synagogue services today, the Torah portions having to do with the dedication and rededication of the Temple are read. We also read the words of the angel who spoke to Zechariah saying, "Not by might and not by power, but, by my spirit (symbolized by oil), says The Holy One of Hosts."

(Zechariah 4:6). We are reminded that the flow of the Holy Spirit (Ruah Hakodesh) is in the Divine Order of God.

Hanukkah is a holiday for having fun and taking joy in life by playing games together. There is a traditional game which is played with a *dreydle*, a little top for spinning. On each of the four sides of the top is a letter, *Nun, Gimel, Hey, Shin,* standing for the first letter of the words, *nes gadol haya sham,* "a great miracle happened there." (In Israel, the last word is changed to *po,* "a great miracle happened *here*). Pennies or peanuts are usually used in the "pot" in the center of the table. A player spins the dreydle and when it drops on one of the four sides the player is instructed by which letter is showing what to do on their turn. Nun does nothing, Gimel, put one in, Hey, take half of the pot and Shin takes the entire pot. The game is fun, but also teaches the lesson that we all have our part in bringing a miracle, whatever that part is, from total commitment to doing nothing. However, if we do nothing, we gain nothing; when we have total commitment, we reap the most. Whatever part we play in the community, we contribute our part (put one in).

Hanukkah is also a time of rededication. It is easy to become deplete of energy by the lack of light and warmth in the deep winter. So too, we can be worn down by the daily activities of life if we do not take time to bring light and joy into our lives. Hanukkah reminds us to treasure our freedom to practice our faith and to bring light and joy into every day, that we do not become discontent in the most difficult times when we see the least light and experience the cold. Hanukkah is a time to rededicate ourselves to being our light, to join our light with others (symbolized by the light of the Hanukiah) to bring light to the world. It is an opportunity to rededicate ourselves to bring joy into the practice of our faith; that we can rejoice in The Holy One and be content in Spirit.

The Shamash, the servant candle, symbolizes the light of the Holy Spirit of God that shares its light with us. (See the section on spirit and the symbolism of oil). It is the light of The Holy One of Blessing that moves through us by Spirit, setting our Souls aglow and enlightening all which is around us. This, too, is the symbolism of Hanukkah.

Because we are reminded of the miracle of oil, we use oil to make special treats for traditional foods eaten at this season. Most traditional is the making (and eating) of latkes, a type of potato pancakes made from shredded potatoes, onions, eggs and spices. They are made into patties and cooked – of course, oil. In Israel, it is traditional to have *sofganyot*, dough fried in oil and filled with fruit jelly.

In centuries past Eastern Europe there was a tradition for children to be given Hanukkah *gelt*, pieces of money. In the US this tradition has evolved to the giving of gifts, chocolate and candy during the eight-day celebration. While this may, in part, be reactionary measures to enjoin the gift giving of Christmas, it is also fair to say that we celebrate the gift of light at this season when the sun sets early and the nights are long. The light is a gift. It is a gift that is within each of us and is the most valuable gift we can give one another. The gift of the light we carry within our own Being and express as our loving actions, words, gifts and talents is a light that shines brighter than day and illumines the night.

Hanukkah is a holiday rich with meaning. It is part of your heritage to celebrate the freedom of your faith and the miracles that God brings into your life. It is a time for the rededication of your life to share your light and honor the miracle of the Holy Spirit illumining your Temple, the dwelling place of your Soul. It is a fun and joyous holiday.

Since the events of the first Hanukkah happened from 169 to 166 BCE, the celebration of Hanukkah was already within the culture and society in Jesus' time. Hanukkah carried special spiritual significance and encouragement during the oppressive rule of Rome over Judea at that time. Jesus would have celebrated the Festival of Lights in a very special way, for he used the symbolism of the light as his message to the world, his sacred pathway and to encourage others to use their light from within.

> Ye are the light of the world. A city that is set on a hill cannot be hidden. Neither do men light a lamp, and put it under a bushel, but on a lampstand and it gives light unto all that are in the house. Let your light so shine before men, that they may see your good works, and glorify your Father Who is in heaven. Matt. 5:14, 15, 16 After this the Feast of Dedication (Hanukkah) was taking place in Jerusalem. It was winter, and Jesus was walking in Solomon's porch in the Temple area.
>
> JOHN 10:22

If Jesus celebrated Hanukkah, do you imagine it is your holiday as well? It is part of your Hebrew heritage. Explore what Hanukkah means to you. This year bring the light during the dark winter months by lighting a Hanukiah in your home. Place the lights near the window as a light to the world. Give gifts, play games and enjoy foods cooked in oil to remind you of the anointing of the Holy Spirit and the joy of God's miracles in your life. Retell the story of those miracles to your children. This year, celebrate Hanukkah, and receive the message of the light in your heart.

Purim
The Mysterious Story of Queen Esther

"And Mordecai wrote these things, and sent letters to all the
Jews who were in all the provinces of the King Ahashverush,
both near and far to enjoin upon them that they should keep
the fourteenth day of the moon Adar, and the fifteenth day of
the same, year by year, as the days on which the Jews rested
from their enemies, and the month which was turned to them
from sorrow to joy and from mourning to holiday: that they
should make them days of feasting and joy and of sending
choice portions to one another, and gifts to the poor."

ESTHER 9: 20-22

Purim occurs in the early spring on the 14th and 15th of the
Hebrew month of *Adar*. This holiday focuses on courage to
follow your sacred pathway and trust in God to accomplish
your life work. The powerful story of Queen Esther teaches
us that we are each purposefully and wonderfully placed in
the world with a sacred mission; and yet we have a choice as
to whether we will accept the challenge. This holiday awakens
our spirit from the long winter hiatus and prepares us for the
experience of deliverance during the next Festival, which is
Pesah (Passover).

The story of Esther is one of secrets. It is filled with clues as
to the deep and mystical secrets through the use of meaningful
names of the characters. The most important of all names, the
name of God, is curiously never used. The plot is intrigue upon
intrigue.

The word Purim means "lots" – which were cast by the
Haman, the villain, to see which day to choose to wipe out the

Hebrews living amongst them. The Hebrew word Haman means "to do ill".

You can find this story in the book of Esther. She is chosen to be Queen by King Ahasuerus, who does not know she is a Hebrew. When a plot is made by Haman, the villain, to eradicate all of the Hebrews, it is up to Esther to reveal the truth to the King and intervene for her people. This story is brimming with secrets to share with us. Queen Esther's Hebrew name is *Hadassah*, meaning "myrtle", which is the fragrant branch used in the lulav at Sukkot. However, she chooses to be presented to the King with the Persian name of Esther to help conceal that she is Jewish. The name Esther is a play on the Hebrew word, *seiter*, which means "hiding place" or "secret." It is from these root words that we get the word "*star*". In ancient times astrology was highly developed. The Persians would have believed the stars to be the place where secrets are held. In modern times the name *Esther* is usually translated to mean "Star". To the Persians in the story, the name *Esther* was a queenly name because it was from the names of goddesses of the ancient world, *Ishtar* and *Astarte*. What are the secrets of Esther's story, the spiritual truths which speak to you personally to guide and help you fulfill your sacred missions in life?

Queen Esther's life teaches us what incredible power our intentions hold. She faced the fear of death and transformed it into the power to overcome fear through setting her intention (kavennah) to act out of her love for the people; for her love was greater than her fear.

When faced with the decision to go before the King on behalf of her people, Esther experienced the same human emotion of fear and thoughts of "What if..." that we experience in our lives. However, she showed us a way to transform the energy of those doubts and fears. She considered the consequences of entering the throne room of King Ahasuerus uninvited. The law required the death of the offender, even if it was the Queen herself. She voiced that fear to her uncle and advisor, Mordecai. He called forth the faith within her by advising her, "For such a time as this have you have been raised up (made Queen)." While not naming God, this alludes to God's Divine plan unfolding in the life of the young woman, Esther.

Queen Esther was wise. She determined in her heart to go before her husband the King, trusting that The One who gave her the opportunity of her position would fulfill Divine Will in her destiny. Her wisdom led her to unify the Energy of all of the people by asking Mordecai to have the community fast for her. (Fasting is part of a spiritual state of Enlightenment for heightened prayer).

She brought the people together with a united purpose, thereby increasing exponentially the power of her intention to carry out her life's mission of rescuing the people without regard to the consequences. "If I die, I die", she said. For her, life meant living in faith, in trust and in love. She set her intention to act out of her love for people rather than her fear of possible consequences.

While we enjoy celebration with abandonment at Purim, antithetically, this holiday also reminds us that we all face frightening situations in our lives. We experience times that call forth a deeper faith within us than we have previously known. Like Queen Esther, it is a time to go within to receive Divine Guidance and to set our intention to fulfill our destiny, ordering our actions out of love. There remains one more step; coming together with others for mutual spiritual support. We increase the Energy of our intentions through our focused unity. Then all of us are increased in our faith as we see the Divine Will moving amongst us in the answered prayers of our lives. We experience loving and being loved in community. We know more deeply that The One who powers the Universe is also our Intimate Friend.

Just as in Queen Esther's life story, we cannot control what happens around us, but we can take every situation as an opportunity to act from our love rather than our fear and to join with others in spiritual prayer to see our lives transformed. The story of Esther teaches us that control is an illusion – there truly is no such thing as control, even though we all tend to buy into it in some degree. Haman thought he could control the King. The King thought he controlled the kingdom. But, the story is about the choices they made.

While we do not have control in life, we do have choice. Control is the illusion, choice is the reality. When we feel others are controlling us we can ask ourselves, "How am I giving away my empowerment by letting others choose for me?" Sometimes we become convinced by the words of others (usually fear-provoking) and choose without conscious decision weighing of what that person is proposing. However, we do each have choice. Our freedom of choice is what empowers us. Esther weighed her decision, and made a choice of action. She went into the Throne room of King Ahasuerus uninvited, allowing for the freedom of the King to choose how to respond. He could have had her executed; however, he chose to act from his love for her, even offering her half of his kingdom. We do not have control, but we do have choice. This is another powerful Divine Secret that is alluded to in the story of Esther.

Would you like to have this experience of opening to the Divine Secrets in your Life? Do you desire to act from your love rather than your fears? Purim is the season (the early spring) for planting seeds in your life that will grow and bear its fruit.

The story of Purim has its grim sections; however, in the end there is a joyous celebration as the people triumph. It is in this spirit of celebration that Mordecai decrees that this shall be a celebration for all generations. Again, God's name is not evoked here, it is a decree from God, but given from the mouth of Mordecai, the human agent, faithfully carrying out God's ways. We have been "commanded" and feel compelled to celebrate with mirth and merriment to this day. This was a celebration that was held in Israel during Jesus' time as well.

Today, we read the scroll of Esther in the synagogue at sunset. The more creative and interactive the reading is the better. Every time the name of Esther is read everyone claps and cheers, but every time Haman's name is read everyone shouts boos, hisses and scuffles their feet, erasing the name of Haman written in chalk on the soles of their shoes. We spin hand-held noise makers called "graggers" to blot out even the sound of the name of Haman every time it is said in the story, as well. It becomes a cacophony of noise, laughter and the full range of human emotions as we read the twists and turn of events of the story. Spoofs and clever word plays are included in the night's fun, as well as music and dancing. It is traditional to dress up in costumes of the personalities of the story of Esther or as favorite characters from the Bible. The more cleverly devised the costume, the better.

One year when my son was very young he planned his own costume. He said he wanted to go dressed as a car. He described the very powerful kind of car he wanted to go as. When I asked what that had to do with a Biblical character he grinned and answered, "I am going as 'Aaron's rod!'" Purim is a joyous and riotous celebration!

Purim reminds us that the faith in God that our ancestors held turned their "sorrow to joy and their mourning to holiday: that they should make them days of feasting and joy, the sending of choice portions and gifts" (Esther 9:22). This is still true today. This is the truth that Mordecai wanted all of God's people to not only remember, but experience for themselves by celebrating this holiday in merriment.

To fulfill Mordecai's edict, at Purim we send gifts of treats, *mishloah manot*, (literally "send gifts") to one another and to the needy. It is a way of sharing our joy, for joy bubbles from the Fountain of Life within us, but it must be shared with others around us to be fully enjoyed.

Purim reminds us of the power of joy and laughter. When we can laugh at ourselves, we are able to let go of self-promotion and fear driven attachments. Joy enables us to "back up" and look at the bigger picture with renewed perspective. It is in this frame of mind that we emerge from the long winter and move into the joy of renewed life in the spring, ready to leave behind our "bondage" in Egypt with the coming of the next festival in the year, Passover. Each holiday focuses upon the truth of the "now" in our lives, while weaving the energy from the previous months to the energy of the months ahead. Purim is our celebration that awakens us to life, all of life – with joy and merry hearts. It helps us accept all of life, knowing that in the joy of The Holy One is our salvation. For these reasons there are those who say the Messianic Age will begin at Purim season. Some say it will be the time of the Messiah.

Decorations for Purim symbolize some of these themes. Paper cut and other forms of artwork depict scenes of a wolf, (Mordecai), uprooting a bramble bush (Haman) while a bear (Ahasuerus, for Persia is symbolized by a bear) sits beneath the spreading branches of a Hadas (myrtle) tree bearing fragrant flowers (Queen Esther, Hadassah in Hebrew), spreading her influence over all. This is the commentators' picture of the story of Esther in symbols.

Other symbols used at Purim are the fish, for Pisces, the

astrological sign of the Hebrew month of Adar (when Purim occurs) and the ram, the astrological sign of the month of Nissan (when Passover occurs). The ram depicts spring and the slaughter of the innocent, and submission of our own will to the Divine Will as Queen Esther was willing to do.

Of course, there is symbolic food to be eaten at Purim. The most popular food – a must to have at Purim – is the triangular shaped cookie with fruit in the center called *Hamentaschen* (the tri-cornered hat of Haman). These tasty delights by tradition come in a variety of fillings: poppy seed, apricot, prune, and raspberry. In our generation we have added the favorite filling of our times – chocolate!

Try celebrating Purim this year with your family and friends. It is a holiday that children love and our inner child gets to "come out to play". To maintain our ability to play and be child-like (not childish) is also an important part of life. This too, is part of your Hebrew heritage.

How do all the paradoxes teach us about God? Why are there so many twists and turns of truth to this story? The mystical understanding is that paradox leads us to ask questions and our questions bring us into dialogue with The Holy One to learn the *Sod*, "the mystery", of Life. Sod is not "intellectual understanding" for the Sod cannot be taught; only received by Grace. It is an "opening of the understanding". It is the moment of the Divine "A-haaa!" It is when you "know because you know" what God has revealed to you. This is the deeper meaning of Purim. It is the hilarious, the vulgar, the tender, the precious, and the violent all mixed together. God's name is not mentioned, yet God is evident. This is life. This speaks to us that all of life is Divine, the good, the bad and the ugly. It is all life and it is all God, even though there is not an appearance of God on the surface. It teaches us that what appears as hopeless can in a flash become hopeful; that which appears as certain death can, in an instant, can become new life. It teaches us that we cannot manage our lives by the illusion of control, but we can direct our own actions and reactions through choice. We can keep ourselves stable in a changing world by letting go of judgment and clinging to our integrity with courage. In some ways it is the same message that *Hanukkah* speaks to us; that we are in partnership with God (seen or unseen) in that we work like it is all up to us, and we pray like it is all up to God. Then by Grace and action, God moves through us in the world.

What secrets and lessons does Purim bring to you? How do you live life in a society that does not hold your beliefs as sacred, or which even tries to destroy you? What paradoxical twist of events in your life has shown you that God is there guiding and caring for you?

Make plans with your faith community for next Purim. If you have a masquerade party for Purim who would you dress as? Who would you choose as your favorite from Genesis through Revelations? Why? Maybe you would like to have a costume parade (adults and children alike) and let each person tell why they chose their character.

And – don't forget the Hamentaschen!

4
Worship through Blessings, Meditation and Prayer

Worship in the Hebrew Traditions

Blessings, meditation and prayer are forms of worship within Judaism. Study is also another form of worship. *Avodah* is the Hebrew word for "worship." It also means "work." It is the root from which we get the word "servant." How do these ideas come together to teach us what it means to worship God?

In the Hebrew tradition, we worship God when we serve God. We serve God with the words of our mouths, the love and devotion of our hearts, with our minds (learning and discerning spiritual principles) and by our actions (keeping the Sacred Ways). We are guided in our worship by the Shekhinah, the Feminine Presence, and by Ruah HaKodesh, Divine Spirit. We worship The Holy One when we bless, meditate, and pray. We study in order to expand our consciousness and awareness of the Oneness of all life and we express that consciousness through meditation, prayer and blessing.

Our sages tell us that when we pray, bless or meditate we must do so with intentionality, kavvenah, in Hebrew. It is our kavvenah which gives wings to our words in transcendence. Our kavvenah requires the focused attention of our mind, the devotion of our heart, and the actions and words which bring our body into worship.

We often use terms of prayer, blessing and meditation, as if they were interchangeable. However, there is a difference between a blessing, a prayer and a meditation. They are distinctly different modes of worship in the Hebrew traditions. They each serve a different purpose on our lives.

100 **Blessings Every Day**
Jewish Mindful Living

Bless The Holy One of Blessings,
O my Soul, and all that is within me
bless The Source, The Holy Name.

PSALM 103:1

The idea of "making a blessing" in Judaism is our way of constantly centering our consciousness in the Presence of the Holy One in our daily lives. It is the Hebrew way of "mindful living". In fulfillment of this way of living we are told by our sages that we are to make 100 blessings every day. That seems like a lot; however, it is amazing how quickly they add up if we count the blessings we have the opportunity to utter from our first thoughts upon awakening to our last thoughts before drifting off to sleep at night.

Blessing offers us a personal consciousness-raising practice, a spiritual adventure bringing sensitivity and gratitude into the foreground of our lives. While we all have moments when a blessing rises spontaneously to our lips, the path of blessing can become a way of life.

THE PATH OF BLESSING, RABBI MARCIA PRAGER

Blessing becomes a way of life, rather than an involuntary response to life. Blessing brings a potent meaning to the every day occurrences of our lives, making us cognizant of their hidden Divine essence.

When we speak of blessings we use the phrase "make a blessing" rather than "say a blessing." In Judaism a blessing is an action, not a thing. It is an act of evoking divine intervention, setting aside something as sacred or giving praise to God. Therefore, we "make" a blessing.

By stopping for one moment and making a blessing we keep ourselves centered and grounded in what we are doing, while at the same time we are reminded to keep "one foot in Heaven." When we make a blessing we place ourselves fully in the "now" of the moment, while at the same time we expand our awareness to The Infinite. We become deeply aware of the Divine in everything around us, while staying fully present to what we are doing or who we are interacting with. We become more fully aware of "other" as related to us in the Oneness of All Life. By making a blessing we do not seek to remove ourselves from the world but we become witness to God <u>in</u> the world. We become aware of our unity with the Divine in the world. We open ourselves to the flow of God's love in all that is around us, and in every person we meet.

When we utter a blessing, we establish true meeting. True meeting means to fully open your Self to engage with "other."

It means to open your Self fully to experience the whole "other" person, place, thing or experience without distraction, preoccupation or preconceived ideas or assumptions. Martin Buber taught this concept of meeting with full Presence in his book, *I and Thou*. He teaches that God is present in the "in between," that is, in what goes on <u>between</u> you and me that is where God is present. His idea of meeting God within the "other" is expressed as "the Divine meeting the Divine." We have the opportunity to experience God, the intangible, in the tangible world when we open our receptors within to receive from "other." When we do this we are open to the abundant love flowing through Creation from the Source of Life. By pausing long enough to say a blessing, we open ourselves to God and to receive God in "other" in every moment.

The Hebrew word for blessing is *"bracha"* (*"brachot"* in the plural). It is derived from the root *"berech"* which actually means "knee". The word *"barach,"* which means "to kneel," is also from this same root. Kneeling is the appropriate position when approaching The Holy One of Blessing. When we kneel we show the flexibility of our will to The Holy One. By kneeling, we draw down then energy of God's Presence.

There are many blessings that are traditional to make for different reasons throughout our day. These formulated blessings come down to us from the Great Assembly, a group of elders of the faith who were from around 400-300 BCE. While these blessings were handed down to us in Hebrew, they can be said in any language, so that you can use your *kavvenah*, your intentionality, knowing what you are saying. Therefore, I will use mainly English translations for the blessings I will share with you in this section for your daily use. As well, these blessings must be followed by the action which is the object of blessing. You say the blessing over bread, and then you break and eat it. Remember, blessing is an action; by blessing the action of eating we are separating it from an everyday act and making it a holy act.

The men of the Great Assembly also crafted a formulation for the structure for blessings to follow. This formulation is intended to focus your kavvenah and make the blessing powerful. You make the blessing, and then do the action of the blessing.

A blessing always begins:

"Blessed are You, O Holy One our God, Guide of the Cosmos ..."

The next line is almost always included:

Who sanctifies us with your Sacred Ways and instructs us to ..."

In Hebrew transliteration these two lines are:

"Ba-rukh a-tah Yah, El-o-hei-nu, Me-lekh ha-Olam, a-sher kid-sha-nu b'mitz-vo-tav v'tzi-va-nu...."

The blessing ends with the words describing the point of the blessing:

Blessing over the wine:

"... Who creates the fruit of the vine."

"... bo-rei pe-ri ha-ga-fen."

Lighting of Shabbat candles is:

".... to kindle the lights of Shabbat."

"... l'had-lik ner shel Shabbat."

This is an ancient formulation for blessing. Each word carries power and meaning. From the first three words, "Blessed are You" we are put on notice to be conscious of Whom we are addressing. We are talking to the Divine One, Our Creator, the One Who powers the Universe and Beyond, our Intimate Friend and Lover. By focusing on these first three words the one who is making the blessing first focuses upon the power of Whom he or she is calling forth. While this power is "dear friend God" it is also not to be forgotten that we are addressing The One Who has hung the stars in space, who keeps the planets in their orbit, who is beyond all knowing in the farthest reaches of our minds' imaginations, God of the Cosmos. We are then ready to finish our blessing acknowledging the sanctity of the action of the blessing.

Jewish mystics and those using spiritual practices meditate upon these three words, "Blessed are You," to gain a higher consciousness of God. Sometimes their meditation may take hours preceding the pronunciation of the rest of the blessing. Meditations on this blessing formulation itself yield new and beautiful relationships which develop as a result of uttering these words with *kavvenah* (intentionality).

Try to meditate upon each phrase of the Lord's Prayer. After doing so over days, weeks, and years, you will have a new relationship with "Our Father, Who art in Heaven," and you will never again say that prayer in quite the same way as you did before. In your meditation, your prayer will become a blessing to you.

In his book, *God In Search of Man*, Abraham Joshua Heschel, a twentieth-century sage, advises us: "[When we drink a glass of water] we remind ourselves of the eternal mystery of creation, 'Blessed are You ... by whose word all things came into being.' A trivial act and the reference to the supreme miracle. Wishing to eat bread or fruit, to enjoy a pleasant fragrance, or a cup of wine ... on noticing trees when they blossom; on meeting a sage in Torah (Biblical scholar) or in secular learning ... we are taught to invoke His great name and our awareness of Him ... this is one of the goals of Jewish living; to feel the hidden love and wisdom in all things."

The wisdom literature of the oral traditions, the Talmud, advises us: "Whoever enjoys this world's pleasures without reciting a blessing is tantamount to one who steals from God" (Berachot 35a). God gives, and we bless God by giving thanks through the sanctifying act of our blessing.

You may notice that the blessings you see here do not have the word *AMEN* at the end. The reason is that the word AMEN is actually an acronym that is not said by the one saying the blessing, but only by those hearing and enjoining the blessing. The acronym, AMEN, is the first letter of each word in the phrase: *Eil Melech N'eman*, which means, "God is a faithful Sovereign." A-Mein is how it can be transliterated into English letters with the accent on the last syllable. The person saying the blessing never says, "A-mein". The other people present say "A-Mein" as if to say "I second the motion" or "I agree." In so doing it is as if those who say, "A-Mein" have actually said the blessing as well. One person says the blessing and the community says "A-Mein." Everyone is covered.

To further understand the powerful practice of making a blessing we can turn to Maimonides who lived in Egypt from 1135–1204 CE. He was a brilliant and prolific writer, commentator, and codifier of Sacred Text, a physician to the Sultan of Cairo, (at the end of a long day at the palace he gave free medical treatment to the people of his home town of Fostat). He was also the leader of the Jewish Community of Cairo. In his writings Maimonides placed brachot, blessings, into one of three categories:

1. Blessings recited prior to enjoying food, drink, or fragrances – anything that is experienced by one of the five senses of the body.

2. Blessings recited prior to the performance of a mitzvah (loving deed of kindness) or the Sacred Ways.
3. Blessings recited in praise, gratitude, or petition of God.

BERACHOT 1:4

The first category of blessings elevates the experiences of enjoying our five senses. In fact, a great many of our blessings involve food and the sense of taste:

Taste

We say a blessing before we eat or drink anything. God provides food to all creation and when we acknowledge this provision we receive it as a gift. Food taken without making a blessing is as if it had been taken without the owner's permission.

When we make a blessing before eating, we are not making the food fit for consumption, or even acceptable or holy, but, we are blessing the act of eating. The table becomes our altar and the food becomes the sacrifice in order that we may live. Consuming food provides energy to use in our bodies for energy to perform sacred acts in our life. We are blessing the act of eating, and acknowledging The Holy One who provides this sacrifice for our life.

Before we eat we make the blessing called *HaMotzi*, "The Bringing Forth." In English it says: "Blessed are You, O Holy One our God, Guide of the Cosmos, Who brings forth bread from the earth."

This simple blessing reminds us of the partnership we share with The Holy One, by Whose power the grain exists and grows. Our part of the partnership is to make bread to feed the hungry.

We are in partnership with The Holy One to sustain life. The wheat represents human life, but the bread we make with the wheat represents community. God gives us human life, but we are the ones who make community. This is the hidden wisdom and love within the blessing.

There are specific blessings for the different types and categories of food which we eat. The question of which blessing to use can become complicated and distracting to the meaning of making the blessings. However, if we are having bread at the meal, then we only make the blessing over the bread, HaMotzi; for bread is considered to be the most humble of all foods. It is the most humble because regardless of how poor a family is they should at least have flour and water from which to make bread. Therefore, since it is the most humble it is elevated as the highest of all foods. All foods come beneath bread. If you make a blessing over the bread all the other food on the table is covered under this blessing. So you hold up the bread, make the blessing, break off a portion, dip it in salt (salt represents the "permanence" of the Covenant you make with God, thus it was used on the sacrifices in the Temple), and then you feed that bite to the person next to you, give to yourself and hand portions of the bread to those at the table with you.

Once you have experienced this tradition, I invite you to explore the depths of the words Jesus speaks to you according to John 6:48, "I am the Bread of Life." Look up "bread" in your concordance and read all the passages having to do with bread. What is the deeper meaning that these passages now hold for you in the light of your experience? Remember, through the doing comes the understanding.

After the meal there are more blessings that are said according to the Sacred Ways given to us in Deuteronomy:

When you have eaten and are satisfied then you shall bless
the Holy One, Source of All, for the good land which God has
given you.

DEUT. 8:10

When we sit down at the table and we are very hungry it is easy
to remember to say, "Thank you God for the food before us!"
However, after we have eaten and are satisfied it is easy to forget
to thank The One Who has furnished this nourishment. We tend
to finish our meals and then dash off to the next activity at hand.
However, Deuteronomy 8 reminds us of the spiritual principle
that God is our ultimate Source of the Divine Plenty that flows to
all areas of our lives. We remember that it is The Holy One Who
provides food for us and for all creation. When we remember
to thank God in such a basic life function as eating, then we are
more likely to remember to thank God as our Source for the more
complex areas of our lives, such as our livelihood and the ability
to gain wealth justly and without causing scarcity in the world.
The opportunity and ability to increase our wealth of household is
according to the covenant made between our ancestors and God.
Gaining wealth is not in order to be sure we have enough, for
having enough is a matter of trust in God, the Source of Life. Nor
is the gain of wealth in order to hoard wealth out of a fear of lack.
Wealth gives us the increased ability to bless all who are around us
with the Divine Plenty of God. Abraham trusted God with his life
and amassed great wealth. Many people joined him as part of his
household, believing in his God, and following him wherever he
went. This is the blessing of creating community and the prosperity
of community from wheat, life, the gift of God. Remembering to
make a blessing after we have eaten and are satisfied teaches us to
remember that God is the continuing Source of All.

Our ancestors trusted God in both the desolate conditions of the Sinai wilderness, and in the great wealth of King Solomon to provide the Divine Plenty that sustains life, and blesses life with abundance. As we awaken to this spiritual principle in our consciousness, we are reminded from Whom all blessings flow as they manifest in our lives, year after year. When we eat and we remember to say a blessing **after** we are satisfied, we are also reminded to thank God when we have much wealth and are well satisfied in all of the other areas of abundance in our life.

Other blessings for our sense of taste:

Before drinking wine or the "fruit of the vine":
"Blessed are You, O Holy One our God, Guide of the Cosmos for creating the fruit of the vine."

Before eating tree-grown fruit:
"Blessed are You, ... Who creates the fruit of the tree."

Before eating produce that grew directly from the earth:
"Blessed are You...... Who creates the fruit of the ground."

Before eating or drinking other foods:
"Blessed are You...... through Whose word everything came to be."

Smell

When we smell fragrances we make a blessing: perfume or fragrant spices, shrubs or trees, or their flowers, herbs, grasses, fragrant edible fruits (such as a lemon) and nuts, and when we light incense. Have you ever walked into a store and smelled the fragrance of candles or potpourri? That is an opportunity to make a blessing.

Upon kindling incense for sacred purposes:
    "Blessed are You, O Holy One our God, Guide of the Cosmos, Who sanctifies us by Your Sacred Ways and instructs us to kindle the sweet smelling savor."

Upon smelling various spices or fragrances:
    "Blessed are You, O Holy One our God, Guide of the Cosmos, Who creates all manner of spices (perfumes)."

Upon smelling shrubs and trees or their flowers (your Christmas tree):
    "Blessed are You,...Who creates fragrant trees."

Upon smelling fragrant herbs, grasses or flowers (a bouquet):
    "Blessed are You..... Who creates fragrant herbage."
    Have you ever smelled apples in the fall?

Upon smelling fragrant edible fruit or nuts
    "Blessed are You.... Who places a good aroma into fruits."

Sight

We are given blessings to make upon seeing natural phenomenon or a frightening sight. By making a blessing, we are drawn into the miracle of nature, the rainbow set in the sky, the rain falling on thirsty ground, the silent purity of snow. We are also given courage when we make a blessing when we see a fearsome event such as a flood, a tsunami engulfing everything and everyone, or lightening splitting the dark sky at night. These blessings include us in Creation and bond us to the Creator.

Upon seeing lightening, experiencing an earthquake, seeing a comet, exceptionally lofty mountains, exceptionally large rivers, great deserts, or a sunrise:

"Blessed are You, O Holy One our God, Guide of the Cosmos, Maker of Creation."

Upon seeing a rainbow in the sky:

"Blessed are You, ...Who remembers the Covenant, and keeps Your Promise.
Have you ever seen a really good-looking guy, or a beautiful woman? Make it a sacred occasion by acknowledging beauty and saying a blessing.

Upon seeing exceptionally beautiful people, trees, or fields:

"Blessed are You.....Who has such in Your Universe."
When you see something which is strange or out of the ordinary find the Divine hidden within it by saying this blessing.

Upon seeing exceptionally strange-looking people or animals:

"Blessed are You...... Who makes creatures different."

Upon seeing an outstanding Biblical scholar (or Holy person):

"Blessed are You.....Who has given of Your knowledge to those who are in awe of You."

Upon seeing an outstanding secular scholar (or very intelligent person):

"Blessed are You..... Who has given of your knowledge to human beings."

These last two blessings serve to remind us that God is the source of all knowledge and wisdom and to avoid elevating a person for what we admire in them as if it is separate from the Divine. Each of us has Infinite Value in the fact of our Being, rather than in what we do or produce. This is an important theme throughout Judaism. We are all a spark of the Divine. Our actions open our consciousness to the Divine, but our value is intrinsic to our existence. Therefore, we bless that which we see in each other as Divine, ever directing our eyes to God Who emanates us.

Sound

Sound creates vibrations, which we not only hear, but feel in the core of our being. It reverberates within us, setting a pattern in our own vibrations and moving us to various emotions and thoughts. Sounds include the awe of thunder rumbling and bouncing off the mountains and down the valley, or it can be the sound of good news, or bad news. Think of a time you heard some exceptionally exciting news in your family. How did you feel? Think of some really bad news you have heard. How did you feel at that moment? Making a blessing at that moment can bring your feelings back into balance and elevate your Spirit. It helps you find the hidden Divine in the moment.

Upon hearing thunder, an earthquake, rushing waters, an avalanche:
　　"Blessed are You, O Holy One our God, Guide of the Cosmos, Whose strength and might fill the world."

Upon hearing good news:
　　"Blessed are You...... Who is good and does good."

Upon hearing bad news:
　　"Blessed are You.....Who is the Power of Truth."

Your acknowledgement of God's Presence through your blessing at a difficult time is comfort to your Soul, gives peace to your mind, and imparts courage to your heart. Your actions are ordered from a state of balance.

Touch

The blessing that the sense of touch gives us is through the nerve endings in our skin. We touch and feel "other", whether it is a person, creature or thing. Without touch, our scientists tell us, our young do not thrive. The bereaved know only too well the power of touch as they long for their loved one's arms to enfold them once again. This gift of touch is covered quite symbolically in the blessing of putting on a garment, for our body is considered the "garment of the Soul." It is through this garment of the body that all touch, the oneness through contact, comes to our Soul. This blessing reminds us Who has made and given us touch, and clothed our Soul with the garment of our body.

When putting on a garment:
   "Blessed are You, O Holy One, our God, Guide of the Cosmos, Who clothes the naked."

Maimonides' second category of blessings is those we make before doing a mitzvah (loving deed of kindness), one of the Sacred Ways. Remember, blessings are a way of setting our intention. When we awaken our sages tell us to let our first thought be the Shema: "Hear O Israel, The Infinite is our God, The Infinite is Oneness itself." In this way we remind ourselves as we leave our dream state and enter back into the consciousness of this world that we are not separate, but that we are all one and one with The Divine. We are then able to set our intentions for the day to bring this unity to all that we do. The Shema is also the last words we utter before going to sleep at night to comfort our Soul in the unity of The Oneness.

Upon getting up in the morning the first thing we do is to wash our hands in a ritual manner, and make a blessing. This sets apart the act of washing our hands as a sacred act. It is reminiscent of the washing of the hands of the Priests at the laver in the Temple before they made offerings to God. As your day begins you will be offering your service to God in what you do and say. As you let the water run over your hands lift up your hands in holy service through the following blessing:

"Blessed are you, O Holy One, our God, Guide of the Cosmos, Who sanctifies us by Your Sacred Ways and instructs us to lift up our hands in Holy Service to You."

This blessing does not say in Hebrew "...Who instructs us to wash our hands," but says, "Who instructs us to **lift up** our hands (in Holy Service)." Each morning we bless the **act** of serving God throughout the day. We set an intention that the work of our hands should be of the highest "lifted up" order.

We also make this blessing, and then wash our hands before each meal as well, setting our intention to eat (the sacrifice from the altar of our table) in order to have the energy to live and do the Sacred Ways. We do this with celebration and rejoicing in the goodness of the bounty.

This blessing can be used whenever you wash your hands. In the medical world it can be an especially meaningful blessing when you are washing your hands between ministering to patients or scrubbing for surgery. How would you feel as a patient if you knew your surgeon made this blessing with kavvenah, to lift up her or his hands, before going in to operate on you? How meaningful this blessing is for the midwife or obstetrician as he or she washes in preparation of bringing a new life into this world. How much more so then should these first hands to touch this new little Soul's body be lifted up in blessing!

We make a blessing whenever we prepare to do a mitzvah (Sacred Way) such as: lighting the candles to mark the beginning of Shabbat or any Holy Day or Festival, when we go into the Mikveh (for sacred immersion), when we blow the Shofar (Ram's Horn), eat the symbolic foods at the Passover Seder, put a mezuzah on our doorway, put on a Tallit (prayer shawl), read the Torah, or begin a study session of Torah, to name only a few times.

Using the ancient formulation, try to make a blessing when you prepare to study or read your Bible. Notice the blessings that are traditionally said when you prepare to do the Sacred Ways and rituals of your Christian denomination. At the beginning of your Sabbath make a blessing and light a candle to mark the beginning of your Sacred Day with God.

Maimonides' third category of blessings is blessings we make when we are praising, glorifying or petitioning God. One of my favorite blessings falls into this category. It is called the *Shehechiyanu*.

The She-hech-i-ya-nu is a blessing we make every time we do something for the first time, or for the first time that season, such as when we taste a food for the first time during its season. We make this blessing over the first strawberry we eat in strawberry season or our first bite of watermelon in the summer. We make a Shehechiyanu when we light the candles on the first night of holidays such as Passover or Chanukah. Even when we put on a new skirt or coat or article of clothing that is new we say this blessing! It reminds us of the miracle of life and the constant renewing of our lives. This is the Shehechiyanu in English:

> "Blessed are You, O Holy One, our God, Guide of the Cosmos, Who has given us life, Who enables us to fulfill our lives, and Who has brought us to this happy day."

In this blessing, we are not only thanking God for the event, but we are actually acknowledging that our life has a plan and a purpose and that God is enabling us to fulfill that sacred destiny. This blessing is not only a thank you to God, but it is a comfort to the person who makes it. Try saying this blessing the next time you do something for the first time in its season, or the first time in your life.

Even from ancient times there have been blessings for having consciousness, being made in the Divine image, having the gift of freedom of choice, and in thanksgiving for God setting the angels over us to guard and protect us on our journey. During your life, whenever you become newly aware of something or gain a new level of consciousness, make a blessing. When you are making a life decision or choice, make a blessing over it. When you feel you want to become more aware of the angels that are around you (even when you are unaware of them or do not feel they are there), make a blessing over God's gift of their presence. You may find you become powerfully aware of their company.

Some of the most powerful blessings we utter are the blessings we say with love for other people. We bless our children and one another after we light the candles on Shabbat. We bless each other during the day when we meet and when we part with the blessing: "Shalom Aleichem" to which we reply "Aleichem Shalom." "Peace (wholeness) be upon you." – "And upon you may there be Peace (wholeness)." When said and received with kavvenah (intentionality) we are reminded of the Divine within each other and our connection within The Divine.

There is a blessing for literally every daily human activity. This is our way of remaining fully present in this world, and fully conscious of The Divine Presence in us, around us, and through us. When we live the Path of Blessing we see the Divine One everywhere. It is a way of "lifting the veil" of physicality to find God hidden within it. This inheritance from your Hebrew roots gives you a rich background of blessing and compels you to continue on the Blessing Path.

There is a blessing that is one of the most powerful experiences of evoking God's blessing upon us. In Numbers 6: 22 – 26, God tells Moses to have Aaron the High Priest and his descendants after him to evoke the blessing of God upon the people with the words of the Birkat Cohanim, the Priestly Blessing. It is this ancient blessing that I make for you this day that you may be among the blessed of The Holy One of Israel:

יברכך יהוה וישמרך:

יאר יהוה פניו אליך ויחנך:

ישא יהוה פניו אליך וישם לך שלום.

Y-va-re-che-cha Yah, v'ish-ma-re-cha.

Y'air Yah p'nav e-lei-cha v'i-hu-ne-cha.

Y'sa Yah p'nav e-lei-cha, v'ya-seim l'cha sha-lom.

May The Holy One bless you and keep you.

May the countenance of The Holy One shine upon you and be gracious unto you.

May you be lifted up into the Presence of the Holy One and be given the most precious of all gifts, the gift of Shalom, the gift of Peace.

There are many more blessings. They have been formulated and collected for thousands of years by our people. They are part of your heritage. You can say a blessing at any of the occasions listed above or at other times that the Holy Spirit moves you within to say a blessing – even a hundred blessings a day!

Meditation
Transcendent Consciousness

"And Isaac went out into the field to meditate at evening time..."

GEN. 14:63

As this verse indicates, our ancestors made it a practice to meditate through the millennia. The book of Psalms is filled with passages that speak of the practice of meditation. The psalms themselves are a type of meditation and are usually about meditating on God's word or the precepts that Torah presents. The word *selah* is a little word placed at the end of many of the Psalms (see Ps. 24). It indicates that the very nature of the psalm is meditative. "Selah" means, "Pause and think upon these things." It calls the reader to come to silence, to an interlude, to allow the meaning of the words to open their secrets of illumination. This is meditation. Selah means to move the mind and consciousness to the empty space of silence in which there is infinite possibility.

There are many stories in the Bible that do not literally say that a person is meditating, however, it is evident from the action in the story that they are in a special place of consciousness; an altered state of consciousness beyond the awareness of waking life. Often a vision is the experience of meditation.

It was during a higher state of consciousness that Abraham met with the unseen God with the inaudible Voice, Who instructed him to "... go to a land which I will show you ..." (Genesis 12:1). Later, when Abraham was in dialogue with God about his lack of an heir, he was told, "Look now toward heaven, and count the stars, if you are able to number them... So shall your seed (descendants) be." This call came to Abraham at a time in his elder years when he had no children at all. It was only in the context of meditation that Abraham could receive this promise.

Abraham passed his spiritual and mystical practices such as meditation on to the next generation of Covenant makers, the fulfillment of God's promise, his son, Isaac.

In the quotation from Gen. 14 which appears at the beginning of this section on meditation, Isaac was meditating in a field when he "lifted his eyes" and saw camels coming which were carrying his future wife, Rebecca and her entourage. This phrase "lifted his eyes" has two meanings. In the plain meaning he lifted his eyes from his meditation and saw the caravan approaching. But why, then doesn't the text read "he opened his eyes" or "he looked and saw her coming"? The answer lies in the hidden meaning; the mystical meaning buried in the use of the words "lifted his eyes". Isaac was in meditation and saw the vision of her coming in his meditation. His spiritual eyes saw her as he was guided in a visual meditation to see his coming bride – even seeing her Soul. He then physically opened his eyes and saw her caravan.

The special love story between Isaac and Rebecca continues. When Rebecca (*Rivka*, in Hebrew) saw Isaac, "she alighted from her camel." However, the Hebrew word translated as "alighted," is *tipol*, which literally means "she fell" from her camel. The mystical play on words is that she too "lifted her eyes" and saw his "beauty" his bright aura or beautification in his meditative state.

When she saw his beauty of Spirit she was smitten, or "fell" in love. She inquired of Eleazar, Abraham's servant who was guiding their caravan, as to who this man meditating in the field was, and found out that this was his master's son, the man whom she will marry. She covered herself with her veil. This is a play on the mystical "sight" each of them has already had of the other. The spiritual work of the meditation having been done within both of them, the action of the story moves quickly forward and in one quick sentence she is taken to Sara's (his mother's) tent. This indicates that Rebecca is now the matriarch of the Tribe. Isaac loves Rebecca. She is destined to become the Mother of the next generation of Covenant makers. The action on this physical plane quickly follows the vision of the meditation.

There are other times when the sacred text merely hints that the person in the story is in a powerful meditative vision state. Whenever the text says: "I dreamed a dream" we can be suspicious that this "dream" was a special vision in some type of meditation or altered consciousness. It was Joseph, the favored son of Jacob, who had meditative sleep states and received visions during his meditation. One such "dream" was his celestial vision of stars, representing his brothers, and the sun and moon, representing his mother and father, Jacob and Rachel. Because of his gift and the personal nature of the dream he could interpret its meaning. This was a spiritual gift he had from childhood, which was essential to his story and destiny. He understood the symbols used in the dream as they were symbols coming from within his own Soul working with his mind. He honed this gift and the understanding of how to interpret dreams. As you become more accustomed to working with the symbols of your meditations and dreams you will understand their meaning in your life. Joseph did this often throughout his lifetime. He was even able to do this for others as he did with the Pharaoh and his dream about the seven cows by the river, (Genesis 41). These dreams were in the symbolic language of the Pharaoh's higher consciousness. Joseph had the gift and practice of transcending to that higher consciousness, even for others.

King David wrote many meditations and put them to music. Some of these meditations are found in the Book of Psalms that we use today. They are another mode of meditation. Certainly the prophets, Isaiah, Ezekiel, Jeremiah and others were accustomed to meditating and receiving their visions and words of prophecy while in an altered state of consciousness.

Do you suppose Jonah was literally swallowed by a great fish, or was this special fish, "appointed by God to swallow up (consume) Jonah" a vessel of his meditation? The seemingly innocuous information that is provided in the text, "appointed by God" is a transcendent tip-off to the mystics of future generations that Jonah was on a meditative journey. There may well have been a storm, but he was also going through the emotional storm of his Soul as he ran away from God's call. According to the story, he went down to the bilges of the ship and lay down. This is an odd place to lie down to take a nap. The bilges are at the bottom of the ship. They are generally a dark, cold, wet, dank and smelly place. This is the belly of the ship; a place of solitude, for no one would be there. This "belly of the ship" and the "belly of the Great Fish" can be understood as vessels of the meditation. Within the three days and nights in the belly of the great fish, or three-part meditation, Jonah experienced a vision/meditation that led him to sweet surrender to his mission, his Sacred Pathway. At God's word the "Great Fish" projects Jonah back to "dry land" or consciousness in this dimension.

God's word came to Jonah a second time, (another

meditation), instructing him once again to go to Nineveh. Jonah went to Ninevah – which was a three-day journey. There are no coincidences in these sacred stories. Three was the number of days that Jonah spent in the first meditation on the darkness, death and solitude that result when we turn away from God and our Soul's life mission. Now Jonah experienced <u>three</u> days of traveling, moving forward to fulfill his Sacred Journey. Three is considered the number of perfection in the spiritual practices. Three is considered a perfect number because it is the only number that has a beginning, middle, and an end: one – two – three. Meditation "takes us" somewhere on our spiritual journey. It takes us toward the perfection (fulfillment being considered "perfection" regardless of flawlessness) of our destiny. In an altered consciousness, in quietness of mind we are able to hear the inaudible Voice. We are able to follow the spiritual symbolism as it applies to our "waking" life for guidance in our physical world life. Just as our ancestor, Jonah, we expand our understanding through the practice of expanding our consciousness in meditation.

In the sacred Christian texts, specifically in Matthew and Luke, there are several instances when a key person in Jesus' life had a visitation from an angel or an archangel, just as did Abraham, their ancestor. As we discussed in the section on angels, Abraham was visited by the angels of God on several occasions. In the story opening the first chapter of the Gospel of Matthew, Joseph, who was to be father to Jesus, was considering what he would do about Mary, his fiancée, who was found to be pregnant before the final covenant of their marriage. He was "thinking this over" when an angel of The Holy One came to him "in a dream" and brought him the message that he (Joseph) was not to be afraid to take Mary as his wife. Joseph most likely experienced the angel visitation in the altered consciousness of meditation. Later he is visited by an angel with the message to take the child out of the country and go to Egypt because of the danger from the political ruler Herod. Again, an angel lets him know when it is safe to return. Surely, this man Joseph was a man accustomed to meditation of a high level.

Mary, the mother of Jesus had a visitation from the Archangel GabriEl, messenger of The Holy One, as well. Surely this faithful woman was accustomed to meditation. That seems evident when the angel appeared to her with the message of her bearing a very special child in the opening chapter of the Gospel of Luke. The book of Luke also tells us of other family members, devoted people such as Zachariah, husband of Elizabeth, who had spiritual visions and angel visitation through his spiritual practices.

Mary went on holiday to spend some time with Zachariah and Elizabeth, relatives of hers. Zachariah and Elizabeth were of the priestly line of Aaron; they were *Cohanim*. As devout servants of the God of Israel, they were both acquainted with prayer, blessing and meditation. It was Zachariah's turn to serve as a Priest of the Temple. He entered the Temple to light the incense (meditation tool) before The Holy One. Everyone outside was praying. This was a powerful time of meditation, and Zachariah did enter the "Temple" of the Higher Dimensions of his meditation. He received a visitation from the Archangel GabriEl telling him of a son to be born to his wife, Elizabeth, (in answer to their prayers for a child). The angel instructed him to name his son John (in English). Zachariah was there in the Holy Place of meditation a long time. He was a man accustomed to sustaining this level of Divine Presence as he heard and accepted the special role of father to this new prophet in Israel.

Later, when Mary visited Elizabeth, she spoke prophecy as she heard Mary's voice in salutation. Elizabeth and Zachariah, Joseph and Mary, accepted their missions as seen in their visions and meditations. According to Christian sacred story this is the family of spiritual practitioners and meditators who raised Jesus, cared for him and nurtured him in the Sacred Ways.

The stories of the life of the Rabbi from Nazareth reveals that he was also given to meditation, prayer and the path of blessing as a way of life. Throughout his ministry, Jesus practiced *hitbodedut*, which is the Hebrew word for "separating oneself for meditation and prayer." He learned at the knee of meditating parents, his mother and father, for they were powerfully imbued and guided by meditation in their stories.

Meditation is a spiritual practice that varies slightly from one spiritual pathway to another. However, one of the main threads of continuity across the traditions is that meditation relaxes the body, calms the emotions and quiets the mind. In the mystical traditions, it is a way of lifting the veils of consciousness to allow you to experience differing and ascending dimensions or realms. While these "higher realms" and the beings of those realms are integrated into this dimension and present in our everyday lives, we are not always aware of them.

The usefulness of meditation is to move within your Self to go beyond your Self. Focusing on your breath is a way of quieting and transcending. It is as if you follow the Source of your breath to places beyond this world.

Meditation is also done in preparation for powerful prayer. When you become heightened in awareness of the imminent Presence of The Divine your prayer dialogue becomes the dynamic exchange of thought beyond your thoughts and wisdom beyond your wisdom. In this quieted state of meditation you can hear the Still Small inaudible Voice that guides you and teaches you the "*Sod*," the secret that you seek.

In the deep state of meditation you visit "*HaMakom*," "The

Place." HaMakom is the Hebrew name we use for God when we are in "The Place" that is "No Place." When you meditate your body does not leave the room; however, "you" are not there. Where are you? You are in HaMakom. It is the meditator's sweet and intimate name for God. It is here you know The Holy One Who is beyond all knowing. This is "the secret hiding place of the Most High God." It is the "cleft of the rock." It is where you find God, and in so doing find your own Soul's home.

As you return from the consciousness of HaMakom, to this physical world of action, you bring the light (enlightenment) you received there within you. You are not always intellectually aware of new knowledge; but within your consciousness is a shift that will surface in the days and events to come. Some things will just "come" to you. Your mind will bring up things that you didn't even know were stored there. They are in the mind of your Soul with the "mind of God." Other times you may remember key things or feelings from the heightened state of consciousness. It is good to write anything you remember in your journal, for like a dream, it can fade in your memory quickly. Whatever you may or may not remember, there will be a deep sense of peace, centeredness and calm. Many people use meditation daily simply to gain this balance of calm in their lives.

While meditating, you may have other-worldly experiences; see or speak with an angelic being or see colors in vividness beyond normal sight. You may even smell fragrances, not with your physical nose, but from your "Soul's sense of smell." For instance, you may smell gardenias and yet know there are no gardenias in the room. Gardenias may not even be in bloom. Yet, you can unmistakingly smell gardenias. There is always meaning in these experiences. They are an invitation to seek God's council through the experience and its meaning for your life.

Through the many ways and reasons to meditate, you learn to shift your consciousness and activate your spiritual receptors. The more you practice meditation the longer you are able to sustain that consciousness for worship purposes.

It is a traditional practice to learn to meditate with a trusted Guide, to help you explore and understand the symbols and experiences of your journey from within yourself. If you are the meditator, then the symbols of your meditation are locked within you. The trusted Guide will help you call forth the understanding of the meditation from within your Self. The trusted Guide will also teach you how to leave "marks on your trail" of meditation to move easily and smoothly back to physical world consciousness. It is like leaving a breadcrumb trail of markers to follow on your way back. You can ask Ruach HaKodesh, the Holy Spirit to be your Guide in all truth on your meditations. Jesus has been a trusted Guide to thousands of Souls. However, it is also very helpful to have a spiritually mature person in the flesh to speak with, who understands the sacred nature of the Soul contract of walking with another on their spiritual journey. If there is no mature and trusted spiritual mentor in your life you can ask God to send that person into your life who has a Soul contract to help you. You may then feel that you want to read a particular book, go to a class or attend services at a particular place and there you may find your spiritual companion. Other times a Guardian Angel may enter your prayer life in human or angelic form.

Some people like to hold or use an object that carries a particular energy to help them focus. This may be an object sacred to you. Some people use a ritual object such as a rosary, a prayer cloth, a prayer shawl, a crystal or prayer beads. Repeating a memorized prayer over and over is a way of moving into meditation. When you are really getting bored with the recitation is when you are getting somewhere; for that is when your mind chatter is quieted and you are open to receiving. Receive what, you might ask. That is what you will find out in your meditation! No two journeys are ever alike.

Throughout the ages humanity of all cultures has moved into meditation through various ways. Certainly meditation has been and continues to be practiced among our ancestors and the spiritual seekers of the Hebrew traditions today.

What are some of the methods of meditation that are used? Below is a listing of many ways that meditation is entered into during the past 4000 years in your Hebrew heritage.

Meditations Pathways

Visual meditation – A *shiviti* (a work of art or drawing that includes the four letter name of God, Yud, Hey, Vav, Hey), is a common object for visual meditation. The idea of meditating on the name of God comes from Psalm 16:8, "I have set The Holy One before me always." The first word of this verse in Hebrew is "shiviti" which means, "I have set." The tetragrammaton, the four-letter name for God used in the Hebrew is a powerful name of God. The letters are the *Yod, Hey, Vav Hey*. These letters are written in many styles, often with other inspirational scripture around them. Sometimes the letters of God's power name are written as white flames on black for a visual meditation. In the visual meditation you gaze into the visual piece rather than simply looking at it. The visual piece becomes a doorway for the mind, a portal to the Higher Dimensions for your consciousness to enter.

The tallit, prayer shawl, has fringes on each corner. The Hebrew word which is translated fringe is tzitzit from the root that means "to gaze." It is easy to understand that the fringes of a tallit are also an aid to visual or gazing meditation, since they would be worn every day and easily in sight.

Another visual meditation is gazing into the flame of a candle. The menorah in the Temple was a gazing object. Its flames, branches, and flowering knobs represented the Tree of Life, and the Sephirot or ten attributes of God flowing into all of existence. By the time you realize you are not looking at anything, but seeing visions with your "third eye" (Soul vision) you are already coming back to physical plane consciousness. Using a menorah for meditation is powerful as it is beautiful. The multitude of dancing flames is always a joyous path of Divine Light unto the Soul.

Auditory – An auditory meditation uses sound to move the consciousness. The sound could be your voice repeating a phrase (usually in Hebrew) over and over (like a mantra). The sound has transcendent vibrations for the Soul to become attuned to and to follow.

The sound of the shofar is called the "wakeup call to the Soul," for it sets up a vibration calling your consciousness of this world to a higher plane in sacred time and sacred space. Sacred time and space are the time and space which are not geographical or chronological as are the time and space of the physical world.

Some meditations repeat different permutations of the letters of some of God's names or the names of angels evoked in a specific order. This is not angel worship, but is a call to the hosts of Heaven to witness before God, the Father. Again, reciting scriptures such as the Psalms is a form of audio meditation, for the vibrations of the words carry you into transcendence. This is actually the power of reciting liturgy such as the "Our Father" prayer or the "Hail Mary" prayer for transcendence prior to prayer in the Christian church.

Singing is also a form of meditation. Especially meditative are the *niggunim* (*niggun*, singular) or wordless songs repeated over and over. The tune "takes you somewhere." The church is especially attuned to using hymns of praise to move worshippers into the Holy Place. This is an audio meditation. The mind is quieted in peace and tranquility, the emotions are smoothed and heightened and the Soul soars through song.

Walking – There are several ways to experience a walking meditation. Sometimes you simply walk in a quiet beautiful place – and walk and walk. You will notice your consciousness shifts. Your thoughts become expansive. You begin to feel a oneness with the nature around you. Mother earth seems to sing within you in one accord to the glory of your Maker. Another practice is to recite psalms or scripture as you walk, picking up the rhythm of the psalm's words. As you begin walking in that rhythm, your body becomes involved in the meditation, picking up the vibrations of the rhythms of the words and your mind shifts to a new awakening. Try this when you are simply walking in your everyday life – from the parking lot to the store or work, down the hall at your work place or in the shopping mall.

Walking in rhythm to recited psalms can also be led by a spiritual leader of a group who is reciting psalms to a particular rhythm or melody. The students or those following the meditation may form a line or group around the leader. This is done at particular occasions of Holy Days by the Yeshivot (religious school) students in Jerusalem on their way to the Kotel (Western wall of Temple Mount) for prayer. This type of walking meditation is not to be done to gain attention, but by way of invitation to join the meditation. *Kavvenah*, intentionality, must be maintained by the members of the group.

Guided – Most meditation is free of form and simply goes

where Spirit takes you. However, a guided meditation leads you on a type of journey that is intentionally pre-set. A spiritual leader speaks words that you listen to as you enter meditation which guide you into a story or journey. You follow the "visual" story unfolding with the leader's words, allowing your meditative journey to show you the answers to questions the leader asks. Each meditator in the group will have a unique experience, even though they are each following the leader's words. Remember, the answers as they appear in your meditation are symbolic of something in your life. For example, the leader may say, "You are approaching a door. (pause) How does the door appear to you? (pause) As you open the door you recognize the figure on the other side who is waiting for you. Who is it? (pause) That person begins to speak to you. What does that person say to you?" (Pause), etc. As you allow the meditation to unfold you answer the questions within your Self. After returning to the presence of the room at the end of the guided meditation it is good to write down anything you remember. You may not remember specifically anything, but you may remember a feeling. Write what you feel. Like dreams, the impressions of the meditation may fade or dissipate with time. You can call upon your inner guidance to help you remember what you need to know. The Holy Spirit is especially good at this, for that is one of its jobs as Jesus tells his disciples in John 14:26, "And He will cause you to recall everything I have told you."

Although many people may go on a guided meditation together, no two people will experience the same journey, although some events of the journey may be shared. I have led guided meditations when it has occurred that two people on different sides of the room smelled oranges in the meditation when there were no oranges in the room. One had experienced smelling fragrances in meditation before and the other had not.

The previous experience of the one meditator served to confirm the validity of the event for the one experiencing it for the first time. She was able to discuss it and know that she had opened to a new spiritual phenomenon of meditation that was unusual, but safe and normal. She had experienced the "higher nose" and needn't doubt her experience further. The meaning of the experience was personal and individual to each of them.

Guided meditations can be a wonderful way to become more experienced in meditative journeying. You can be part of a group sharing your experiences afterward as a group or one on one. The enjoyment and value of group and shared journeying is that each person's journey will be unique, yet as a group they are also complimentary to a common theme that emerges through the sharing of the details of each journey. When each person shares the details of their journey, the group gains a larger and clearer picture of the meaning of the meditation for the group as a whole. This is especially true for groups who meditate together regularly. This is also true for husbands and wives or partners who meditate together. It is up to the individual to use discretion as to how much of their meditation to share, according to their own inner guidance and their own comfort level with sharing this intimate experience.

Guided meditations can also be done by way of a CD or tape. My CD entitled *Walking with Your Angels* has four guided meditations which are intended to help you learn how to interact with the ministering spirits which work with you to the Glory of God. The CD method can be used individually or by a group. It is not recommended to listen to meditation CDs when driving your car. You need to be fully present to the physical world while driving!

Another unique experience of the guided meditation is that you may find that you do not always follow the script or story of

233

the leader. Your meditative journey may lead you elsewhere. The more adept you become at meditative journeying the more this may happen, for you transcend and may not need or be aware of the human voice in the physical world. Your Soul will still take you according to your highest intention set.

If you find you are uncomfortable with someone who is leading a group, either go on your own meditation journey or leave the room, removing yourself from the presence of the disharmony. It is always good to ask God why you were uncomfortable and to use the message for your higher good and spiritual development.

Guided meditation can be fun. It is also very useful and brings healing for your life. My guess is that the men and women following Jesus had more than one group meditation session which helped them connect with him, especially after he was gone. They were certainly doing so at the Pentecost experience!

Silence or breathing – Entering meditation by focusing upon your breath or upon silence can move you quickly through the veils of consciousness. Many people use breath-work for a healing state as well. This is another way to use the four-letter power name of God.

The power name of God; Yod, Hey, Vav, Hey, is said to be unspeakable or ineffable. This is not because it has been forgotten as many suppose. It is because this name of God is **breathed**, not vocalized. The Yod, Hey is the breath as it is drawn in. The Vav, Hey is the breath released. This is the first and the last acts a human being makes on this earth. A baby draws in the breath – Yod, Hey – before it does anything else. A person breathes out the last breaths as the Soul transcends the body, leaving behind the earthly life and human form. This is the Vav, Hey. From birth to death life is a series of breaths, Yod, Hey, – Vav, Hey, God's power name. This is life. When we focus on that breath for meditation, we enter God's name, we enter the life-force of God! Is it any wonder that it is so powerful for transcendence and healing in our lives? Each moment that we breathe we utter the power name of God. Yod, Hey, Vav, Hey. Life.

Sweet smelling savor – Aromatherapy is a modern day term for allowing a fragrant essence to "take you somewhere" in healing or in meditation.

Incense is often used for meditation in many spiritual traditions. Opening yourself to meditation by way of the sense of smell is a most pleasant way of transcending.

Have you ever noticed that smells carry memory with them? What are some of your favorite smells? What memories are connected to them? The ability to connect us to our memory is part of the power of meditating with incense, fragrant oils and spices.

When you use a particular scent for meditation you are immediately transported into the mode of meditation. The aroma is the trigger. Just as the smoke of incense or the fragrance rises, so does your consciousness ascend to the Higher Realms of the hidden places of the Higher Realms.

Incense made from a special formula given to Moses by God and written in the Torah was used in the Temple. Each fragrance used in the formula had its' own particular power and gave the incense a unique essence from the blended aroma. This aroma filled the Temple. It lifted the spirits of the priests and the people to the Sacred Space.

The traditions tell us that the sense of smell is the only one of the five senses that is strictly for the benefit of Soul. Think about that in terms of how you use your five senses. Sight, sound, taste and touch all serve the body in some way. Only smell is solely for the benefit of the Soul.

Try using the same incense, your favorite fragrance or oil for one month during your meditation time. From then on notice how easily you will move into meditation whenever you smell that scent.

When you light incense you can say a blessing over the act of kindling the sweet smelling savor unto The Holy One. By saying a blessing you are separating this kindling of incense from an everyday act. You make it a sacred act for your meditation time. Look back in the section on Blessings to find an appropriate blessing over kindling incense, or make up your own blessing.

Vision quest – There may be a special time in your life when you seek spiritual growth or guidance through opening to a vision of spirit. To do this set yourself apart from everyday life and the influences of others in a secluded spot for an extended period of time in retreat, in order to focus life solely on receiving your vision through meditation. This solitude allows you to receive clarity and a vision and a sense of your own unique Self, who you have been created to be in this lifetime. It gives you time to connect with the symbols that are personal in meaning to you in your life and which are giving your Soul guidance from your Creator. It is a time to hear the inaudible Voice, and see the invisible One through your life.

Once you have received this life vision your path is forever changed, rooted and grounded in who you truly are and who you are growing to become. It gives you guidance for steps in your life to fulfill your destiny. Your vision gives you a foundation of integrity to act as the keel of a boat, steadying you in the waves of life that might otherwise take you off course. Your vision meditation is for clarity, truth and to follow with integrity your Authentic Soul.

Meditation on the Alef-Bet – The letters of the Hebrew alef-bet (alphabet) are each symbols representing mystical powers. When you put these symbols together you can form words that carry the combined powers. When you combine the words you create in the physical world through the power of your words. There is a spiritual tradition of meditating on the individual letters of the alef-bet to unlock their power and meaning for your life.

When you meditate upon a particular letter you open to the creative power that it represents. For instance, if you are beginning a new venture or phase in your life you might meditate on the letter "dalet" "ד". The name of the letter, "dalet" comes from the same root as "delet" which means door. It is the doorway of transcendence and deliverance for information and wisdom in your new venture. It becomes a way for you to open yourself to receiving God's wisdom in spirit for you.

Jesus used this symbol of the delet (door) in his teachings when he said, "I am the door..." John 10:7. Look up this story of Jesus and find the new meanings it holds for you as you begin to understand more about "delet" the doorway, through meditating on the letter "dalet".

Meditate on each letter of the alef-bet to allow that letter to "speak" the secret of its symbols to you for your life at that time.

Text Meditation – You can meditate on by reciting or reading repeatedly, a phrase or section of the Bible to allow its secrets and personal meaning to open to you.

Singing Meditation – We touched upon this form of meditation in the audio meditation section. Psalms, hymns and songs of Praise raise our consciousness to a higher level, lifting away the veils of the Dimensions. This is what is meant by the teaching that, "God is present in the praises of the people." (Ps. 22:3 "You are Holy, dwelling in the praises of Israel.") This does not mean that God is only Present when people are singing praises

– as if God needs our adoration for ego building. It means that the veils of our consciousness shift as we lift our voices in praise. We become more fully aware of the Presence of God through our praise. We move our consciousness from the finite of this world to the Infinite worlds beyond. In our songs of praise we ourselves truly become present to God's eternal Presence.

This listing is but a few types of meditation. There are many more that bring us to a state of mindfulness and deliver us into another dimension.

Jewish meditation is not a way of escaping the difficulties this world. Jewish meditation is not focused on attaining a state of "nothingness" for its sake alone. What Jewish meditation does is to prepare us for prayer. It is a way to quiet the chatter and "noise" of our busy minds. It is a way to allow the sea of our emotions to calm. It is a way to lift the veils of our conscious mind and prepare us to shift into a state of "eminent awareness" of God. It prepares us to be "face to face" with The Holy One, creator of the Universe who is as close as our very breath; our Intimate Friend, the one who knows our heart. It is a powerful time of "traveling" in spirit to HaMakom, "the place which is no place." **Selah** – Pause and meditate upon that!

What are ways that you like to meditate? What practices in your church support a meditative state? Does your church use incense, song, visuals (such as candles and sacred art), or text recitation? What are you using in your private meditation time? Enjoy using some of the new ways that you may have learned in this section on meditation. Keep a meditation journal. May your meditations be a journey of blessings.

For further reading on meditation you might find the following books to be helpful:

Minyan, Rabbi Rami Shapiro

Meditation and the Bible, Rabbi Aryeh Kaplan
Jewish Meditation, Rabbi Aryeh Kaplan
The History and Varieties of Jewish Meditation, Mark Verman
Mystical Journey Into The Alef-Bet, (video) Dr. Ed Hoffman.

Prayer
Private Talks and Communal Conversation with God

Prayer is talking to God; but in Judaism it is talking to God in a specific way. *Tefillah* is the Hebrew word for prayer. Tefillah comes from the root, *Pi-lel*, and it literally means "to think, judge, or to intercede." *Hit-pa-lel*, the reflexive and intense form of the verb means "to pray". As always, the Hebrew language reflects our ways of relating to God. Prayer engages our consciousness to God's Presence in such a way that we may be thought about, judged and interceded for, adding ideas such as "much", "often" and "eagerly". **In other words, prayer is *intense* conversation with God.**

Prayer must be fervent to be prayer. This is why we are often reminded by our sages to use our kavennah, "intentionality" when we pray. The Psalms of David are an example of this intentionality. These meditative prayers are usually intense and fervent in mood and emotion, concept and spirituality.

There are two types of prayers in Hebrew. First, there are communal prayers that were formulated thousands of years ago and which we still use today in worship services. Many of these prayers were formulated in ancient days by the same council of elders in 300-400 BCE who formulated the order of blessings. In the same way as the blessings, these prayers carry much power from the way in which they are formulated. These prayers also carry with them the spirit of the many people who have uttered them over thousands of years. The second form of prayer is *tefillah b'lev*, the prayer of the heart, which may arise spontaneously from our lips at any time.

To reprint the formulated prayers of our people would go beyond the scope of this book. You can find Jewish prayers and worship services in a siddur, a Jewish prayer book. The prayers and services for the High Holy Days, Rosh Hashanah and Yom Kippur are in a special prayer book called a mahzor. You can find these prayer books in a synagogue or Judaica store where Jewish books and objects are sold.

If you look at the prayers in a Siddur, you will find many of them are familiar to you because the services and prayers of the early church were based upon prayers that were used in the synagogues by Hebrew worshippers of that time.

The prayers of a worship service follow a set pattern. Formulated prayers are said three times a day: morning *Shacharit*, afternoon, *Mincha*, and evening *Maariv*, by a prayer group usually of at least ten people called a *minyan*. Communal prayers are said at morning, afternoon and evening because the sacrifices were offered up in the Temple at those times. Since the destruction of the Temple in 70 CE, prayer has replaced animal sacrifice. Now we sacrifice our will on the altar of our hearts in the bended knee of our prayers. The blood covenant of sacrifice has evolved to the higher level of the Covenant of our sacred words in prayer. As the Prophet Isaiah said, "My house shall be a house of prayer for all peoples." (Isaiah 56:7).

Since these prayers are communal it is traditional to have at least ten people present to say the prayers. Each person represents one of the ten fruits or attributes of God that make up the Tree of Life. The ten persons represent the Ten Commandments, the sacred principles of God entrusted to us. The ten people represent the hands, or ten fingers bringing right action from God into this world.

The communal prayers are rarely phrased in the first person singular, "I", but most commonly use the first person plural, "we", including all of those present and those not present. These prayers are for the community of humanity and for the prosperity and fulfillment of all creation.

The culmination of the prayer service is the *Amidah*, or the Standing Prayer. During this prayer we stand for after entering with praise and worship we are at the point of standing in the "throne room", the intimate Presence of the Holy One. It is there that we make our petitions.

Traditionally, there are a few moments of silence at the end of the Amidah, in order for each person to hear the still small Voice and have their moment of sacred dialogue with God. After our petitions are made known and we have been silent we move to thanksgiving in the prayer. It is as if we are backing out of the throne room, never turning our backs on the "King". We acknowledge by our thanks that our prayers have been heard.

At the end of the prayer service we recite a prayer called *Kaddish*. It is said in honor of our loved ones who have died. It is actually a poem written in Aramaic, the everyday language during the time of Jesus that he would have spoken, reserving Hebrew as the Holy Language of the Temple service and prayer life.

The Kaddish speaks no words of death, but is only the highest praises we can imagine to utter to The Holy One of Life. The poem was originally written by the students of a beloved Rabbi. At his death they honored him and all he taught them by reciting this poem at his grave. It has since become the custom to honor a loved one's Soul by saying Kaddish for them every day for eleven months after their death. It is not said for salvific purposes, but as a witness to the love and *mitzvot* (loving deeds) they brought to the world and to our lives. It helps the mourner to integrate the ongoing relationship of their love with the one who has died, transferring the emotions of their relationship from the physical to the spirit. It confirms God's love and God's presence in life in the midst of death. Every year at the anniversary of the loved one's death this poem is recited in their honor and in memory of them. Even though this poem is a communal prayer it is also a prayer of the heart.

In Biblical times our greatest leaders prayed to God in ways that indicated their relationship of intimacy with the God of their Covenant. These are *tefillah b'lev*, the prayers of the heart. Abraham "hondled" (bargained) with God over how many righteous residents would be enough to keep Sodom and Gomorrah from destruction. Moses argued with God over the fate of the complaining Israelites. Gideon asked God for confirmation of his mission to save Israel in battle, by putting out a fleece of wool on the threshing floor overnight with the condition that the fleece would have dew on it while all around it the ground was dry if the battle would go well. In the morning he wrung a bowl full of dew out of the fleece while the ground around it was dry. Then he asked God for a second test, just to be sure he had heard God correctly. This time the fleece would be dry while the ground all around it would be wet with dew. Read Judges 6:37 to learn the outcome!

These instances of personal dialogue with God show us that while we might think of these leaders as superhuman in the great stories and feats of faith told about them, they are also shown to be quite human. Their prayers are the dialogue they hold with The Holy One, Creator of the Universe, who is their Intimate Friend.

This is our invitation to experience God in all our humanness, as well.

Jesus used prayer constantly to accomplish his mission. Remember the humanness of his prayer in the Garden of Gethsemane? In that prayer he is shown to be very human in the cry of his heart. Prayer is the catalyst of the human Soul reaching to the Highest Source beyond; beyond Self for Divine intervention in the "here and now". Prayer is the spiritual wave of energy-exchange, which manifests through the actions of humanity and nature on Earth. Prayer is the dialogue of the Emanator of Life and Life itself speaking heart to heart.

Tefillah b'lev, the prayer of the heart, is the conversation you have with God without preset formulation, according to the flow of your Soul. You may be talking with The Holy One in your everyday activities, or you may be secluded in your quiet spot, meditating on that which leads you to deeper prayer. You may be thanking God for a particular event in your life, or you may be asking for help or beseeching God for wisdom and guidance when faced with making a difficult decision. Whatever the topic, *tefillah b'lev*, the prayer of the heart, is coming from your Soul and is spontaneous. When you have poured out your heart in joy or in sorrow, always remember to be quiet and still at some point – just be – and listen with the ears of your Soul to hear The Voice – God speaking to you. Don't be surprise if God asks **you** a question. It is through questioning God that we learn. It is by God questioning us that we learn also. This too is prayer; the dynamic dialogue between The One and The Many, which is all God.

Creating Your "God Trap"

While it is true that we can meditate and pray anywhere and anytime, there are spiritual practices within Judaism that our people have used throughout the centuries that help us "transcend" by moving our consciousness beyond this dimension. Some of these spiritual practices might include lighting candles, wearing a prayer shawl and/or *Tefillin* (black boxes worn on the forehead and arm that contain small scrolls with Deut. 6:8 written upon them), burning incense, playing meditative music, using fragrant oils, and or facing East, the direction of the Temple in Jerusalem. It is also traditional to have a place of solitude to go to for prayer and meditation. This becomes your sacred place of meeting where you have intimate visits with The Holy One, the Creator of the Universe. This is the place where you use whatever helps you to transcend in consciousness. Jesus often went into seclusion away from the crowds and even his disciples to meditate and pray, to go to "the secret hiding place of the Most High" for intimacy with God.

Reb Zalman Schachter-Shalomi refers to this place as your "God Trap." This is a playful idea that by using the spiritual practices we set the "trap" for God and bring The Holy One close to us. In fact, Reb Zalman is bringing to our attention the fact that just the opposite is true; we capture (trap) **our** scattered energy and focus on God to transcend. We lift the veils of **our** consciousness to gain a "closer proximity" toward The Source of All Life. After transcending to the Higher Realms of consciousness we can recognize The Divine Presence already in our midst in this world.

The place of quietude we use becomes our *Ohel Moed*, or "tent of meeting" as the Tabernacle in the Wilderness was called. The

Ohel Moed was the place that the people gathered to "meet" with God; the place that Moses would "meet" daily with God. Your Ohel Moed is the place where you can "meet" with yourself, discovering before God the deepest parts of your Soul; the most intimate "you."

If you do not have such a place, try different areas of your home or yard. Maybe it is a place of solitude out in nature or the woods. Maybe it is in a garden or by the seashore. Once you are in your Ohel Moed, experiment with some of the spiritual practices you have learned and see which ones feel comfortable and powerful to you.

After your prayer and meditation time write your enlightenment experiences, thoughts, and feelings you may have retained in a journal. Many times after coming out of deep prayer we begin to lose some of the details of what we experienced, just as we do with dreams, so it is helpful to take a few moments to write down your journey. Date your entries so that in years to come you can look back at your spiritual journey. Keeping a spiritual journal enables you to look back over the years and see how you were prepared and grew spiritually in the events of your life. You may even see how your prayer life has directed those events.

Saying 100 blessings everyday for mindful living, meditating for a transcendent shift of consciousness, and praying in dynamic dialogue with God are all part of your Hebrew heritage. Enjoy integrating the ideas you have read in this chapter. Let your inner guidance lead you on your Blessing Path. May you have a wonderful adventure through your Spirit-led journeys in meditations. Stay constant in prayer, for God is always praying through you!

Worship through Sacred Dance!

"And David leaped and danced before The Holy One with all his might ..."

SAMUEL II 6:14.

King David brought the Ark of the Covenant into Jerusalem with great joy and gladness. David and all of the people accompanied the Ark of the Covenant with singing, shouting, the sound of the shofar and dancing. In the verses following this passage we read that Michal, daughter of King Saul and David's first wife, looked out of a window and despised David for his public display. After placing the Ark of the Covenant in the Holy Place and blessing the people in joy and celebration, David returned home to Michal's biting remarks about his having danced in his *ephod* (equivalent to today's underwear) before the women of Israel. David unapologetically proclaims to her that he was dancing before The Holy One, the God of Israel, Who chose him to rule over her father King Saul. Further, he announces that he has only yet begun to "abase" himself before the people and God in worship and praise to the Source of All Life. King David is a passionate man who is not afraid to express his love and joy to God in singing (Psalms), dancing and celebration to the God Who is his Creator.

Another form of avodah, worship, is spiritual dance. There are times in our lives when God so overfills our hearts that we must enter into worship and praise with our whole hearts, minds *and* bodies. Then it is that our feet must leave the ground in dance, our arms lift our hands to the skies and our faces reflect the Glory of God in our ecstasy.

The followers of the *Baal Shem Tov* (Master of the Good

Name), who were called the *Chassidim* (faithful ones) transcended and connected with God through joy and the practice of ecstatic dancing and whirling. They celebrated life through joy. They danced and sang to lift the veils of their consciousness to a state of loving union with The Holy Presence.

As the Spirit of God moves among worshippers they dance with joy before The Holy One, abandoning self-consciousness to be in God – consciousness, removing the sense of self and others and embracing The One. This is a powerful experience which connects you with the Spirit and energy of our ancient roots. It frees your Soul and brings your body into praise and worship.

Do you suppose Jesus ever danced? While we do not read any accounts of it, I can imagine his joining into the joy at the wedding of Cana, (John 2:1-11). As a Rabbi, I understand the deeply rooted tradition of dancing at weddings, to celebrate the Divine union of the bride (Creation) and the groom (Creator). This wedding would have been a celebration filled with dancing. If Jesus was to do his first miracle of turning water into wine there at the wedding of Cana, we understand that he was joined with the community in this celebration. The joy of The Holy One celebrated in bride and groom would have moved his feet with joy and the glory of the Creator of bride and groom!

If you feel you are not quite ready for that level of public expression, you may want to play some of your inspirational music while you are alone with God in your "God Trap" corner, or in the privacy of your own home. Learn to dance "as the Spirit moves you" to experience this beautiful and freeing form of worship.

You may also enjoy learning some Israeli dances, some of which are very ancient and date back to Biblical times. Israeli dance classes are usually offered at Jewish Community Centers. Maybe your church could arrange to have someone (from the community) who knows Israeli dances come to your church to teach classes. A few dances you may enjoy include: *Zimer-atik,* (Little Song), which is said to have come out of Egypt with the Children of Israel at the time of the Exodus; *Hora Medura* (Dance around the Campfire), which is a dance that interprets the experiences of battle and *Hineh Ma Tov* (Behold How Good), which is a line dance that choreographs the scripture "Behold how good and how pleasant it is for brethren to dwell in unity...". As you become freer to move in dance, the music will "take you on a journey" and before you know it, you will join King David, leaping and dancing before The Holy One with all your might. This is joy! This is joyful worship!

5

The Call of the Burning Bush, The Sacred Fire of Your Soul

Now Moses kept the flock of Jethro his father in law, the Priest of Midian: and he led the flock far away into the desert, and came to the mountain of God, to Horev. And the angel of the Holy One appeared to him in a flame of fire out of the midst of a bush: and he looked, and behold, the bush burned with fire, but the bush was not consumed. And Moses said, I will now turn aside, and see this great sight, why the bush is not burnt. And when The Holy One saw that he turned aside to see, God called to him out of the midst of the bush, and said, Moses, Moses. And he said, "Hineni, Here am I."

EXODUS 3: 1-4

The men and women in the stories of our ancestors are always depicted in very human terms. Their frailties, as well as mistakes, are recorded along with their heroic faith and triumphant deeds. This makes them real to us. It encourages us to reach toward the ideals their lives set before us. They had their doubts and fears the same as we do. They struggled with their decisions and commitments just as we do today. Your Hebrew heritage does not call you to a higher walk than you are capable of attaining; but it gives you ancestors whose shoulders you can stand upon to see farther and to enable you to fulfill your own unique destiny. Moses teaches you how to turn aside (let go of the busy-ness of your life) in order to see the miracles of God (the burning bush); thereby experiencing the true miracle of God's Voice speaking to you and calling you to action.

Moses was tending the flock of the High-Priest of another nation, the nation of Midian. He had grown up in Egypt, in the household of the Pharaoh and was trained in the Egyptian ways. When he left Egypt he spent the next forty years of his adult life living in the family of Jethro, married to Zipporah, the daughter of Jethro, the High Priest of Midian. He learned the ways of a shepherd and he learned to meet with The Holy One on the mountain of God, *Har Khorev*, Mount Khorev. The name *Khorev* comes from the root *Kharav*, which means a dry or desolate place. In this place of desolation in his life, God met with Moses to call him to his mission of bringing the Children of Israel out of Egypt to the land flowing with milk and honey. God meets each of us in our most desolate times as well, to call us to a place of nurturance in our lives; to call us to the purpose for our lives.

Moses was prepared by the events of his whole life for the fulfillment of his sacred pathway, his mission of bringing the Children of the God of Abraham out of their bondage in Egypt. Even though his early life in Egypt did not seem to be preparation for such a great and holy mission, it was a vital part of it. His forty years in Midian were years of preparation, as well. The events of Moses' life taught him how to be not only a strong ruler, a Pharaoh, but also a compassionate leader, a caregiver, a shepherd. The leaders of God's people need both attributes.

King David learned to be a shepherd as a young boy, and was later anointed to be a king. By contrast, Moses learned how to be a king as a youth when he was raised in the palace of the Pharaoh; then he learned how to be a good shepherd as an adult from his Midianite wife, Zipporah, and her father, Jethro. Only then was he prepared to be the shepherd of God's flock, the people of Israel.

The pivotal point of Moses' life was his burning bush experience, when he heard God call him by name, "Moses, Moses" and he answered, "Hineni, here am I." He was on holy ground before God. He was given his choice to follow his heart and his Soul toward God, or not. The story tells us how he doubted his own ability and voiced his fears to God. But, finally, when he answered God with "Hineni," in his heart, as well as in his words, his consciousness came into unity with his Soul's sacred pathway and he fulfilled the destiny to which he was born. In his answer, "Here am I," he truly found himself.

Jesus found this moment of fulfillment in his prayer at the Garden of Gethsemane, "…. nonetheless, Your will be done."

What is your sacred fire, the special purpose for your Life?

Each of us has a destiny for which we came into the world. Each of us has a sacred pathway, a mission to which we were born. We are all prepared and enabled to fulfill our sacred destiny by the events of our lives. The experiences of our early years, youth and adult life are all vital to our preparation and ability to fulfill that mission. We each have that moment in our life when we stop and see the miracle of God; the "fire on the mountain." We each hear the call of our name from deep in our own heart, echoing from the Source of our Life, God. Will we answer, "Hineni, Here am I" to consciously commit ourselves to our Soul's purpose? In that

251

sacred moment before God, there is a space of silence in our lives while the Universe pauses to wait and hear our reply. We each either say, "Hineni, here am I" or we choose not to answer the call. It is almost always a moment of awe, for there looms before us the inexplicable joy of the mission as well as our fear of failure. Moses experienced this conflict of emotions and raised his objections to God. God's answer to him was, "Certainly, I will be with you; and this will be the token for you, that I have sent you." (Ex. 3:12). God's Presence never left Moses in all of the years of his ensuing journey. God's promise extends to you in your journey, echoing, "Certainly, I will be with you..."

What is your service to God that brings you joy?

Just as it was with Moses, so it is with each of us. We stand on sacred ground before our personal "burning bush." We hear God's call our name and our heart desires to answer it in the face of our fears of rejection or possible failure. These fears are only a signal flag waving to remind us that we have a choice. We can choose to stand in our fears and be paralyzed by them, or we can act out of our love for God, our Source, our intimate Friend, and move forward assured that God's Presence will be with us – no matter what. We are not assured that our path will always be easy, but we are assured that God will be with us, guarding and guiding us all the way; for The Holy One is emanating us, how can it be any other way? We are each emanated and created uniquely, with purpose and fulfillment, yet as One.

This was the wisdom that Jesus taught in John 8 when he said that he speaks only what The Holy One has taught him to speak and that The Holy One has never left him to be alone. Even in the Garden of Gethsemane, this truth rang true as Jesus also struggled with his fears. God does not leave us. The Holy One and all which emanates forth from The Holy One are One. The illusion is that we are alone. The truth is that all is One, as the Shema says: "Hear O Israel, The Infinite One is our God, The Infinite One is Oneness itself." We are all One in The One, the Creator of the Universe. We are called according to the purposes of the light of God and we are infused by the Divine Light. When we answer "Hineni, Here am I," the light flows forth through us in full illumination to all who are around us through our unique sacred fire, the gifts we offer to the world.

> How have the events of your life prepared you for your sacred mission?

What are the events of your life that have prepared you? The most difficult parts of your life, and often the parts of your life that you try to keep hidden from others the most are the very areas that hold the valuable treasure of the preparation of your calling. Are you still seeking the calling that God has for the fulfillment of your life; that special gift of work to bring God's light into the world for which you have been prepared by the events of your whole life? If so, open your will to seek out the miracle of the burning bush, God's sacred meeting place with you. Try "The Burning Bush" meditation.

The Burning Bush Meditation

- Go to a quiet place where you meet with God (your Ohel Moed, Tent of Meeting).
- Visualize the burning bush in Moses' story in the distance before you. Draw closer and closer to it to experience the miracle of its

warmth radiating out in rays of white light around you.

- You are standing on Holy Ground. Take off your shoes and stand with your bare feet planted solidly on Mother Earth before the fire of God's Presence.
- Look at the fire of the bush until you are looking into the fire, moving your consciousness deeper into God's Sacred Presence.
- Listen quietly for the familiar Voice of God speaking your name from within your own heart. When you truly sense The Presence of God, speak **your** presence to God with your answer: "Hineni, Here am I."
- Allow God to speak the calling of your life to you in your heart.
- Ask God any questions you have and listen to the answer from out of the Divine Silence.
- Speak your fears about your calling. Hear God's reply to each fear.
- Ask God to show you how the experiences of your life have prepared you for this mission.
- When you are ready, speak from your heart your answer to God. If you consciously desire to fulfill your destiny as God created you, say the words of sweet surrender, "Hineni, here am I."
- You may suddenly experience an exhilarating joy and a new perspective on your calling that brings you into true celebration. Hosts of angels and all of the ministering spirits who are there to help you in your mission will celebrate with joy in the Heavens! By Grace you shall succeed!
- In great thanksgiving thank God for the opportunity to be God's Love made manifest on Earth through your life.
- What first step can you take to "bring your sacred fire?"
- When you are ready, come back to this time and space. Open your eyes, take a deep breath, and become present to everything

in the room again.
• Take another deep breath! Stretch your arms out to the sides and fully inhabit your body consciousness once more.

Write your experiences as you remember them in your sacred journal. Look back over your life and review the areas that relate to the development of your special gift to the world, your sacred fire. What events have prepared you to be able to give what you have to offer?

Write down the first steps you can take to put an action to the calling you have received. You will have this entry to re-read anytime you doubt yourself or become discouraged. Return to the place of the Burning Bush, to HaMakom, whenever you need to hear God's Voice assuring you of your pathway.

> Where does your spiritual journey lead you from here?
> "And you will love The Holy One, your God, with all your Soul, with all your heart, with all your strength."
>
> DEUT. 6:5

The words of Torah in Deut. 6:5 are not a commandment, but a statement of the result of being in the imminent Presence of the Holy One. The result is a total fulfillment of love. Bliss overcomes and leads your heart in the pathway of your destiny. This bliss is renewed as you think about and act upon the sacred fire that you offer. What is the passion of your heart? This is your sacred pathway. Can you give it a name, or title it as if it is the book of your life? This is the Divine Destiny that your Soul has become embodied to fulfill. What is your answer to The Holy One every day? What are the first steps, the actions that you can take today to start your journey of fulfilling your Destiny? Put these steps into your appointment book, for once they are committed in your schedule you have taken at least one step of the journey.

When I started the rigorous five-year program of rabbinic seminary I asked my Soul-mate, "How am I going to do this?" His wise answer was, "You are going to do it the same way you eat an elephant, my dear – one bite at a time." Your pathway may seem enormous to you at the outset, but you will be the fulfillment of God's love through each step you take ... "one bite at a time."

When you choose to consciously begin your Sacred Path and answer God from your love, then you walk alongside our matriarchs and patriarchs of the Hebrew traditions of 4000 years. God's promise to you is, "I will be with you. You are not alone; we are One." You will more deeply understand the heart of Jesus. You will gain the Hebrew treasures of your spiritual inheritance. You will know the greatest of all gifts in your life, the gift of Shalom, the gift of peace.

Welcome home to your Hebrew heritage.

THE END